CONSTRUCTIVE CONSCIOUS CONTROL
OF THE INDIVIDUAL

CW00553088

Also by F.M. Alexander
and available in Gollancz Paperbacks

THE USE OF THE SELF

CONSTRUCTIVE CONSCIOUS CONTROL OF THE INDIVIDUAL

by

F. MATTHIAS ALEXANDER

With an Introduction by Patrick J. Macdonald

LONDON
VICTOR GOLLANCZ LTD
1987

First published in Great Britain 1923
by Methuen & Co. Ltd

This edition first published 1987
by Victor Gollancz Ltd,
14 Henrietta Street, London WC2E 8QJ

First published in Gollancz Paperbacks 1987

British Library Cataloguing in Publication Data
Alexander, F. Matthias
  Constructive conscious control of the
  individual.
  1. Physical fitness
  I. Title   II. Alexander, F. Matthias. Man's
  supreme inheritance
  613.7   RA781

  ISBN 0-575-03938-8

Printed and bound in Great Britain
by Cox & Wyman Ltd, Reading

Dedicated to the Memory of My Mother

INTRODUCTION
by Patrick J. Macdonald

Most people think that education brings continued improvement, but while everyone seems to agree that we should have more of it, there does not seem to be a great deal of agreement about the kind of education that is needed. Alexander pointed out that the vital thing in education was that people should be taught not to go on destroying themselves through misuse of themselves by overlooking the essential thing which he had discovered, or rather re-discovered.

We consider our century the most enlightened, yet violence and inhumanity are not diminishing, and though many theories exist as to what is wrong, the offered solutions often seem to disappoint. Acquired information and knowledge might not benefit us all that much, unless they are put to use through a well-functioning and integrated being.

Alexander postulated that proper use was essential for survival. This was once instinctive and effective while the needs of life were unchanged, but with the fast-changing environment which occurred with civilization, man's coordination began to falter – demands came to him more rapidly but his responses did not change equally rapidly. Man grew apart from nature.

Alexander offers us the means to use our intelligence to re-direct ourselves towards a proper response to living, allowing for further growth. Aldous Huxley wrote in *The Saturday Review of Literature:*

"Alexander's fundamental discovery was this: there exists in men, as in all other vertebrates, a primary control conditioning the proper use of the total organism. When the head is in a certain relation to the trunk, then (it is a matter of empirical fact) the entire psycho-physical organism is functioning to the best of its natural capacity. When, for any reason whatsoever, the proper relations between head, neck, and trunk are disturbed, the psycho-physical organism comes to be used improperly."

"Wrong" and "failure" are synonymous in the minds of the young, and accordingly remain blocks to their development. Alexander pointed out that trying to do the "right" thing is a trap into which most of us readily fall, because we try to do it without investigating what really happens in the attempt. What usually happens is that we just do the same thing again but with extra tension; in other words, we do it as before, only worse. Man's supreme inheritance (Alexander's phrase and the title of his first book) is the ability to choose whether to act in one way, or another, or not to act at all. If we are really to do what is needed, we must change the "normal" concept as to what has to be done, and choose means whereby we act in a different, yet coordinated and appropriate manner. Professor John Dewey claimed:

"The technique of Mr Alexander bears the same relation to education that education itself bears to all other activities. It contains to my judgment the promise and potentiality of the new direction that is needed in all education."

Being taught how to change our habitual thinking patterns takes time and effort and can be difficult, for change is what most people dislike, and what they tend to shy away from rather than welcome or seek out. Education about how to learn and not just what to learn may lead to increased knowledge. Excessive trust in thinking and reasoning might be an impediment on the path to truth and, in my experience, teaching intellectuals is not necessarily easier; they assume they know how to learn but often they do not, as they find it difficult to stop their reasoning to allow instead for a completely new and unknown experience to take place.

This book, the second of Alexander's four books, is concerned with education both in the broad and in the narrow sense. My father, Dr Peter Macdonald, after having been helped by a series of lessons with Alexander, fully grasped that Alexander did not give people who came to him a kind of medical treatment, but rather what he gave them was a re-education through a process developing their awareness about their behaviour. In 1923 he stated in his address at the BMA Conference in the Section of Neurology and Psychological Medicine: "His [Alexander's] work should be incorporated in the education of our young, if only as a matter of preventive medicine."

PATRICK J. MACDONALD
London, December 1986

CONTENTS

INTRODUCTION

by Professor John Dewey

THE principle and procedure set forth by Mr. Alexander are crucially needed at present. Strangely, this is the very reason why they are hard to understand and accept. For although there is nothing esoteric in his teaching, and although his exposition is made in the simplest English, free from technical words, it is difficult for anyone to grasp its full force without having actual demonstration of the principle in operation. And even then, as I know from personal experience, its full meaning dawns upon one only slowly and with new meanings continually opening up. Since I can add nothing to the clear and full exposition that Mr. Alexander has himself given, it has occurred to me that the most useful form this introductory word can take is an attempt to explain wherein lies the difficulty in grasping his principle.

The chief difficulty, as I have said, lies in the fact that it is so badly needed. The seeming contradiction in this statement is just one instance of the vicious circle which is frequently pointed out and fully dealt with in the pages of the text. The principle is badly needed, because in all matters that concern the individual self and the conduct of its life there is a defective and lowered sensory appreciation and judgment, both of ourselves and of our acts, which accompanies our wrongly-adjusted psychophysical mechanisms. It is precisely this perverted consciousness which we bring with us to the reading and comprehension of Mr. Alexander's pages, and which makes it hard for us to realize his statements as to its existence, causes, and effects. We have become so used to it that we take it for granted. It forms, as he has so clearly shown, our standard of rightness. It influences our every observation, interpretation, and judgment. It is the one factor which enters into our every act and thought.

Consequently, only when the results of Mr. Alexander's lessons have changed one's sensory appreciation and supplied a new standard, so that the old and the new condition can be compared with each other, does the concrete force of his teaching come home to one. In spite of the whole tenour of Mr. Alexander's teaching, it is this which makes it practically impossible for anyone to go to him with any other idea at the outset beyond that of gaining some specific relief and remedy. Even after a considerable degree of experience with his lessons, it is quite possible for one to prize his method merely on account of specific benefits received, even though one recognizes that these benefits include a changed emotional condition and a different outlook on life. Only when a pupil reaches the point of giving his full attention to the *method* of Mr. Alexander instead of its results, does he realize the constant influence of his sensory appreciation.

The perversion of our sensory consciousness of ourselves has gone so far that we lack criteria for judging the doctrines and methods that profess to deal with the individual human being. We oscillate between reliance upon plausible general theories and reliance upon testimonies to specific benefits obtained. We oscillate between extreme credulity and complete scepticism. On the one hand, there is the readiest acceptance of all claims made in behalf of panaceas when these are accompanied by testimonies of personal benefits and cures. On the other hand, the public has seen so many of these panaceas come and go that it has, quite properly, become sceptical about the reality of any new and different principle for developing human well-being. The world is flooded at present with various systems for relieving the ills that human flesh is heir to, such as systems of exercise for rectifying posture, methods of mental, psychological, and spiritual healing, so that, except when there happens to be an emotional wave sweeping the country, the very suggestion that there is fundamental truth in an unfamiliar principle is likely to call out the feeling that one more person, reasonably sensible about most things, has fallen for another one of the " cure-alls " that abound. " How," it will be asked, " can the teaching of Mr. Alexander be differentiated from these other systems ? " " What assurance is there that it is anything more than one of them, working better perhaps for some persons and worse for others ? " If, in reply, specific beneficial results of Mr. Alexander's teaching are pointed out, one is reminded of the fact that imposing testimonials of this kind can be produced in favour of all the other systems. The point, then, to be decided is : What is the worth of these results and how is their worth to be judged ? Or, again, if it is a question of the theories behind the results, most of the systems are elaborately reasoned

out and claim scientific or spiritual backing. In what fundamental respect, then, do the principles and consequences of Mr.
Alexander's teaching differ from these?

These are fair questions, and it seems to me that probably
the best thing that this introduction can do is to suggest some
simple criteria by which any plan can be judged. Certain other
questions may suggest the path by which these criteria may be
found. Is a system primarily remedial, curative, aiming at
relief of sufferings that already exist; or is it fundamentally preventive in nature? And if preventive rather than merely
corrective, is it specific or general in scope? Does it deal with
the "mind" and the "body" as things separated from each
other, or does it deal with the unity of man's individuality?
Does it deal with some portion or aspect of "mind" and "body"
or with the re-education of the whole being? Does it aim at
securing results directly, by treatment of symptoms, or does it
deal with the *causes* of malconditions present in such a way that
any beneficial results secured come as a natural consequence,
almost, it might be said, as by-products of a fundamental
change in such conditioning causes? Is the scheme educational
or non-educational in character? If the principle underlying it
claims to be preventive and constructive, does it operate from
without by setting up some automatic safety-device, or does it
operate from within? Is it cheap and easy, or does it make
demands on the intellectual and moral energies of the individuals
concerned? Unless it does the latter, what is it, after all, but a
scheme depending ultimately upon some trick or magic, which, in
curing one trouble, is sure to leave behind it other troubles
(including fixations, inhibitions, laxities, lessening of power of
steady and intelligent control), since it does not deal with causes,
but only directs their operation into different channels, and
changes symptoms from such as are perceptible into more
subtle ones that are not perceived? Anyone who bears such
questions as the above in mind whilst reading Mr. Alexander's
book will have little difficulty in discriminating between the
principles underlying his educational method and those of the
systems with which it might be compared and confused.

Any sound plan must prove its soundness in reference both to
concrete consequences and to general principles. What we
too often forget is that these principles and facts must not be
judged separately, but in connexion with each other. Further,

whilst any theory or principle must ultimately be judged by its consequences in operation, whilst it must be verified experimentally by observation of how it works, yet in order to justify a claim to be scientific, it must provide a method for making evident and observable what the consequences are; and this method must be such as to afford a guarantee that the observed consequences actually flow from the principle. And I unhesitatingly assert that, when judged by this standard—that is, of a principle at work in effecting definite and verifiable consequences—Mr. Alexander's teaching is scientific in the strictest sense of the word. It meets both of these requirements. In other words, the plan of Mr. Alexander satisfies the most exacting demands of scientific method.

The principle or theory of Mr. Alexander and the observed consequences of its operation have developed at the same time and in the closest connexion with each other. Both have evolved out of an experimental method of procedure. At no time has he elaborated a theory for its own sake. This fact has occasionally been a disappointment to " intellectual " persons who have subconsciously got into the habit of depending upon a certain paraphernalia of technical terminology. But the theory has never been carried beyond the needs of the procedure employed, nor beyond experimentally verified results. Employing a remarkably sensitive power of observation, he has noted the actual changes brought about in individuals in response to the means which he has employed, and has followed up these changes in their connexions with the individual's habitual reflexes, noting the reactions due to the calling into play of established bad habits, with even greater care than the more obvious beneficial consequences obtained. Every such undesirable response has been treated as setting a problem—namely, that of discovering some method by which the evocation of these instinctive reactions, and the feelings associated with them, can be inhibited, and, in their stead, such acts called into play as will give a basis for correct sensory appreciations. Every step in the process has been analysed and formulated, and every changing condition and consequence, positive or negative, favourable or unfavourable, which is employed as a means for developing the experimental procedure, has been still further developed. The use of this developed method has, of course, continuously afforded new material for observation and thorough analysis. To this process of simultaneous development of principles and consequences, used as means for testing each other, there is literally no end. As long as Mr. Alexander uses the method, it will be a process tending continually towards perfection. It will no more arrive at a stage of finished perfection than does any genuine experimental scientific procedure, with its theory and supporting facts. The most striking fact of Mr. Alexander's teaching is the sincerity and reserve with which he has never carried his formulation beyond the point of demonstrated facts.

It is obvious, accordingly, that the results obtained by Mr. Alexander's teaching stand on a totally different plane from those obtained under the various systems which have had great vogue until they have been displaced by some other tide of fashion and publicity. Most of those who urge the claims of these systems point to " cures " and other specific phenomena as evidence that they are built upon correct principles. Even for patent medicines an abundance of testimonials can be adduced. But the theories and the concrete facts in these cases have no genuine connexion with each other. Certain consequences, the " good " ones, are selected and held up for notice, whilst no attempt is made to find out what other consequences are taking place. The " good " ones are swallowed whole. There is no method by which it can be shown what consequences, if any, result from the principle invoked, or whether they are due to quite other causes.

But the essence of scientific method does not consist in taking consequences in gross; it consists precisely in the means by which consequences are followed up in detail. It consists in the processes by which the causes that are used to explain the consequences, or effects, can be concretely followed up to show that they actually produce these consequences and no others. If, for instance, a chemist pointed, on the one hand, to a lot of concrete phenomena which had occurred after he had tried an experiment and, on the other hand, to a lot of general principles and theories elaborately reasoned out, and then proceeded to assert that the two things were connected so that the theoretical principles accounted for the phenomena, he would meet only with ridicule. It would be clear that scientific method had not even been started; it would be clear that he was offering nothing but assertion.

Mr. Alexander has persistently discouraged the appeal to
" cures " or to any other form of remarkable phenomena.   He
has even discouraged keeping records of these cases.   Yet, if
he had not been so wholeheartedly devoted to working out a
demonstration of a principle—a demonstration in the scientific
sense of the word—he would readily have had his day of vogue
as one among the miracle-mongers.   He has also persistently
held aloof from building up an imposing show of technical
scientific terminology of physiology, anatomy, and psychology.
Yet that course also would have been easy in itself, and a sure
method of attracting a following.   As a consequence of this
sincerity and thoroughness, maintained in spite of great odds,
without diversion to side-issues of fame and external success,
Mr. Alexander has demonstrated a new scientific principle with
respect to the control of human behaviour, as important as
any principle which has ever been discovered in the domain
of external nature.   Not only this, but his discovery is necessary
to complete the discoveries that have been made about non-
human nature, if these discoveries and inventions are not to
end by making us their servants and helpless tools.

A scientific man is quite aware that no matter how extensive
and thorough is his theoretical reasoning, and how definitely it
points to a particular conclusion of fact, he is not entitled to
assert the conclusion as a fact until he has actually observed the
fact, until his senses have been brought into play.   With respect
to distinctively human conduct, no one, before Mr. Alexander,
has even considered just what kind of sensory observation is
needed in order to test and work out theoretical principles.
Much less have thinkers in this field ever evolved a technique
for bringing the requisite sensory material under definite and
usable control.   Appeal to suggestion, to the unconscious and
to the subconscious, is in its very description an avoidance of
this scientific task ; the systems of purely physical exercise
have equally neglected any consideration of the methods by
which their faults are to be observed and analysed.

Whenever the need has been dimly felt for some concrete
check and realization of the meaning of our thoughts and
judgments about ourselves and our conduct, we have fallen
back, as Mr. Alexander has so clearly pointed out in his writings,
on our pre-existing sense of what is " right."   But this signifies
in the concrete only what we feel to be *familiar*.   And in so far

as we have bad habits needing re-education, that which is familiar in our sense of ourselves and of our acts can only be a reflection of the bad psycho-physical habits that are operating within us. This, of course, is precisely as if a scientific man, who, by a process of reasoning, had been led to a belief in what we call the Copernican theory, were then to try to test this reasoning by appealing to precisely those observations, without any addition or alteration, which had led men to the Ptolemaic theory. Scientific advance manifestly depends upon the discovery of conditions for making new observations, and upon the re-making of old observations under different conditions; in other words, upon methods of discovering *why*, as in the case of the scientific man, we have had and relied upon observations that have led into error.

After studying over a period of years Mr. Alexander's method in actual operation, I would stake myself upon the fact that he has applied to our ideas and beliefs about ourselves and about our acts exactly the same method of experimentation and of production of new sensory observations, as tests and means of developing thought, that have been the source of all progress in the physical sciences; and if, in any other plan, any such use has been made of the sensory appreciation of our attitudes and acts, if in it there has been developed a technique for creating new sensory observations of ourselves, and if complete reliance has been placed upon these findings, I have never heard of it. In some plans there has been a direct appeal to " consciousness " (which merely registers bad conditions); in some, this consciousness has been neglected entirely and dependence placed instead upon bodily exercises, rectifications of posture, etc. But Mr. Alexander has found a method for detecting precisely the correlations between these two members, physical-mental, of the same whole, and for creating a new sensory consciousness of new attitudes and habits. It is a discovery which makes whole all scientific discoveries, and renders them available, not for our undoing, but for human use in promoting our constructive growth and happiness.

No one would deny that we ourselves enter as an agency into whatever is attempted and done by us. That is a truism. But the hardest thing to attend to is that which is closest to ourselves, that which is most constant and familiar. And this closest " something " is, precisely, ourselves, our own habits and ways of doing things as agencies in conditioning what is tried or done by us. Through modern science we have mastered to a wonderful extent the use of things as tools for accomplishing results upon and through other things. The result is all but a universal state of confusion, discontent, and strife. The one factor which is the primary tool in the use of all these other tools—namely, ourselves—in other words, our own psycho-physical disposition, as the basic condition of our employment of all agencies and energies, has not even been studied as the central instrumentality. Is it not highly probable that this failure gives the explanation of why it is that in mastering physical forces we have ourselves been so largely mastered by them, until we find ourselves incompetent to direct the history and destiny of man?

Never before, I think, has there been such an acute consciousness of the failure of all external remedies as exists to-day, of the failure of all remedies and forces external to the individual man. It is, however, one thing to teach the need of a return to the individual man as the ultimate agency in whatever mankind and society collectively can accomplish, to point out the necessity of straightening out this ultimate condition of whatever humanity in mass can attain. It is another thing to discover the concrete procedure by which this greatest of all tasks can be executed. And this indispensable thing is exactly what Mr. Alexander has accomplished. The discovery could not have been made and the method of procedure perfected except by dealing with adults who were badly co-ordinated. But the method is not one of remedy; it is one of constructive education. Its proper field of application is with the young, with the growing generation, in order that they may come to possess as early as possible in life a correct standard of sensory appreciation and self-judgment. When once a reasonably adequate part of a new generation has become properly co-ordinated, we shall have assurance for the first time that men and women in the future will be able to stand on their own feet, equipped with satisfactory psycho-physical equilibrium, to meet with readiness, confidence, and happiness instead of with fear, confusion, and discontent, the buffetings and contingencies of their surroundings.

JOHN DEWEY.

PREFACE

THE demand for this book has been an insistent one for some time past, particularly from the American readers of *Man's Supreme Inheritance*, and, out of gratitude, I have a keen desire to make a contribution to our knowledge worthy of the written encouragement I have received from a large circle of readers, from the Press, and from scientific men in Australia, England, and America.

This mass of correspondence is of the greatest interest and value to me, for every letter contains a request for further enlightenment on some particular point, or points, of special interest to the writer of the letter. Of course, it is quite impossible to answer all these queries in this volume, but, whenever possible, I shall give practical illustrations to show, in a general way, the fundamental principle or principles which are involved in these queries, in the hope that these illustrations will help my correspondents to a better understanding of the practical side of their problems. I have sufficient matter for several volumes, and in making my selections I have been influenced by the relative importance of this matter to each portion of my subject. It may, therefore, be a source of satisfaction to any reader who may be disappointed in this respect to know that I have given due consideration to this essential part of my work.

In *Man's Supreme Inheritance* I have set down my thesis, together with practical procedures and illustrations, and, if I may judge from the correspondence received from readers, the way has thus been cleared to a new outlook and to the desire for a better understanding of the *means whereby* life may be lived sanely in the environment of twentieth-century experiences and rapid changes. In this book I am most anxious to answer such oft-repeated questions as: " Why are our instincts less reliable than those of our early ancestors? " " At what stage of man's evolution did this deterioration begin? " " What is the cause of our present-day individual and national unrest? " " Can you set down principles which will enable us to decide as to the best methods of educating our children?" "Evidently your conception of conscious control, co-ordination, and re-education differs from the usual conception; if so, will you explain the difference in your next book?" I am of opinion that if I succeed in answering these questions, I shall have made a distinct step forward in helping to clear away, once and for all, the doubts of any person who, in the midst of world-wide unrest and dissatisfaction, is seeking honestly for truth amidst the mass of methods, systems, "cures," and treatments in what are called "physical," "mental," and "spiritual" spheres. In this connexion, it is important to note that the enthusiasts for these different methods point to excellent *specific* results (that is, according to their idea or conception of results) in support of their contentions and beliefs, but the fact remains that in spite of these results, associated with human effort during the past five hundred years in all spheres of remedial and curative activity, the standard of sensory appreciation, of general co-ordination, and of reliable use of the mechanisms of the organism has been and still is being gradually lowered, with the associated serious conditions which are apparent to-day on every hand.

I intend to deal with a wide range of more or less generally accepted statements and principles laid down by experts in these spheres, in an attempt to show my readers how they may arrive at a definite and reliable decision as to which method, system, or "cure" may prove satisfactory.

To a certain point I am in sympathy with all workers in either "physical," "mental," or "spiritual" spheres, for I believe that "there are more things in heaven and earth than are dreamt of in our philosophy," but it has always seemed to me that the first duty of man was and is to understand and develop those potentialities which are well within the sphere of his activities here on this earth. For this reason I intend, in this volume, to adhere to my earlier scheme of practical illustration, endeavouring, as far as possible, to give a demonstrable illustration in connexion with statements and arguments. This formula, I venture to predict, will prove to be more and more the rule and not the exception as we progress towards a plane of constructive, conscious guidance and control. It has two advantages over other formulas. In the first place, it forces the philosopher or teacher to give to the world practical procedures, which may be applied to the actual activities of life, instead of theoretical conclusions which too often have no practical bearing upon life. In the second place—and this is all-important—it transfers his work from the doubtful field of individual or collective opinion to the more reliable field of demonstrable conclusion, inasmuch as he is in duty bound to devote years of labour and investigation to the valuable but difficult process of converting to practical use each and every original idea (opinion). This is a process of years, but if at the end of each experiment he gives to the world only those ideas which he has succeeded in reducing to practical procedures, rejecting all others, he will be making a great contribution to humanity : he will be offering practical experiences in a field where for centuries we have too often been offered little but personal opinions. As the thesis of *Man's Supreme Inheritance* is unfolded, volume by volume, it will be found that it covers ground that has been smoothed or roughened, as the case may be, by numberless combats among adherents of the various theories which tend in practical application towards the separation instead of the unity of human potentialities; and that, on the constructive side, it provides principles which are fundamental to that condition of unity which we all agree should be inseparable from the processes of living. The subject matter of this book represents an endeavour to show that the great problems involved in the present condition of individual and national unrest demand for their solution a recognition, not only of their unity, but also of the unity of their underlying causes.

This reference to my thesis gives me an appropriate opening to lay before my readers the difficulty I have encountered in my attempts to set down, in a sufficiently clear and direct way, the results of my experiences in unfamiliar fields. This difficulty lies in the fact that the adequate description of these experiences, for purposes of practical application, calls for new and more comprehensive words than we have at our command. It is obvious that the most appropriate word (or words) chosen in order to convey an idea, will prove inadequate to express the aggregate, after an element that is new has been added to the idea. In such a case, we are forced either to use a word (or words) which is inadequate, or to coin one in an attempt to express adequately the expanded idea.

Expanding ideas are the forerunners of human advancement. The conveyance of the knowledge concerned with expanding ideas, whether by the written or spoken word, calls urgently for the recognition of the fact that expanding ideas demand new words which will adequately express the original as well as the new thought or thoughts involved.

This book is really the second volume of *Man's Supreme Inheritance* and I have named it *Constructive Conscious Control of the Individual*. I am offering constructive arguments and a constructive plan, and the fact that I have indulged freely in destructive criticism does not affect this statement, for a consideration of the needs and aims of such a book reveals at once that this is a necessity. It will be found that my criticism is directed solely towards what I believe to be the impeding factors in our progress towards a constructive plan of life and education.

The preparation of the subject matter of this book has proved a very difficult task, in which I have needed considerable assistance, and I take this opportunity to express my gratitude to Professor John Dewey for the invaluable suggestions he made after reading the manuscript; to my assistants, Miss Ethel Webb and Miss Irene Tasker, for their valuable help in and their untiring devotion to the work of revising and preparing the subject matter for publication; to Dr. Peter Macdonald and to the Rev. W. G. Pennyman for assisting me by reading the manuscript and offering criticism; to Miss Mary Olcott for undertaking the responsibility connected with the correction of the proofs; and to Miss Edith Lawson and Miss Carla Atkinson for their help in connexion with proofs and typescripts. To each and all of these I owe a deep debt of gratitude.

F. MATTHIAS ALEXANDER.

16 *Ashley Place,*
   Westminster, London.

PREFACE

(reprinted from the 1955 Edition)

MANKIND to-day stands at bay. In the world outside himself his plans and schemes have not worked out as he expected. Theories and beliefs faithfully held have failed when brought to the test of actual practice. Hence it is not unreasonable to conclude that even if the bases of these theories and beliefs were sound, man's reaction in translating them into practice has led him into error and consequent failure.

One thing is certain. The bridging of the gap between theory, with its associated beliefs, and practice, depends at every step upon the human element, for it is the nature of the reaction of the individual engaged in the task of this bridging—the carrying-out of the plan or theory—that will determine the measure of success or failure. The all-important consideration, therefore, in bridging the gap between theory and practice is the make-up of the individual, particularly the sensory make-up. The manner of the use and functioning of the psycho-physical mechanisms responsible for his reactions in carrying out the activities required for this bridging (as for all his activities) depends upon the nature of the registering of sensations and experiences, and, where this registering is trustworthy, the beliefs and judgments which result may be correspondingly trustworthy, but not otherwise.

The high estimate I hold of the part played by the human sensorium in the use and functioning of the self will be clear from this book, for its four parts are devoted to Sensory Appreciation in its Relation to Man's Evolutionary Development, Learning to Do, Man's Needs, and Happiness. In an interesting passage quoted in my book *The Use of the Self* (pp. 105–6), Sir Arthur Eddington points out that religious belief is based upon experience, but goes on to admit that " there is such a thing as illusion," and that not " every experience is to be taken at face value." Hence it may be of interest and value to give consideration to the use and functioning of the human self that makes possible the registering of experience upon which religious and other beliefs are based. Certain it is that without the functioning of the human sensorium this registration would not be possible, and hence it will be seen how all-essential it is that the human sensorium should function as a reliable register in order to minimize the effect of sensory illusion in the forming and assessing the validity of the beliefs upon which our judgment of reality depends.

The nature of this functioning determines the nature of this registration, and this in turn determines the nature of the experience upon which belief is based, and is, therefore, the forerunner of all we finally accept in arriving at our judgment in the matter of reality. If the Leaders in the religious life of the past and the Prophets had given due recognition to this in assessing the nature and value of the experiences upon which they believed religious and other beliefs should be based, their followers would not have been so frequently led into error by mistaking illusion for reality. Instead, they might have been led to unknown experiences far beyond the present limit of human conception of experience, as they passed from the instinctive to the conscious in changing and improving the use and functioning of the human self.

In this connexion I think it may be of general interest to quote the following passage from *The Thought and Character of William James* * by Ralph Barton Perry which shows the attitude of William James towards sensory experience. Professor Perry writes :—

> " In speaking, first, of James's sensibility, I do not mean his susceptibility to feeling or emotion, but the acuity of his *senses*—the voluminousness and richness of the experience which he received through them, and the prominence of that experience and of its underlying motive in his life as a whole. . . . His psychological writings testify to his discrimination of organic sensations.
> " Having a high sensuous endowment and being avid of sensory experience, it is not surprising that he should have felt such experience to convey the authentic revelation of reality. It is the unsaid but fundamental premise of his whole metaphysics that only he can speak authoritatively of the universe who is most sensitively attuned to it. Metaphysics is an apprehending of reality in its most immediate and lifelike aspect, or a listening to hear ' the pulse of Being beat.' When he said that he found ' no good warrant for even suspecting the

existence of any reality of a higher denomination than that
distributed and strung-along and flowing sort of reality which
we finite beings swim in,' he was placing his ultimate reliance
on the human sensorium." *

This is of particular interest to me because a member of the
medical profession, a close friend of William James, had interested
him enough in my work to persuade him to come to me in
London for a course of lessons. Unfortunately, unforeseen
circumstances interfered with this plan, so I did not have the
pleasure and honour of numbering him among my pupils. For
me this has been a lifelong regret, because, from what this friend
told me, there can be little doubt that much could have been
done to help him to enlarge his experience by means which would
tend to restore trustworthiness to the sensory processes which
were more or less untrustworthy, and bring the psycho-physical
processes which activated his "high sensuous endowment"
under conscious control, thus enabling him to bridge the gap
between the instinctive and the conscious way of living.

I am emboldened to make this claim because of the knowledge
I have gained through the evolution of my technique, first in
teaching myself and then in my long experience of teaching
others. As my technique evolved it became increasingly clear
that by its procedures provision is made for coming into contact
with the unknown, because the improved condition of psycho-
physical functioning brought about is not the result of working
for a previously conceived and directed end (the known), but
emerges as the indirect result of the employment of reasoned
means whereby improved conditions in the use of the self are
brought about (the unknown). This result does not come about
by inducing self-hypnotism, or because of some chance happen-
ing, as, for instance, the coming into contact with an outside
influence, personal or otherwise, or the possession of some natural
aptitude (habitual reaction) which is fitted to produce a certain
desired result. In all these cases instinct rather than the thinking and reasoning processes is relied upon, whereas " reasoning
from the known to the unknown," as in my technique, depends
upon the conscious employment of means that conform to
biological, physiological, and other laws known to us; in which,

* Vol. II, pp. 682–3. Quoted by the courtesy of Little, Brown & Co.,
Boston. (1935.)

also, the observation of phenomena in cause and effect can be tested according to strict scientific method, so that, as Dr. Dewey writes in his Introduction, " the causes that are used to explain the consequences, or effects, can be concretely followed up to show that they actually produce these consequences and not others."

To-day I do not know of any person who doubts that if man is to evolve in the right direction, the gap between instinctive and conscious control of the self must be bridged, in order to bridge " the gap between idealistic theory and actual practice." During the past fifty years I have had a unique experience in helping men and women in many walks of life to do this, by employing their conscious reasoning processes in changing and improving their human sensorium as they pass from known (wrong) to unknown (right) experiences of their use of themselves. Moreover and all-important, the prerequisite to each step in this process was the restoration of trustworthiness to the human sensorium without which a human being could not register experience so as to be able to test its validity.

The untrustworthiness of the sensory appreciation of the people of this age is demonstrable, and will be found to be extreme in the rapidly increasing number of people afflicted with so-called " mental " and criminal tendencies. Few people would accept as trustworthy the experiences related to them by any person who was a so-called " mental " case, and by the same token we should be wise not to accept " at face value " the experiences of anyone else, or place implicit confidence in the judgment and conclusions based on these experiences, unless we have good reason for believing that the sensorium of that person is a trustworthy guide in functioning and in registering impressions.

Summed up, the foregoing meets the well-known point at issue between the adherents of science and of religion, the scientist finding fault because of the want of what he calls " operational verification " of the experiences of the unknown upon which religious faith is based, and the adherents of religion claiming that many of their experiences, although not verifiable objectively, should not on that account be rejected by the scientist, for they are none the less real.

My earnest plea is for the unprejudiced consideration of the education that I have advocated for the gaining of unknown experiences in the improvement in the use of self. This is an education equally for the adult as for the child, and involves improvement of the nature of their sensory appreciation as an essential training for a more trustworthy registration of any other experiences which may come to them, so minimizing their present liability to fall into error even if they inherit a " high sensuous endowment " such as Professor Perry tells us that William James possessed.

It is true that dependence upon instinctive reaction meets the needs of the animal kingdom, but the world crisis of our day serves to show that such dependence no longer meets man's needs when he tries to translate into practice his idealistic theories with regard to self-improvement, growth, and progress.

F. Matthias Alexander.

16 *Ashley Place,*
  London, S.W. 1.

PART I

SENSORY APPRECIATION IN ITS RELATION TO MAN'S EVOLUTIONARY DEVELOPMENT

Inadequacy of Subconscious Guidance and Control to Meet the Rapid Changes of Civilized Life

IN the interest of readers who may not be familiar with the thesis of my earlier book, *Man's Supreme Inheritance*, I wish to point out that in the arguments therein set forth it was contended that human beings cannot progress satisfactorily in civilization whilst they remain dependent upon subconscious (instinctive) guidance and control; for the reason that in civilization—that is, in a plan of life where changes of environment have occurred and continue to occur more rapidly than in the uncivilized state—man's continued dependence upon precisely this subconscious guidance and control has resulted, either directly or indirectly, in the gradual development of imperfections and defects in the use of the human organism.

The effect of these rapid changes upon a creature, who heretofore had experienced only slow and gradual changes of environment and was still subconsciously guided and controlled, could hardly fail to be harmful, inasmuch as many of his instincts,[1] in consequence of these changes, came to survive their usefulness, whilst many of those new instincts which were developed during his *quick* attempts to meet the new demands of civilization proved to be unreliable. This degree of unreliability increased as time went on, until an observant minority became aware of a gradual but most serious deterioration, a deterioration, however, which unfortunately they recognized as a physical deterioration only, and which, at what

---

[1] The word "instinct" is used in this work to indicate established habits, inherited or developed. As I wrote in *Man's Supreme Inheritance* (chapter vi): " I define instinct as the result of the accumulated subconscious experiences of man at all stages of his development, which continue with us until, singly or collectively, we reach the stage of conscious control."

must be considered a psychological moment in human development, they attempted to set right by the adoption of " physical exercises."

For all who are concerned with the urgency of present-day problems the point of interest in the foregoing lies in the fact that man has been and still is unable to adapt himself quickly enough to the increasingly rapid changes involved in that plan of life which we call civilization. It will be generally conceded, I think, that the results of man's attempts to adapt himself to this plan of life, as they are manifested to-day in the general make-up of the organism of the human creature and in the application of this organism to all the activities of life, are unsatisfactory and most disappointing. It is only necessary to read the daily papers and note the records of crime, of unbalanced human thought and activity in all spheres, of the " trial-and-error " methods of our leaders in their efforts at reform in politics, social conditions, industry, religion, and education, in order to be firmly convinced of the comparative failure of our plan of life, and of the shortcomings of the different institutions which are part and parcel of it.

In order, then, to arrive at correct conclusions concerning man's comparative failure to adapt himself satisfactorily to the changing conditions of civilization, it will be necessary to make an examination and comparison of the evolutionary processes which obtained in the savage state and those which are operative in the civilized state to-day.

At this juncture I wish to make clear the sense in which I use the word *psycho-physical*. The term *psycho-physical* is used both here and throughout my works to indicate the impossibility of separating " physical " and " mental " operations in our conception of the working of the human organism. As I wrote in *Man's Supreme Inheritance*, " In my opinion the two must be considered entirely interdependent, and even more closely knit than is implied by such a phrase." Hence I use the term *psycho-physical activity* to indicate all human manifestations, and *psycho-physical mechanism* to indicate the instrument which makes these manifestations possible.

Psycho-physical activity must not, however, always be considered as involving equal action and reaction of the processes concerned, for, as I hope to show, the history of the stages of man's development reveals manifestations of human activity which, at certain stages, show a preponderance on what is called the " physical "

side, and at other stages a preponderance on what is called the
" mental " side.

I am forced to use the words " physical " and " mental " here
and throughout my argument because there are no other words at
present which adequately express the manifestations of psycho-
physical activity present at these various stages, not in any sense
because the " physical " and the " mental " can be separated as
such.   I wish, therefore, to make it clear that whenever I use the
word " mental," it is to be understood as representing all processes
or manifestations which are generally recognized as not wholly
" physical," and vice versa the word " physical " as representing all
processes and manifestations which are generally recognized as not
wholly " mental."

Comparison of Evolutionary Processes in the Savage and Civilized States

In the first place, it is important to remember that during
the animal and savage stages of evolution [1] the processes concerned with development were processes which operated very
slowly; indeed, experts assure us that it took millions of years
of the evolutionary process to produce the animal, not to speak
of the savage.   Each later stage of development was the result
of the experiences undergone by the creature in the process of
satisfying the new and varying needs arising during his progress
from the savage to the civilized state, and years of repetition of
these experiences were probably needed to establish them as
part and parcel of what is understood as instinct, for, on a
subconscious plane of development, continuous repetition is
essential to the establishment of instinctive accuracy.

In obedience to the fundamental law of self-preservation, the
animal and the savage were forced, day by day, to make use of
their mechanisms in securing the food and drink necessary to
their existence and in attempting to thwart the designs of their
common enemies.   The evolutionary processes associated with
these varying experiences, essential to the continued existence

---

[1] In this book the word evolution is used to indicate all processes
which are involved in the quickening of the potentialities of the creature
at the different stages of growth and development, and which are
necessary to the success of his attempts to satisfy the varying needs of
an ever-changing environment, and to reach a plane of constructive
conscious control of the individual organism.

and development of the organism, ensured that comparatively desirable combination in human activity, namely, an adequate and correct [1] use of the psycho-physical organism *as a whole*, together with an adequate use at the same time of the parts of that organism.

This meant that the creature reached the stage of his development to which we shall refer as the beginning of civilization, endowed with mechanisms functioning subconsciously in accordance with the dictates of instinct, which was the product of experiences gained at an earlier stage in connexion with the evolutionary processes we have outlined. At this earlier stage the demands made upon the creature were such that he could meet them satisfactorily by the subconscious use of the mechanisms involved, for his environment rarely changed, his needs remained practically the same, and in this comparatively static environment he would be able to meet a need satisfactorily by the slowly operating forces at his command.

But the attempts of the creature to meet the demands of the civilized state called for a higher and still higher standard in the development of his potentialities. Here his most trying problem arose from the fact that his environment continued to change at an increasingly rapid pace, and that these changes brought about a more rapid development of new needs. The response to the stimuli resulting from these new needs had to be a much quicker response than any in his previous experience, for progress in growth and development under the civilizing plan involved ever-increasing needs and called for a correspondingly increasing speed in the matter of response to stimuli.

Furthermore—and this is all-important—the demands thus made upon the psycho-physical processes, generally called mental processes, which were comparatively unused in his case, were destined to increase very rapidly, whilst the demands made upon the psycho-physical processes, generally called physical processes, which were comparatively highly developed in his case, were destined to decrease, and their spheres of activity actually to become more and more limited with the

---

[1] When I use such terms as " adequate " and " correct " in connexion with the manner of use of the psycho-physical organism, it must be understood that they indicate conditions of psycho-physical functioning which are the best at any given time for the working of the organism *as a whole*.

advance of time. These experiences indicate that in order to meet satisfactorily the new demands of civilization, *it was essential that man should acquire a new way of directing and controlling the mechanisms of the psycho-physical organism as a whole*, mechanisms which in the savage state had been kept up, of necessity, to a high standard of co-ordination by their use in securing the creature's daily food and in meeting the great " physical " demands of this mode of life. This serves to indicate that at some period of his evolutionary progress the human creature must have reached a psychological moment to pass from the subconscious to the conscious plane of control.

The change from a subconscious to a conscious plane of control would have involved a knowledge on man's part of the *means whereby* he would be able to command a conscious, reasoning direction and control of his psycho-physical mechanisms in all activity. With this knowledge the human creature would have had some chance of meeting satisfactorily the increasing demands of his ever-changing environment, and of commanding a continuous growth and development of the organism itself, that marvellous psycho-physical instrument which holds within itself the potentialities for the satisfying of such demands.

Unfortunately, the process of reasoning out the " means-whereby " in connexion with the gaining of his " ends " [1] was

---

[1] I judge from the numerous queries received from readers of *Man's Supreme Inheritance* that many people are not quite clear as to what is meant by the expressions " means-whereby " and " end-gaining." In the endeavour to make my meaning clear, I would point out that whenever a person sets out to achieve a particular " end " (whether this " end " is the development of potentialities or the eradication of defects, peculiarities, or misuse) his procedure will be based on one of two principles which I have called the " end-gaining " and the " means-whereby " principles.

The " end-gaining " principle involves a direct procedure on the part of the person endeavouring to gain the desired " end." This direct procedure is associated with dependence upon subconscious guidance and control, leading, in cases where a condition of mal-co-ordination is present, to an unsatisfactory use of the mechanisms and to an increase in the defects and peculiarities already existing.

The " means-whereby " principle, on the other hand, involves a reasoning consideration of the causes of the conditions present, and an indirect instead of a direct procedure on the part of the person endeavouring to gain the desired " end." This indirect procedure is that psycho-physical activity, associated with constructive conscious guidance and not and evidently could not have been adequately established as a habit in the human creature at this psychological moment in his development, else a consideration of the "means-whereby" of his development under savage conditions would have led him to a due consideration of these "means-whereby" in their relation to satisfactory development under civilized conditions, and he would then have realized that the demands made upon him in the civilized state must necessarily be different in many ways from those made upon him in a savage state.

Hence, whilst it was desirable that the change from the subconscious to the conscious plane of control should have taken place, it is evident that man had not reached that advanced stage of evolution which would have made it possible for him to effect it, for experience shows that, although, with the advance of civilization, conditions have continually changed and become more and more complex, man's fundamental psycho-physical method of adapting himself to these changing conditions has remained the same, with the unsatisfactory and disappointing results to which I have referred.

Complexity and Complications of Civilized Life

People attempt to account for the difficulties of civilized life by saying, "Life is so complex!" This means that, though they are conscious of the presence of an undue stress and strain, they are prepared for the most part to accept the position, and consequently live on with the conviction that a growing complexity is the natural result of civilized life. What they fail to recognize is that this condition is the result of their own or others' ill-considered, end-gaining attempts to surmount the difficulties encountered during the progress of civilization. This serves to show how the egotism of the average human being is developed out of all proportion to the degree of successful endeavour that he can legitimately claim for himself. This

control and with the consequent satisfactory use of the mechanisms, which establishes the conditions essential to the increasing development of potentialities. Under these conditions defects, peculiarities, and misuse are not likely to be present within the organism.

In this connexion I wish it to be understood that throughout this book I use the term conscious guidance and control to indicate, primarily, a plane to be reached rather than a method of reaching it.

fact, however, rarely seems to reach his sphere of consciousness, and hence the improbability of his awakening to his own individual shortcomings, an awakening which would lead him to attempt to reach that desirable stage of consciousness and reasoning where he would have the conviction borne in upon him that

> The fault, dear Brutus, is not in our stars,
> But in ourselves,

not in the complexity of the civilizing plan, but in our un-reasoning attitude towards its demands, an attitude associated with a continued dependence upon subconscious guidance and direction in our " end-gaining " attempts to meet these demands.

The prevailing condition of stress and strain caused by these attempts is harmful to the organism as a whole, and if it con-tinues to increase as rapidly as in the past, it is likely so to undermine our reserve forces that the most serious forms of organic derangement and kinæsthetic perversion may be pre-dicted. Indeed, we might say that a dangerous stage of per-version and delusion has already been reached, when the attempts at solution of all the problems of life seem to call for complexity rather than simplicity in procedure. We even reach a stage when the most simple " means-whereby " in accomplishment become the most difficult. A very interesting instance in this connexion occurred in my teaching experience. A well-known man of scientific attainments had great difficulty for some days with a simple, practical problem of psycho-mechanics concerned with his re-education. When he came to his lesson one morning he said : " I know now what is the matter with us all. This work of yours is too simple for us ! "

In fact, the complexity needlessly introduced into the act of living in general is equalled only by the complexity which we build up individually in our attempts at accomplishment in specific spheres, as, for instance, in the sphere of education (taking this word in its widest sense, whether in learning some-thing or in learning to do something), and also in any process of self-instruction. All acts concerned with learning something or learning to do something call for psycho-physical activity, and the standard of efficiency in these spheres depends in every case upon the standard of the creature's satisfactory employ-ment of his psycho-physical self in the performance of these acts. The imperfectly co-ordinated [1] child or adult, for instance, will not be likely to reach the standard of effective functioning enjoyed by the satisfactorily co-ordinated child or adult. The former will experience difficulties with which the the latter will not be beset.

In the case of the imperfectly co-ordinated child or adult, there may be said to be serious complications in his psychomechanics; in other words, the mechanical working of the structures of the organism is out of order, and complications and difficulties, therefore, are inevitable. On the other hand, in the case of the satisfactorily co-ordinated child or adult, the mechanical working of the structures of the organism is not complicated but complex, in the sense that, although there are present a large number of factors or means which are related to one another (like the different parts in the mechanism of a motor car), the act of using them (like the act of driving a car or any other machine in running order) is one and simple. Satisfactory psycho-physical activity depends upon psychomechanical structures which are complex, but of which the mechanical working does not become complicated until the mechanism get out of order.

Take, for instance, the simple act of learning to write. In the case of the average badly co-ordinated pupil there will be present certain impeding factors (into the detail of which we

---

[1] The word *co-ordination* is ordinarily used at the present time in as narrow and limited a sense as the words relaxation, readjustment, re-education, etc. In view of this fact, I consider it necessary to give some idea of the more comprehensive sense in which it is used in this work.

I use the word *co-ordination*, both in its conception and in its application, to convey the idea of co-ordination *on a general and not a specific basis*. Specific co-ordination of any specific part of the organism, such as the muscles of the arm or leg, may be brought about by means of a direct process, during which process, however, new defects in the use of the organism in general will certainly be cultivated, whilst others already present will become more pronounced. These harmful conditions will not be cultivated if the specific co-ordination is brought about by means of an indirect process involving, primarily, the general co-ordination of the psycho-physical organism—that is to say, an integrated condition in which all the factors continue to make for satisfactory psychomechanical use.

This distinction between the specific and the general applies also to the terms readjustment, re-education, and relaxation as I use them in this book, for in general re-education specific defects are eradicated in process.

will enter later on) on account of which learning to write becomes a comparatively complicated proceeding. However expert the teacher may be, the pupil does not possess the psycho-physical equipment which would enable him to take adequate advantage of the instructions given to him. His first attempt to carry these out will reveal defects, and the subsequent attempts new defects. Each request from his teacher to do something, and each injunction not to do something else, means a building-up of a series of specific psycho-physical acts to-wards the given " end "—namely, learning to write. This means that although the " end " may be gained, the result *as a whole* will not be as satisfactory as it might be, for nothing will have been done in the way of re-education on a general basis to correct the mal-co-ordinated conditions connected with the use and control of the mechanisms when employed in the act of writing. In the endeavour to overcome the impeding factors concerned, the teacher builds up for the pupil a complicated procedure in order to gain the specific " end." For the act of writing demands correct direction and control in the use of the fingers, wrist, and arm, and the standard of success reached in these particulars depends upon the co-ordinated use of the mechanisms *in general.*[1]

Co-ordinated use of the organism means that there is satis-factory control of a complex mechanism. In a reasoned plan of life the human creature would be in the enjoyment of a co-ordinated use of the whole organism and, comparatively speak-ing, there would not be any impeding factors, such as we have indicated, to be overcome. The pupil would have at command a satisfactory psycho-mechanical organism—that is, he would

---

[1] As I wrote in *Man's Supreme Inheritance* in connexion with drawing :—

"Any attentive and thoughtful observer who will watch the movement and position of these children's fingers, hand, wrist, arm, neck, and body generally, during the varying attempts to draw straight or crooked lines, cannot fail to note the lack of co-ordination between these parts. The fingers are probably attempt-ing to perform the duties of the arm, the shoulders are humped, the head twisted on one side. In short, energies are being pro-jected to parts of the mechanism which have little or no influence on the performance of the desired act of drawing, and the mere waste projection of such energies alone is almost sufficient to nullify the purpose in view."

possess the psycho-physical equipment necessary for the ready assimilation of the teacher's instructions—and, if these instructions were correct, their assimilation would enable the pupil to reason out the " means-whereby " to the desired " end," which would then be gained in that simple and easy manner characteristic of all successful accomplishment.

Recognition and Satisfaction of Essential Needs in Relation to Evolutionary Progress

In the foregoing I have attempted to indicate the urgency of the problems concerned with the evolutionary progress of the human creature—an urgency which will be generally conceded —and a consideration of the psycho-physical " means-whereby " of such progress may be helpful at this point.

Satisfactory evolutionary progress demands a continuous advancement, in individual psycho-physical activity, from stage to stage of cultivation and development.   The primary desire or need in this connexion is that individual desire or need which is the stimulus to the development of those psycho-physical potentialities which enable the creature to meet satisfactorily the demands of the processes essential to the satisfaction of the need.   *The adequate development of these potentialities connotes a satisfactory standard of the co-ordinated use of the organism.*

It is obvious that a person who is satisfied with his present position on the evolutionary plane, with his present ideas, opinions, ways of life, etc., will not have the desire or feel the need for changing conditions which, consciously or subconsciously, he deems to be satisfactory.   All advancement, however, is associated with the discovery and acceptance of ideas, principles, ways of living, etc., which are new to the individual. Anyone who has established a desire to live on, influenced only by past psycho-physical experiences, and who refuses to seek consciously for and to acquire new experiences, cannot expect any real advancement on the evolutionary plane.

In such a case there are present impeding factors, such as a narrow outlook, a condition of rigidity, an undue dread of psycho-physical changes, a lack of reasoning in the sphere of guidance and control, etc., all of which tend to prevent the subject from conceiving of or seeing or accepting anything outside his present experiences, these experiences being the sum total of the experiences which he has inherited (represented by his race instincts) plus his comparatively limited individual experience in every-day life.

The establishment of psycho-physical conditions here indicated means that a number of perversions have been built up subconsciously in the human creature's use of himself in everyday activity, and, as a result, many individuals, sooner or later, become aware of the presence of some shortcoming. It is probable that only one in twenty of such shortcomings ever reaches the sphere of consciousness, and so he continues to exist within a danger zone of psycho-physical shortcomings of which he is not conscious, but which impede his progress at every turn.

Mind-Wandering Recognized as a Shortcoming—Its Relation to Self-Preservation

The shortcoming to which the individual will awaken will be one which interferes with his immediate activities outside himself, in reading, for instance, or when he is attempting to learn something, or to learn to do something, and, as a matter of fact, the shortcoming that has been recognized as interfering more than any other in this connexion is the shortcoming concerned with his inability, as he would put it, to " keep his mind " on the particular work with which he is immediately engaged; in other words, the shortcoming which is commonly known as " mind-wandering."

Now, what is "mind-wandering"? In the attempt to answer this query, we will begin with a consideration of the psycho-physical processes concerned with direction and control within the human creature in the all-important sphere of self-preservation.

In the beginning of things all growth and development must surely have resulted from a form of consciousness [1] of need.

---

[1] Many readers may not agree with me on this point, but it will be seen that all that is necessary to my argument is a recognition of the place of need, the requirement of a new way of linking up with environment, so that the rest of my argument is not affected by belief or disbelief on this point.

For the growth and development of the creature are and always have been associated with new experiences which involve new activities. These activities—the response to some stimulus or stimuli—result from the consciousness of some need or needs within or without the organism, the presence and recognition of need being essential to the evolutionary process.

The recognition of a need denotes a state of consciousness of a need, and the primary activity (or activities) which is the response to this consciousness of a need or needs involves new experiences in the spheres of direction and control. The process of evolution depends upon the continuous repetition of such primary experiences, or group of experiences, this repetition resulting in the establishment of a use (or what is termed habit or instinct) and in the satisfaction of the need or needs.

In connexion with the theory of conscious activity in the early stages of the creature's development, we should recall the time when a pair of eyes, for instance, became a need. It is quite conceivable that after the consciousness of this need had arisen, the growth and development of the organs of sight may have occupied a thousand or more years. It is also conceivable that when the eyes had become developed, it may have needed a conscious effort, perhaps of years, to open the eyelids [1] and likewise to close them, and that the repetition of this conscious effort, week by week, month by month, and year by year, may have caused this function of the eyelids to become habitual and subconscious, and to develop to that wonderful standard of use now enjoyed by the creature.

There can be little doubt that self-preservation (taking the word in its broadest sense) was the most fundamental of the creature's needs, for, first and foremost, the creature itself needed protection and preservation during its attempts to satisfy its specific needs.

This need for self-preservation called for that satisfactory direction and control with which, in this sphere, we find wild animals and savages equipped, inasmuch as, owing to the particular circumstances which obtained in their case, the response to any stimulus arising from a need would be satisfactory in the spheres of direction and control—that is, it would be a response which would enable the creature to employ

---

[1] I am quite aware, of course, that sensitiveness to light, likewise the eyes, developed long before there were any eyelids.

what would be for him the most satisfactory " means-whereby " to securing the essential " end," self-preservation.

Most of us are aware of the marvellous accuracy in the use of the organism manifested by the wild animal or the savage in the various familiar spheres of activity concerned with self-preservation. The civilized creature does not manifest anything like the same standard of accuracy in the employment of the organism in the spheres of activity concerned with self-preservation. In other words, the civilized human being does not enjoy the same standard of effective direction and control as the savage and the wild animal, and it is the lack of this adequate standard in the human creature which manifests itself as a shortcoming in some sphere of activity, and, as I have said, in the sphere of learning something and learning to do something, the shortcoming most frequently recognized is that known as " mind-wandering."

Now there exists a close connexion between the shortcoming which is recognized as " mind-wandering " and the shortcoming which manifests itself as a seriously weakened response to a stimulus to an act (or acts) of self-preservation. To make this connexion clear, we have only to consider the psycho-physical processes involved in these two shortcomings to realize that in both cases these processes are the same.

For the lack underlying these two shortcomings is the lack of an adequate standard of direction and control in the human creature, manifesting itself, in the one case, in the broad sphere of self-preservation and, in the other, in the specific sphere of learning something or learning to do something.

An act of self-preservation is the response to a stimulus (or stimuli) resulting from a fundamental need, and a satisfactory response depends upon the satisfactory direction and control of the psycho-physical mechanisms which are engaged in the act or acts of self-preservation.

An attempt to learn something or to learn to do something is the natural response to a stimulus (or stimuli) resulting from a wish or need to learn something or to learn to do something, and a satisfactory response depends upon the satisfactory direction and control of the psycho-physical mechanisms which are engaged in the acts of learning or learning to do something.

It will thus be seen that the processes involved in the acts concerned with self-preservation, or with learning or learning to do something, are precisely the same, and it follows that, if in the sphere of self-preservation the direction and control are unsatisfactory, the response to the stimuli concerned with the needs of self-preservation will be unsatisfactory; and, by the same rule, if in the sphere of learning and learning to do, the direction and control are unsatisfactory, the response to the stimuli concerned with the wish or needs in connexion with the acts of attempting to learn something or of learning to do something will likewise be unsatisfactory, and this unsatisfactory response is manifested in everyday life in that short-coming, so common in our time, called " mind-wandering."

We have now reached the point where we must consider the origin of the conception which led to our giving to this particular manifestation the name of " mind-wandering."

A person decides to learn something or to learn to do something. The conception involved in this decision immediately starts a series of activities of the psycho-physical mechanisms involved, those concerned with direction and control being of vital importance to a satisfactory result, which, in this instance, is the ability to learn something or to learn to do something.

Where a person succeeds in this connexion, he is not likely to become conscious of such a shortcoming as " mind-wandering," for the success of his attempt means that his conception of the act to be performed involves the employment of satisfactory *means whereby* he will be able to gain his desired " end." In such a case the activities of the psycho-physical mechanisms involved in his attempt will be the result of satisfactory direction and control.

On the other hand, where a person does not succeed in his attempt to learn something or to learn to do something, the failure of his attempt means that there are defects in his conception of the act to be performed, in the sense that this conception does not involve the employment of satisfactory *means whereby* he will be able to gain his desired " end." In such a case the activities of the psycho-physical mechanisms involved in his attempts will be the result of unsatisfactory direction and control, resulting in a *misdirected* use of the psycho-physical mechanisms, and hence his inability to keep them operating on the satisfactory *means whereby* he will be able to gain his desired " end." The whole procedure is an attempt to communicate with points of vantage along lines of communication which are unreliable, resulting in a shortcoming which reaches the consciousness of the ordinary person as an inability to attend to, or, as we say, to " keep the mind upon " the work in hand; and hence it is called " mind-wandering."

As a matter of fact, the defective use of the mechanisms which is responsible for such conditions cannot be adequately described as " mind-wandering," seeing that it is the manifestation of a harmful and misdirected action and reaction, not only in connexion with those processes commonly spoken of as " mind," but *throughout the whole psycho-physical organism*. It is the manifestation of that imperfectly co-ordinated condition which is associated with an unreliable sense of feeling (sensory appreciation) concerned with unsatisfactory direction and control, and which, in the course of its development, has gradually weakened the response of the human creature to stimuli in the sphere of self-preservation.

In this connexion it is important to remember that the savage creature depended chiefly upon the sense of feeling in the spheres of direction and control, and, as his sense of feeling (sensory appreciation) was comparatively reliable, the activities thus directed and controlled would be associated with an *increasing* response to the stimulus for self-preservation.

The civilized creature also depends chiefly upon the sense of feeling in the spheres of direction and control, but, as the sense of feeling (sensory appreciation) in his case has now become harmfully unreliable, the activities thus directed and controlled are becoming more and more associated with a *weakening* response to the stimulus to self-preservation.

This all points to a general weakening in the psycho-physical directing and controlling forces of the human creature,[1] a

[1] The fact that an individual happens to exhibit satisfactory specific direction and control in some particular activity does not confute this statement; indeed, only serves to strengthen it, as I shall endeavour to show throughout the pages of this book.

In this connexion I have found in my professional work that too often a person will consider a psycho-physical experience to be quite satisfactory when I, as an expert, know it to be in reality unsatisfactory. In such a case the supposedly satisfactory experience is a delusive and harmful experience, on the part of the person concerned, of feeling and thinking he is right when he is actually wrong. In fact, the experience is really an unsatisfactory one, but he does not know it; and so, when weakening which has been brought about by the fact that man has continued to depend upon subconscious guidance in his endeavours to meet the demands of the civilizing plan, and to rely upon instincts which have survived their usefulness and upon the harmful guidance of defective sense registers (feeling).

Experience follows experience in the human creature's activities, some of these experiences satisfactory, but the majority unsatisfactory, and the creature may be satisfied for the moment, only to be again dissatisfied, however, with the varying results of attempted accomplishment; and the psycho-physical experiences involved do not make for confidence in regard to any attempts which he may be forced to make in the future to meet the demands of civilization.

When conditions such as these are present in the human creature, success is hardly possible; indeed, failure will be almost certain to result, even though he may devote to the accomplishment of his aims the time deemed necessary to ensure success. The natural result of his experiences of failure or comparative failure is that in time he will come to give consideration to the cause or causes involved in these experiences, and this consideration is of special interest to us, because it practically always leads him to the same conclusion—namely, that his failure is due to " mind-wandering."

Let us now follow out his consideration of the facts in detail. He sets out to learn something or to learn to do something and proceeds, as he would put it, to " give his mind to " his work, in accordance with his conception of this phrase. But he soon discovers that his " mind " is not " on his work," that it has become more occupied, as it were, with some other trend of thought. He therefore proceeds to make a special effort, as he would say, to " keep his mind on " the original task in hand.

Now it is highly probable that he has never given consideration to the " means-whereby " required for such a special effort, for if he had, he would probably have awakened to the fact that he did not have within his control the *means whereby* a special effort of this kind could prove satisfactory. However this may be, the fact remains that in spite of all his efforts to

later he becomes dissatisfied, he does not attribute his dissatisfaction to his own psycho-physical experiences, but to other people, surroundings, " something wrong somewhere," always believing the cause to be without instead of within the organism.

" keep his mind on " what he is doing, the process he thinks of as " mind-wandering " is repeated, with the result that after a certain number of repetitions of this experience, he becomes convinced that the cause of his failure is his *inability* to " keep his mind on " what he is doing.

Just think of the psycho-physical disaster that is here indicated, for it means that the human creature has reached that dangerous stage in connexion with the employment of his psycho-physical mechanisms when the response to a stimulus arising from a need is ineffective, erratic, and produces a state of confusion.

The seriousness of this inability of the human creature to " keep his mind on " what he is doing is widely recognized, and this recognition has led to the almost universal adoption of what is called concentration [1] as the cure for " mind-wandering." Unfortunately, this remedy, as I shall show later, is in itself a most harmful and delusive psycho-physical manifestation, and has been adopted without any consideration being taken of its effect upon the organism in general or of the psycho-physical processes involved in what is called " learning to concentrate."

Consideration of the Mechanism of the Human Psycho-Physical Organism in Relation to the Activities called Learning and Learning To Do

The foregoing will serve to indicate that in the sphere of learning something or learning to do something (as indeed, in connexion with all psycho-physical acts) there is an important problem to be solved if we are to progress to that standard of

---

[1] It is of interest to remember that the recognition of the defect called " mind-wandering " long antedated the conception of concentration as a remedy. I must refer my readers to the chapter on concentration for a fuller discussion of this important question. For the moment I wish merely to point out that I am not here objecting to concentration in the sense which implies a number of things going on, moving at the same time, and converging on a common consequence, a form of concentration which is present in the processes involved in the psycho-physical manifestations of the normal child at play and of the competent artisan or artist engrossed in his work, *and which simply implies a condition of co-ordination*. On the other hand, the form of concentration to which I am objecting is that which implies fixating on one thing, " bringing the mind to bear " on one object, for just the same reason that I object to that conception in education which seems to justify people in consider-

psycho-physical functioning and use which will enable us to meet satisfactorily the ever-increasing demands of an advancing civilization. Since, as we have seen, the standard of functioning in the performance of any psycho-physical acts depends upon the conception which influences the direction and control of the mechanisms involved, it is most essential to give consideration to this all-important matter of conception, in connexion with the understanding of what we wish to learn or learn to do, and also in connexion with that psycho-physical activity by means of which we are enabled to arrive at our conceptions concerned with learning and learning to do.

We will therefore go on to consider the mechanisms of the psycho-physical organism in relation to the activity called learning something.

First, for every form of psycho-physical activity there must be a stimulus. In considering the response to this stimulus, I would remind my readers that I do not separate " mental " and " physical " operations (manifestations) in my conception of the manner (" means-whereby ") of the functioning of the human organism. For how can we prove that the response to any stimulus is wholly " physical " or wholly " mental " ?

On the one hand, in what would ordinarily be considered purely physical spheres (the performance of " physical " acts), the standard of functioning depends

> (1) *upon the degree of correctness of the conception of the act to be performed,* and
> (2) *upon the degree of co-ordinated employment of the guiding and controlling orders or directions, and of the mechanisms involved in carrying out the activities essential to the correct means whereby the act can be performed.*

On the other hand, in what would ordinarily be considered purely mental spheres, the standard of functioning depends

> (1) *upon the degree of reliability of the sensory guidance and direction in the use of the mechanisms involved in conveying the stimuli primarily responsible for the psycho-physical processes concerned with conception,* and

---

ing the essential aim of educational procedure to be the securing of " ends " by *specific* methods (" end-gaining "), irrespective of the *means whereby* the psycho-physical mechanisms are employed *in general* during the attempts to gain these " ends."

(2) *upon the standard of co-ordination reached in the use of the whole organism.*

If the highest standard of so-called physical functioning is to be reached, there must be *co-ordinated employment of the muscular system through co-ordinated guidance, direction, and control by processes so-called mental, involving action and re-action in psycho-physical unity* and an adequate standard at all times of the vital functioning of the organism.

In the same way, as I am prepared to demonstrate later, if the highest standard of so-called mental functioning is to be reached, there must be *co-ordinated employment of those processes which are involved in the co-ordinated use of the so-called physical self, involving action and reaction in psycho-physical unity* and an adequate standard at all times of the vital functioning of the organism.[1]

It is clear, therefore, that no human activity can be said to be wholly " physical " or wholly " mental," but that all human activity, in whatever sphere, is psycho-physical activity, *the standard of individual functioning, both mental and physical so-called, being determined by the standard of co-ordinated use of the organism in general, the standard of this co-ordinated use being determined in its turn by the standard of co-ordinated employment of the psycho-physical processes concerned.*

Now psycho-physical activity is simply the response to some stimulus (or stimuli) received through the channel of the senses, of hearing, for instance, of sight, touch, feeling, etc., and the nature of the resulting conception and of the response, or psycho-physical reaction, will be determined by the standard of psycho-physical functioning present.

It then follows that *the process of conception, like all other forms of psycho-physical activity, is a process the course of which is determined by our psycho-physical condition at the time when the particular stimulus (or stimuli) is received.* We all know that

---

[1] We are all aware, for instance, that a sluggish liver does not make for the best use of the " mental " powers, and we know of people who, through bad habits of over-indulgence, have reached a stage of liver or kidney disorder when their reasoning processes have become seriously impaired and those of remembering practically ruined. If the vital functioning of the " physical " mechanisms and organs is for any reason inadequate, the organism, as a whole, becomes gradually more or less poisoned, with resulting gradual interference with the processes of remembering.

a man's conception of his present or future financial or other condition in life is quite different when he is, as we say, in a good and happy " frame of mind," from what it is when he has a " grouch." Again, the conception as to the outcome of a disaster or piece of good fortune in life will be quite different in the case of a man in enjoyment of good health from that of a man weakened by bad health.[1]

Influence of Sensory Appreciation Upon Conception in All Psycho-Physical Activity

This dependence of the process of conception upon the general psycho-physical condition is a factor of paramount importance. For if, as we contend, all so-called mental processes are mainly the result of sensory experiences in psycho-physical action and reaction, it will be obvious that in our conception of *how* to employ the different parts of the mechanism in the acts of everyday life *we are influenced chiefly by sensory processes* (feeling). Thus we may receive a stimulus through something we hear, something we touch, or through some other outside agency; in every case, the nature of our response, *whether it be an actual movement, an emotion, or an opinion,* will depend upon the associated activity, in action and reaction, of the processes concerned with conception and with the sensory and other mechanisms responsible for the " feeling " which we experience. This associated activity is referred to throughout my work as *sensory appreciation.*

Sensory Appreciation

This sensory appreciation is the factor upon which the baby, like the animal, depends for guidance in his first subconscious attempts to use the different parts of the mechanism, the success of these attempts depending upon the degree of reliability of the child's sensory appreciation, and I assert that wherever we find defects, peculiarities, etc., in children at a very early age, even in their first attempts at crawling, standing, walking, etc., these defects are present because the instinctive processes of such children are unreliable. It is my purpose

[1] The latter may usually be classed as a pessimist and the former as an optimist.

throughout this book to attempt to prove the truth of this contention, which is based on the results of a teaching experience of very many years; also to show that we must be prepared, in cases where the instinctive processes are unreliable, to restore the sensory appreciation to that standard of reliability upon which the adequacy of the functioning of all psychophysical processes depends.

A comprehensive understanding of sensory appreciation, of its enormous influence for good and evil in the development of the creature, and of its future bearing upon the progress of mankind, is therefore of the greatest importance to all, but especially to those interested in education, both in the sense of education in our schools and in the broadest sense of the word.

Sensory appreciation, from our point of view, has a much wider significance than is generally attributed to it. But it will be sufficient at this point to state that, taken even in the most limited sense, it includes all sensory experiences which are conveyed through the channels of sight, hearing, touch, feeling, equilibrium, movement, etc., and which are responsible for psycho-physical action and reaction throughout the organism.

If we raise an arm, move a leg, or if we make any other movements of the body or limbs, we are guided chiefly by our sensory appreciation or, as most people would put it, by our sense of feeling. This applies to the testing of the texture of a piece of cloth between one's fingers, or to the gauging of size, weight, distance, etc.—in fact, to the employment of the " physical " mechanisms in the processes of hearing, seeing, walking, talking, and in all the other activities of life.

The Human and the Inanimate Machine Compared and Contrasted

The function of sensory appreciation will be clear to us if we stop for a moment and consider the human organism as an animate machine, and compare its mechanical processes with those of an inanimate machine. The reliability of both machines is dependent upon the standard of reliability of their controlling, propelling, motor, and other mechanisms, the controlling factor taking first place as causing the other mechanical factors to work co-ordinately and to give the best results in practical use.

But the all-important difference from our standpoint between the animate and the inanimate machine lies in the quality and function of their respective controlling mechanisms. In the inanimate machine, the controlling mechanism is limited by the fixed nature of its own make-up, and by certain fixed conditions in the other mechanisms without which it cannot operate. In the animate machine, or human psycho-physical organism, the controlling mechanism is a wonderful psycho-physical process by means of which an almost unlimited use of the different units which make up the whole may be brought about, so that at one moment a correct use and at another an incorrect use may be commanded.

This psycho-physical process is that essential factor in satisfactory human development which we call sensory appreciation. When functioning adequately, this sensory appreciation has a wide field of operation, and our ability to reach the maximum of our potentialities depends upon the standard of its reliability. This being so, it will be obvious to the most casual observer that, if we are to continue to develop satisfactorily, our sensory appreciation of the working of the mechanisms concerned with the movements of our bodies and limbs in the activities of life must be reliable.

Unreliable Sensory Appreciation a Universal Defect

Unfortunately, we can prove by practical demonstration upon any person, adult or child, that the sensory appreciation of the people of our time is more or less unreliable and in the great majority of cases positively delusive.

Readers of *Man's Supreme Inheritance* will probably be convinced on this point without demonstration. If they are not, and will take the trouble, with the help of some friend, to make tests on themselves in the light of the facts given, they will assuredly be convinced.

Take the case of a person who persists in putting his head back whenever he makes an attempt to put his shoulders back. Ask him to put his head forward and keep his shoulders still, and it will be found that, as a rule, even though he may put his head forward as asked, he moves his shoulders also. Ask him to put his head forward whilst the teacher holds his shoulders still, and the pupil, as a rule, will put his head back instead of forward. In practically every instance, be the pupil adult or child, the attempt to carry out this simple request will be unsatisfactory, owing to the pupil's harmful interference with the general adjustment and use of the organism and limbs, due to unreliable sensory appreciation.

Similarly, if a pupil is asked to turn his toes out, it is my experience that, instead of taking the weight of his body on his heels in order to lift the front part of the feet to turn them out, he will, as a rule, throw the weight on to the balls of the feet and still attempt to lift the front part, or else he will move his heels in towards one another instead of turning out the toes. Point out one or other of these errors to the pupil, and he, as if aware of the delusive sensory appreciation which is responsible for these errors, at once looks down at his feet in order to try to *see how* to move them correctly.

Again, there are very few persons who, when asked to do such a simple thing as open the mouth, will not throw the head back, with the idea, as it were, of lifting the upper jaw away from the lower. This serves to show that they have not given any consideration to the psycho-physical use of the muscular and other mechanisms concerned with this act. If they had, they would have realized that there are subconscious processes continuously operative which keep the mouth closed, and, consequently, the first thing to do is to cause these processes to be inoperative, and so to bring about such relaxation of the muscular tension involved as would allow the jaw to drop. It does, in fact, commonly drop in the case of that type of idiot who is most often open-mouthed; whilst it is common knowledge that if a boxer receives a blow on the head, heavy enough to throw out the controlling gear, his jaw drops of itself and frequently remains dropped for a considerable time. When I ask a pupil to allow me to move his lower jaw away from the upper, he usually increases instinctively the tension that keeps the lower jaw in place. As I have frequently pointed out, an enormous aggregate waste of energy is involved in these constant and irrational tensions.

Many who are brought for the first time face to face with the fact that the sensory appreciation of most of the people of our time is more or less unreliable become unusually disturbed, especially when they realize that this fundamental factor in human activity has been practically ignored by our experts and leaders in educational and other spheres in their attempts to effect reforms in the civilizing plan.[1]

[1] This is indeed a fearful fact to ask the ordinary human being to face, and when in my professional sphere I have been forced to impress

The truth is, we have not given sufficient consideration to this essential matter. We have merely acted on the presumption, in the usual subconscious way, that if we have a potentiality such as sensory appreciation (feeling), it must as a matter of course be reliable.

Consideration of Three Stages of Man's Development in Relation to Deterioration of Sensory Appreciation

I will now endeavour to put before the reader certain facts concerning stages in the evolution of the human creature, when psycho-physical conditions became present which made for the gradual deterioration of sensory appreciation, indicating possible causes of this deterioration in our sense of feeling and in all our other senses.[1] I shall confine this consideration of man's development to three stages :—

    (1) the stage when he was guided chiefly by sensory appreciation ;

it upon my pupils, I have read in their faces the different ideas, opinions, and feelings evoked by my statement. Very often it has been evident that they have looked upon me almost as an enemy. For instance, I was recently discussing the point with a professional friend, who at once denied that our sensory appreciation was unreliable, and asked, " Why should Nature *permit* us to go wrong in such an essential ? " I agreed to answer this if he, on his part, would first explain to me why Nature *should* prevent us from going wrong, seeing that in the process of the creature's development in civilization even the simplest fundamentals of nature have been ignored. It was clear to me that my original statement had been a shock to my friend, and that his question was more an emotional reaction to this shock than the outcome of any process of reasoning, for he admitted later that until I had brought the matter up to him, he had never given thought to this question of unreliable sensory appreciation, and yet had disagreed with one who, as he knew, had not only been considering this subject for more than thirty years, but for more than twenty-five of these had been professionally engaged in demonstrating practically to his pupils the fact of their unreliable sensory appreciation.

[1] The factors which made for the establishment of reliable sensory appreciation, and for a continuously improving standard in this connexion, have been indicated in *Man's Supreme Inheritance*. The matter concerned with the technique of ploughing may suggest the kind of human experiences responsible for that early interference with the standard of functioning and use of the psycho-physical mechanisms, which lowers the standard of reliability of sensory appreciation. See *Man's Supreme Inheritance*, chapter : " Conscious Guidance and Control in Practice."

(2) the stage when he was developing the ability to inhibit in specific spheres, and was still, as we say, " physically fit " ;

(3) the stage when he had still further developed this inhibitory power in specific spheres, but had recognized a lower standard of " physical " fitness which called for a remedy.

Stage I

Uncivilized Stage :—

Standard of Sensory Appreciation Reliable and Satisfactory Conditions Maintained

We are all well aware of the higher standard of sensory appreciation (associated with all the sensory experiences involved in the general psycho-physical activities essential to a healthy existence) in the uncivilized as compared with the civilized state. In the stage we are considering the satisfactory condition of the savage creature was maintained by the constant use of the mechanisms in the limited spheres of activity concerned with procuring food, drink, and shelter, and with preservation of life from human and other enemies. Under such conditions, and at this stage of evolution, subconscious guidance satisfactorily met his immediate needs. He was unaware, that is, of the *means whereby* he employed his mechanisms in the simplest of every-day activities, and this unawareness did not matter at this stage.

The reason for this is not far to seek. It is that, at this early period, the standard of co-ordination and of the accompanying sensory appreciation in both sexes was comparatively high, and the needs of uncivilized existence did not call for the continual adaptation to rapid changes which civilized life demands.

In fact, the physical co-ordination and development of the savage, like that of the animal which he encountered daily, had reached at that period a fine state of excellence. For if we are justified in believing that the two-footed upright creature inherited from its predecessor on four feet a well-developed and healthy organism (and surely there can be little doubt upon this point), we may assume that it reached the human stage in a condition of health which may be described as relatively high.[1]

Since then, during a slow growth of thousands of years, this human creature had been surely and gradually building up a use and development on the so-called physical side in an environment in which changes but rarely occurred, and which, when they did occur, were comparatively slow, so that his activities would generally consist of the daily repetition of the same series of acts of which the standard of difficulty remained about the same.

But on the so-called mental side his use and development had been comparatively limited in an environment where his chief daily effort would consist of hunting down the animals, birds, or fish which constituted his daily food supply—an activity for which his instinct was as sure a guide as that of his prey.

With this relatively high standard of use and development on the " physical " side and the associated development of the organism in general, his experience of ill-health must have been correspondingly small, but if he ever incurred an illness or met with an injury, there can be little doubt that he would apply as a remedy some specific herb or root which he would know to possess the curative qualities he needed.[2]   This act would be a subconscious reaction to the stimulus resulting from the sense of ill-being, in exactly the same way as the act of seeking his daily food was a subconscious reaction to the stimulus resulting from the sense of hunger, and as long *as he possessed a mechanical*

---

[1] This does not exclude the possibility of the creature's experiencing occasional aches and pains or even of suffering from specific diseases, but, barring such specific troubles, the usual level was a normal one.   It is significant in this connexion that primitive man always thinks of disease after the analogy of wounds from arrows, stone bruises, etc.— that is, as coming in specifically from without—and the technique of the medicine man is to drive out the foreign substances that have come in; if he sweats the patient, for instance, it is to expel some foreign substance.

[2] Thus we see that the habit of " taking something " for an ill had a very early origin.   This habit led naturally to the coming of the medicine-man.   For one of the first channels into which man would direct his developing intelligence would be the discovery of the means of remedying or allaying his physical ills or discomforts.   This was bound, sooner or later, to produce men and women who would devote themselves exclusively to the study of such remedies and of the human ills for which the remedies were needed.

*organism which worked with mechanical accuracy, instinctive
procedure served his purpose.* The " specific " cure in these
circumstances was in keeping with sane and natural requirements. For just as the automatic, slowly developing, subconscious process called instinct guided him in his daily life
when he was well, so, when he was ill, this same mysterious but
limiting process would indicate to him the necessary and
specific remedy, through the agency of the only part of his
organism which was as yet highly developed—namely, his
sensory appreciation—which would mean that, in this case, his
senses of taste and smell would be working in co-ordination with
his stomach and his digestive processes.[1]

Thus we see that, whether he were well or whether he were
ill, the subconscious guidance of instinct was reliable in the
practically unchanging routine of his daily life, so that, because
of its association with a reliable sensory appreciation, man
would have no need of recourse to the higher directive processes.

Stage II

Early Civilizing Stage :—

*Development of Reasoning Inhibition and the Beginning of the
End of the Dominance of Instinct as a Controlling Factor*

As time went on, reasoning came more and more to illumine
the creature's dull and limited existence, shown by the fact that
he began to construct rude weapons and to build primitive
shelters. This reasoning process was destined to grow and
develop through the myriad operations of evolutionary build-

---

[1] Incidentally, it is interesting here to draw attention to the fact that
up to this day the majority of people under similar conditions are
dominated more or less by their sensory appreciation, and the practical
proof that this sensory appreciation has deteriorated lies in the difficulty,
known only too well to workers in the curative sphere, of persuading
the patient to give up some particular food or drink which he himself
knows has caused and is still causing his illness. The same thing holds
good in cases where a doctor recommends some food or drink which he
knows will be most beneficial to his patient, but is not pleasing to the
patient's sense of taste. In nine cases out of ten the doctor's advice
will be ignored, and, even where it is followed, it will probably be only
because he has brought considerable pressure to bear upon his patient.
This means that the patient will have allowed his reasoning processes
to be dominated by his deteriorated sensory appreciation.

ing involved in the new and divers experiences concerned with his progress towards a higher plane. With every advance and with every change which he made in his environment, he began to put into practice a reasoning inhibition which enabled him, within certain well-defined limits, to master or modify for his own purposes the desires and tendencies of that sensory mechanism upon which up to that time he had depended entirely for judgment and direction.

The development and use of this reasoning process marked primitive man's differentiation from the lower animals, but it also marked—and this is even more important from the point of view of man's evolutionary history—the " beginning of the end " of the dominance of instinct as a controlling factor in human activity, so that from this period onwards man could no longer satisfactorily live and move by subconscious guidance alone.

Let us see how his newly awakened processes of reasoning would work in the new sphere. In the early stages of his emergence from the savage state, any changes which took place in his environment would be but slow and gradual, and the consequent demands upon his newly developing, higher directive processes would be correspondingly light. As civiliza-tion advanced, however, slowly at first but with increasing rapidity as time went on, man must have been placed more and more in new and untried situations which would inevitably demand from him an increasing use of his reasoning processes. This would be exactly the opposite of what had occurred in the earlier savage state where, as we have seen, conditions had called for a relatively higher development on the so-called physical than on the so-called mental side. It is conceivable, therefore, that the new conditions of civilization would call for a relatively rapid increase in man's use and development on the " mental " as compared with the " physical " side. There can also be little doubt that at this stage he had not become dis-satisfied with the results of this changing process, and that he continued to receive from within and without more stimuli to " mental " than to " physical " activities. The farther he progressed from the savage state, the more frequent would become such stimuli, and the more urgent the call on him to deal with new situations, with the result that he would be forced more and more to develop his reasoning processes, in the constant inhibition of his natural desires to meet the demands of a young and developing society and to make the necessary adjustments to the complex requirements of an advancing civilization.

Man had now arrived at the stage where he had left behind him the environment with which he was familiar and to which his limited experiences had adapted him, and as the pathway of his new experiences inevitably widened out, he was confronted with one of the greatest difficulties experienced in his evolutionary progress on a subconscious basis—namely, that of adapting himself quickly to an environment which continued to change with ever-increasing rapidity, and so continually entailed new psycho-physical experiences.

He did adapt himself, of course, to these new conditions whilst his sensory appreciation was still more or less reliable, else he could not have survived, but it was only in the same way as he had always adapted himself—that is, by trusting blindly to the subconscious guidance of instinct which had served his primitive forefathers in their particular environment. Thus early, it seems, in his civilized career, man presumed subconsciously that he was equipped in every way for any new procedure in life such as sawing, for instance, ploughing, chopping, etc., and even for occupations which, with the progress of time, entailed working more and more in cramped or difficult positions.

We may remember, however, that at this early stage a man had every justification for believing that, if he received either from without or within a stimulus to carry out some new duty, to perform some new evolution, or to adopt some new position in the carrying out of a particular piece of work, he would be able, in all probability, to accomplish his aim with impunity. As far as we can see, nothing as yet had occurred to make him suspect that his sensory appreciation was not reliable, or that his standard of co-ordination was not satisfactory, or that, in adapting his mechanisms to new activities in a *specific* way, he might be injuring them in a *general* way, and thus be leading gradually to a general deterioration. In all his activities hitherto, such as, for instance, the hunting and fighting of his savage days, he had been accustomed to rely upon the subconscious guidance of his sensory appreciation, and so it was upon this same guidance in the use of himself that he continued to rely for all the new and varied occupations of civilization.

This shows that although he had developed his reasoning processes to some extent in inventing crude weapons, implements, etc., during the early stages of his progress towards the civilized state, he did not apply these reasoning processes to the direction of his psycho-physical mechanisms in the use of himself in the various activities of everyday life. With his reasoning processes thus limited in their use, and with no consciousness as yet of any sense of physical shortcoming, it is most unlikely that man could have received even a slight subconscious hint that his instinct would be in any way affected in the new surroundings and amidst the new experiences of civilization, or that he would ever lose a fraction of that satisfactory " physical " use and development which his race had enjoyed for countless ages, which was then his inheritance, and which he never doubted he was to hand down to his successors for all time.

Had he reasoned the matter out, he would have realized that his instinct was built up from very limited experiences, gained in the uncivilized state where growth was slow and changes rare, so that this instinct could not be expected to meet the demands of a mode of life in which growth was much more rapid and changes more frequent and unforeseen. He would also have realized that many of his instincts were being used less and less in the old way, and consequently were becoming less and less reliable. *It would then have been obvious to him that in order to meet satisfactorily the requirements of his new and changing environment, he must employ new guidance and direction, and that, in order to build up this new guidance with the rapidity that his necessities demanded, he must call upon reasoning to supersede instinct (the co-worker of slow development) in the use of his psycho-physical mechanisms. In other words, he would have realized that his primitive psycho-physical equipment must pass from the subconscious to the conscious plane of guidance and direction.*

The centuries passed, bringing with them an increasing scope for the use of man's reasoning processes. Unfortunately, he continued to confine this use of his reasoning processes to the consideration of the relation of " cause and effect," " means and ends " in connexion with his activities in the outside world, both social and physical, and failed to apply this reasoning to the consideration of the relation of " cause and effect," " means and ends " in connexion with the use of his psycho-physical organism. At the same time, the use of his so-called physical mechanisms was being gradually but surely interfered with, partly owing to the change from a standard of daily use to one of comparative inactivity, but chiefly owing to the failure of his instincts to meet the demands made upon them by the activities of the new life.

The results of the failure of man's instincts to meet the new and varied demands of civilization would not manifest themselves at once. For it is reasonable to suppose that, as man emerged from the savage state, his instinct was still working satisfactorily and that there was little need for curative measures on account of his comparatively high standard of health. Up till then the so-called physical self, as being more highly developed, had been the guiding and controlling factor in human activity. It is almost beyond human power to-day to realize that the experiences of millions of years had gone to the building-up of this so-called physical development. The experiences man had gained on the so-called mental side were infinitesimal in comparison.

Henceforward this restless, inquisitive creature, endowed with wonderful potentialities and developing on the so-called mental at a far greater rate than on the so-called physical side, continued to progress in the direction of what we call civilization with ever-increasing rapidity. But his race instincts had not equipped him for such a sudden psycho-physical rush, such a tremendous overbalancing on the so-called mental side, so that he arrived at the new stage breathless, dazed, at a loss, as it were, from the lack of the graduated psycho-physical experiences which had been part and parcel of his earlier growth.[1]

[1] This indicates (1) that conscious, reasoned psycho-physical activity must replace subconscious, unreasoned activity in the processes concerned with making the changes demanded by the ever-changing environment of civilization; (2) that these changes must be made more quickly than heretofore in order to meet this demand satisfactorily; and (3) that, with the advance of time, there will be a corresponding call for quickening in this sphere of psycho-physical activity.

In short, the fundamental difficulty arises from the following facts. Uncivilized man depended upon subconscious guidance and control, and probably hundreds of years were occupied in making simple changes, for subconscious activity is very slow in its response to the stimulus of the need of change. Civilized man still depends upon subconscious guidance and control just as he did in the uncivilized state

Stage III

Later Civilizing Stage :—

Recognition of a Serious Shortcoming which was Called Physical Deterioration

There came at last a time in the history of man when a number of people became aware of a certain serious shortcoming, and the adoption of " physical exercises " as a remedy is proof that they recognized this shortcoming as a " *physical* " deterioration. This was a recognition of the general undermining of well-being that was more or less to accompany mankind from that time right on through the different stages of the civilizing process.

I write " was to accompany " him advisedly, because it has done so. I also write that it should not and would not have done so if man had realized that this sense of shortcoming was the signal that he had reached a psychological moment in his career, and that the time had arrived for him to come into his great inheritance—that is, to pass from the subconscious, animal stage of his growth and development to higher and still higher stages of apprehension (conscious reasoning) in connexion with the use of his psycho-physical mechanisms.

Unfortunately man did not recognize the real significance of this danger signal, for the fact remains that he continued the experiment of guiding himself subconsciously, even though this experiment was already proving a failure, and has since so proved itself, with signs unmistakable which " he who runs may read."

There certainly was some consideration of the position. There was this recognition of a deterioration on the so-called

---

—the tragedy of civilization—but although he has remained satisfied with the form of direction and control by means of which changes have hitherto been made, it would seem that he has become dissatisfied with the time occupied with making changes. It is man's supreme civilizing blunder that he has failed to realize in practice that an adequate quickening of the response to the stimuli, arising from the need for some comparatively rapid change, calls for a corresponding quickening of the spheres of direction and control in the use of the psycho-physical mechanisms involved, such as is possible only on a plane of constructive conscious control.

physical side beyond any previously recognized experience of mankind, whilst on the other there may even have been a distinct sense of gain through the increased use and development of the so-called mental processes. But the point I wish to make clear is that, where this unequal development was concerned, there had been an inadequate co-ordinating process at work—a process, in fact, the very opposite of co-ordination, and one which has continued, with but few exceptions, in human beings until our own time. Indeed, from its beginnings the process of civilizing tended to widen the scope for so-called mental and to narrow the scope for so-called physical activities, and, on a basis of subconscious guidance and control, this process meant for the time being a further development on the so-called mental side, but at the cost of an equally distinct if more gradual deterioration on the so-called physical side, with an accompanying deterioration in the standard of sensory appreciation. But it must be remembered that because of the interrelation and interdependence of the mechanisms and potentialities of the organism in the process we call human life, any deterioration on the so-called physical side must, in time, seriously affect the so-called mental side. Enlargement of the spheres of so-called mental activity does not necessarily denote a growth of healthy " mental " activity.[1] This has been proved by man's experiences in civilization up to the moment, a statement borne out by the events of 1914–18 and 1939–45. In fact, the process of civilization has gone hand in hand with a harmful interference with those co-ordinating processes upon which the satisfactory growth of man's psycho-physical organism depends.

This being so, it follows that from the time that man entered the civilized state, human growth on this subconscious basis was bound to be uneven and unbalanced, and this unbalanced development marked the beginning of a new era in human existence. It marked the beginning of an interference with the co-ordinated use of his mechanism as a whole, and particularly with those muscular co-ordinations so essential to his " physical " well-being.

---

[1] " Mental " growth continued even after a deterioration had been recognized in the " physical " self, and this deterioration caused, as it were, one limb of the tree to grow at such a pace that it overbalanced the tree, bent it too much in one direction, seriously disturbing the roots responsible for its equilibrium and healthy growth.

Interference with the Co-ordinated Use of the Psycho-Physical Mechanism and an Associated Lowering of the Standard of Sensory Appreciation

In the savage state instinctive guidance and control was associated with a co-ordinated use of the human mechanism, and with an accompanying reliable sense of feeling (sensory appreciation) for guidance. This old instinctive guidance, as we have seen, gradually lost its sphere of usefulness under the new conditions, and so became more or less impaired, but man continued to place upon it the same implicit reliance as in his uncivilized days. The inevitable result was an interference with the co-ordinated use of his psycho-physical mechanism, together with a more or less continued lowering of the standard of general functioning and of the standard of sensory appreciation, the harm being intensified by the fact that by leaving himself to blind subconscious guidance in all matters connected with the use of his psycho-physical organism, he continued to depend upon a sense of feeling which was continually deteriorating, with the result that to-day he represents perhaps the most imperfectly co-ordinated type of human creature ever known in the history of mankind.

We can readily understand how this gradual interference with the co-ordination of man's psycho-physical mechanisms would cause a number of disagreeable and alarming symptoms to manifest themselves, and, as a matter of fact, the deterioration of the human creature at last reached a point where the need for a remedy became exceedingly urgent. Man was now faced with a situation which was new to his experience, and which demanded from him, not only a response, but a *quick* response. The problem was complicated by the fact that the human creature on whom this urgent demand was made was already badly co-ordinated and had acquired, by reason of the rapidity with which his experiences had been gained—a rapidity hitherto unknown to the human organism—the habit of re-acting in a certain confident, nay, almost reckless way to stimuli.

When, therefore, this insistent, this urgent call came upon man to find a remedy for his ills, we can easily conceive of the confusion that would of necessity accompany his first experience in making a comparatively hasty decision on a new problem of psycho-mechanics—a problem, moreover, which did not present itself to him until he had reached an advanced stage of psycho-physical mal-co-ordination. We have only to imagine such an experience repeated indefinitely, (1) the increasing sense of shortcoming, (2) the urgent S.O.S. call for a remedy, (3) the hurried haphazard response, to realize that the disturbed condition involved [1] is not conducive to the employment of the reasoning processes.

We all remember Mr. Carlyle's reaction under similar circumstances to the needs of his friend Henry Taylor; how, on hearing that his friend was ill, he became confused and rushed off with a bottle of medicine which he believed had helped Mrs. Carlyle, without any consideration of the nature of his friend's trouble, or even a knowledge of the contents of the bottle. If a man of such attainments, living in a so-called advanced civilization, acted at a psychological moment in such an unreasoning way, we cannot be surprised to find that the poor, subconsciously-guided human being of an earlier period, when faced with the problem of his deterioration, rushed in the same unreasoning way to find a " cure." As far as we can judge, he subconsciously adopted the form of " cure " to which instinct had prompted his ancestors in the past, without recognizing that this form of " cure " was no longer suited to the circumstances of his life owing to the ever-changing demands of civilization, and without any consideration of the effect of these changes upon his organism.

So, because in an earlier stage of evolution the form of " cure " sought by primitive man had always been a *specific* one, instinct guiding him in the choice of the specific berry or root to alleviate some specific pain or hurt, man now followed, as far as we can judge, the example of his more lowly evolved ancestors, and dealt in a *specific* way with his trouble. Recognizing that his standard of well-being was being lowered and that his muscular development was also continuing to deteriorate, he decided that his loss of health was *due* to a deterioration

---

[1] It is easy to see how, under these conditions, unreliable lines of communication can become established, with the associated unsatisfactory psycho-physical actions and reactions, such as will have that general effect upon the kinæsthesia which leads in time to the cultivation of the fixed habit or phobia, so common to-day and so erroneously called nerves or neurasthenia.

in his muscular development.   But he saw this deterioration as a deterioration in his muscular development alone, not as a deterioration in his general psycho-physical co-ordination, and in his sensory appreciation, an interference, that is, with the general adjustment of the organism together with a misplacement of the vital organs and viscera, causing serious pressure and irritation and resulting in a number of disagreeable and alarming symptoms.[1]

Specific Remedy Chosen to Counteract a General Malcondition

Owing to the limited range of the working of his reasoning processes, he must have concluded that his general shortcomings were due to specific muscular shortcomings, and this narrow and erroneous conception led directly to the idea of muscle development by means of *specific* exercises to be performed at *specific* times for the purpose of developing *specific* muscles.   It will be evident that such a process could not satisfactorily check the deterioration in *general* co-ordination and the maladjustments and misplacements to which I have referred.

By way of illustration let us begin with what might be called the " weight-lifting conception " of a remedy.   This was a crude remedy indeed,[2] and one well in keeping with the stage of evolution in which instinct had become impaired and the reasoning processes were as yet employed only in limited spheres.   The era of weight-lifting exercises was superseded by the crudest form of gymnasium where most strenuous exercises were performed.   These primitive mechanical exer-

[1] Unfortunately, the narrow view here indicated is still held by most of our authorities on physiology and anatomy, with results which are only too evident.   It is only necessary to watch the movements of many who are experts in the subject-matter of physiology and anatomy to realize the futility of their knowledge from a practical standpoint For the knowledge of the ordinary anatomical and physiological workings of specific muscles does not enable any person to re-educate or co-ordinate them on a general basis in the acts of everyday life, and it is on this basis of common sense and practice that the value of any knowledge or principle must be judged.

[2] In *Man's Supreme Inheritance* I have pointed out the gradual modification which has taken place in these muscle-building exercises, a modification which is still going on at the present day.

cises were succeeded by others less strenuous, and then again by an increasing number of machines which were destined to become the vogue with enthusiasts for muscle-building. This particular form of muscle-development passed through a number of phases, but it is evident that the results were still unsatisfactory. Whether it was that they considered that the " right " remedy had not yet been found, or that the rapidly deteriorating psycho-physical condition of man was now beyond the power of the most satisfactory muscle-building machine or method to remedy, one thing at least is certain, that all concerned became aware that the results were still discouraging, and that the deterioration was continuing in spite of all efforts to check it. Hence changes in methods were made. Swedish drill became the fashion and also different types of exercisers and dumb-bells which were used in the performance of muscle-tensing movements of all kinds, and succeeding experiences in connexion with posture, calisthenics, plastic dancing, deep breathing, " Daily Dozens," and other specific methods cannot evidently be considered satisfactory, as the search for the " great unknown or unrecognized " still continues.

Another set of people, convincing themselves that civilization was never meant as a mode of life for a human being, decide that in this fact they can see the light in their long " physical darkness," and come to the conclusion that *the remedy* is a " return to Nature," to the " simple life." And so we have the spectacle of these simple, lowly evolved human beings actually trying to return to the scenes of the early triumphs of their prehistoric forbears, where, as they imagine, all experiences will be sufficiently non-varied and slow in development to meet their present capacities on the subconscious plane to which they so tenaciously cling. The picture of early man in his crude but natural surroundings presents a curious but interesting study to those who have evolved beyond that state, but the spectacle of civilized man trying to return to the environment of his prehistoric ancestors would give us cause for laughter, were it not for the tragedy involved in a conception which is so uncomplimentary to our intellectual pride.

Certain Errors of Judgment in Man's Choice of " Physical Exercises" as a Remedy for a Fundamental Shortcoming

Now what I wish to emphasize is that, throughout the long search for the remedy for his deterioration, man overlooked certain most important factors in the case, factors which are still overlooked to-day by the majority of people in their search for health and general uplifting.

In the first place, man completely overlooked the fact that the sensory mechanism, upon which he had heretofore entirely depended for guidance in general activity, was no longer registering accurately, and that he could no longer rely, therefore, entirely upon feeling—that is, on instinctive subconscious guidance—for the satisfactory performance of the ordinary acts of life.   The very fact that at some period " physical exercises " were considered necessary proves that imperfections must have developed to a very serious extent, and the reason for this, as I again repeat, is that the gradual failure of the sense registers to continue to guide men satisfactorily in the use of themselves in the activities of life had finally brought about an advanced stage of mal-co-ordination in the human psycho-physical organism.

It was clearly unreasonable, therefore, to expect " physical exercises," of whatever kind, to bring about any lasting or fundamental improvement in this unsatisfactory condition, when the person performing them would be guided by the same imperfect and delusive sensory appreciation, *dependence upon which had led originally to the very condition he wished to remedy.* What is more, during the performance of " physical exercises " under these conditions there would be an actual development of his original mal-co-ordinated condition, and he would be sure to encounter some new and very baffling psycho-physical problems in himself.[1]   These problems actually arose, and have become since then increasingly complicated, and I should like here to reiterate that, even if they cannot be said to be wholly overlooked to-day, their real significance is still almost entirely misunderstood, in that the majority of people do not realize that human beings are still propelling an already maladjusted

---

[1] In the second part of this book I have dealt with certain of these problems as they occur in educational and other spheres of life.

and damaged mechanism along the difficult road of modern life, whilst relying for guidance upon an imperfect and sometimes delusive sensory appreciation.

Secondly, in choosing " physical exercises " as a remedy for his deterioration, man did not take into consideration the fact that his body was a very delicate and highly co-ordinated piece of machinery, so that there might be many contributing causes other than muscular weakness to account for his deteriorated condition ; further, that the exercises themselves were not correlated in any way to the needs of his organism, either in the practical activities of life or during those periods of rest which are such an important part of the daily round (a point constantly overlooked by enthusiasts for " physical culture ").

If we ask ourselves why man overlooked these important points, the answer may throw light on many of our own problems at the present time. It was undoubtedly because he was aiming exclusively at a method of " cure," not of prevention. In the terms of my thesis, his attention was fixed on the " end " he was seeking (his " physical " amelioration), not on the reasonable *means whereby* that " end " could be brought about.

If he could have thought of his body in the terms of the very intricately constructed machine which it is, he would have seen in his deteriorated condition, not a deterioration in his muscular development alone, but a deterioration in his general psycho-physical co-ordination, accompanied by an interference with the general adjustment of the organism and by a general lowering of the standard of its functioning. He would then have realized that his deterioration must be merely the symptom of some failure in the working of the machinery, *and that the whole machine would need to be readjusted before it could work co-ordinately once more.*

He would have dealt with it as he would have dealt with any other machine—his watch, for instance—that was out of working order. If his watch gained half an hour one day and on the next stopped altogether, or if its small hand worked at the same speed as the big one, he would not trust to its accuracy if he wanted to catch a train, and, still more to the point, he would not start to repair it at random. He would send it instead to an expert who, through his knowledge of the correct working of the machinery, would make good any worn or broken part and readjust the mechanism once more. The watch-maker would then probably suggest, *as a preventive measure*, a periodic overhaul so that wear might be watched, and, when necessary, damaged parts repaired or new ones supplied. By this means a reasonable endeavour would be made *to prevent* another such derangement of the mechanism as had rendered the watch an unreliable guide.[1]

We cannot be surprised, however, that man did not reason in the same way in connexion with the deterioration of his own mechanism. His reasoning processes in connexion with the care of his own mechanisms and with his general well-being had not been employed to anything like the same degree as in connexion with the mechanisms of external nature. He decided that he had discovered a " physical " defect for which he must find a remedy, and there can be little doubt that as soon as he conceived the " remedy " idea, any other possible consideration was shut off, whether of the cause or causes of the " physical " deterioration, or of the psycho-physical principles involved, or (even if the cause or causes had been discovered) of the *means whereby* the desired " end " (remedy) could be secured. His decision, in short, was the result of a subconscious and, therefore, unreasoned procedure, not of conscious reason-ing reflexion. As we have already pointed out, a different result could hardly be expected at this early stage of man's development, seeing that even to-day, in the twentieth century, the problem of psycho-physical unfitness is met with the same primeval " remedy " outlook both in theory and practice.

Man's Conscious Reasoning Processes Applied in Connexion with Outside Activities but Not in Connexion with his Psycho-Physical Organism

The stubborn but unpleasant fact must be faced that civilized man has never progressed personally—that is, in himself—a

---

[1] We must again note the difference that exists between human and inanimate machinery. The human machine, when in a state of co ordinated and adequate use, commands in itself the power of growth and development in each part of the muscular mechanism, and the condition approximating to wear in inanimate machinery may b prevented more or less from becoming present in the human being b nature's method of supply and repair under right conditions in the matter of used and wasted tissue.

he has advanced in matters outside himself. Although he has reasoned out the *means whereby* he can control and turn to his own uses the different forces he has discovered in the outside world, he has not applied this reasoning principle where his own organism is concerned. He has left this masterpiece of psycho-physical machinery, more subtle, more delicate in its workings than the most intricate man-made machine,[1] to the subconscious guidance of his sensory appreciation, unaware that this sensory appreciation is becoming, as we have seen, more and more unreliable with the boasted advance of civilization.

We are all acquainted with the word sacrilege, and we have a knowledge of the acts which come under this category. But the word has not yet been applied, as far as I am aware, in connexion with the use of the psycho-physical organism of the human creature. Yet, is it not a sacrilege that during the experiences of civilization in the past two thousand years, the human psycho-physical organism has been directed and employed in the activities of life on a subconscious and un-reasoned plan, with the result that distortions and defects have been developed and have become established? The adjust-ment of the wonderful psycho-physical machinery has been harmfully interfered with, likewise the co-ordinations which play the great part in the actual working of this machinery, this interference resulting in a lowered standard of general functioning of the organism.

There was a time when the body and limbs of the human being were the "mould of form," an inspiration to sculptor and painter, and a joy to look upon as "a thing of beauty" and symmetry. In our time, however, the organisms of the vast majority of people may be described as more or less mis-shapen, maladjusted, and unsymmetrical. Awkwardness and ungainliness have superseded grace and poetry of motion, shapely limbs have become misshapen, and the psycho-physical mechanisms are employed not to advantage but to dis-advantage.

* * * * *

To sum up, we have seen how, in his choice of "physical

[1] It is well known that a passion for mechanics exists among boys of our time. How very easy it would be to turn this desire towards an understanding of their own mechanisms!

exercises " as a remedy for what he recognized as physical deterioration, man overlooked certain important facts. Firstly, he left out of account the fact that he had developed a state of unreliability in his sensory appreciation, which was therefore no longer a reliable guide in psycho-physical activity. Secondly, he did not think of his body as a co-ordinated mechanism, and was therefore misled into choosing a specific remedy for a specific malcondition, instead of laying down on broad, general lines *preventive principles*, by which a condition of co-ordination of the entire psycho-physical mechanism could be restored and maintained. Above all, he did not apply to his problem the one great principle on which I claim man's satisfactory progress in civilization depends—namely, the principle of *thinking out the reasonable means whereby a certain end can be achieved*, as opposed to the old subconscious plan of working blindly for an immediate " end."

We can now have a clear understanding of a fundamental process which has been in course of building from the early days of the human creature, and is still to-day in course of building among the great majority of people who, at certain psychological moments, still act in the same way as their for-bears of the so-called Dark Ages, and, when faced with similar problems, still work subconsciously for their immediate " ends " (" cure " idea), instead of first thinking out the reasonable *means whereby* their desired " ends " can be achieved (preven-tion idea).

It is quite true that some modification is going on here and there. I am quite willing to admit that we have a small minority of people actually attempting to analyse their own and others' cases, where ills and imperfections are concerned, but, as I shall show later on, they are all attempting to make " cures " by means of a *specific* remedy, instead of dealing with each problem on a *general* basis.

This applies equally to the various forms of so-called mental healing, including Christian Science, Auto-suggestion, New Thought, etc., which have recently come into vogue. These are simply a reaction from the earlier idea of " physical culture," but, like the reactions of all creatures who are sub-consciously controlled, they are but the reaction from one extreme to another. For it would seem that in most of our attempts to progress on a subconscious plane we tend to move

from one extreme to another, and fail to recognize the danger
into which we are drifting, until we are metaphorically struck
on the head by some unforeseen or unknown force of Nature
which makes us pause. We then perhaps retrace our steps,
but only to start off just as blindly in another direction until
we reach the other extreme (a process which amounts to over-
compensation), when Nature again intervenes and forces us
once more to cry a halt. Our progress under subconscious
guidance, in other words, resembles that of a man lost in the
bush, who, becoming oblivious to those signs which, if he were
not emotionally disturbed, could not escape his observation,
wanders round and round in a circle, and after a long and sad
experience finds himself back at the place from which he started.
It is owing to this habit of rushing from one extreme to another
—a habit which, as I have pointed out, seems to go hand
in hand with subconscious guidance and direction—to this
tendency, that is, to take the narrow and treacherous sidetracks
instead of the great, broad, midway path, that our plan of
civilization has proved a comparative failure.

Harmful Concept of Division of the Psycho-Physical Organism

There is yet one other aspect of the case which I will now
put forward, as it epitomizes all the errors which human
beings have made in their attempts to solve the problem of
living in civilization whilst relying upon subconscious guidance. In the adoption of " physical exercises " and of the
various methods of " mental healing " as specific remedies for
human ills, man made an arbitrary attempt to separate the
psycho-physical organism into parts which he defined as body,
mind, and soul.[1]

[1] In *Man's Supreme Inheritance* I endeavoured to leave no room for
doubt that I base my philosophy and practice on the unity of human
potentialities, which, up till now, have been differentiated and represented as " body," " body and mind," or " body, mind, and soul."
The words " mind " and " soul " are in as common use as the word
" body," and we have all been guilty of using them. Now we do know
something about the body, something tangible, but what do we really
know about " soul "? And do we know anything more about " mind "
as such, than we do about " soul "? Yet phrases in connexion with
" mind " still remain in continual use, such as, for instance, to " hold in
mind," to " keep the mind," on something, or when we speak of " improv-

Now to separate any organism into parts and then to expect it to function satisfactorily is an unreasoned proposition, as unreasoned as it would be for instance to expect to obtain the best results from any other machine, by separating the gear mechanism from the explosive and steering mechanism.

It is probable that this unreasoned conception had its origin in that emotional and confused condition which is responsible

---

ing the mind," or of " developing or making a mind," or of a person's " mental " attitude, of " mental " progress, " mental " control, " mental " habits, or of a person suffering from " mental " trouble.

The pages of *Man's Supreme Inheritance* and also of this book abound with arguments and illustrations in connexion with the harmful results which follow the efforts of people beset with unreliable sensory appreciation, when they attempt to follow out written or spoken instructions, with the aim of eradicating defects or peculiarities in the use of their psycho-physical mechanisms. Now of the working of these mechanisms it is possible to acquire some tangible knowledge; if, then, harmful results can follow attempts at improvement or development in a sphere where we can acquire some tangible knowledge, how much more harmful must be any attempts to follow out such specific instructions as " hold in mind," or " keep the mind " on something, when of the working of what we call " mind " we have no tangible knowledge. And when we reach the point where we can suggest the possibility of " developing or making a mind," we must surely be so far removed from concrete realization of facts as to have reached the borderland of mysticism. The history of man's efforts at every stage of his development furnishes proof of the harmful results which accrue whenever the human creature attempts to respond to a stimulus (or stimuli) arising from his conception of a phrase which represents intangible phenomena. How can this be otherwise? How is it possible for him to come into possession of any tangible *means whereby* he may secure an intangible " end "?

It will therefore be understood that I have a special reason for giving so many concrete illustrations in my books. Here we have something demonstrable in simple, practical procedures, and free from those intangible phenomena which are too often inseparable from what is known as " mental " or " spiritual " discussion.

If it were not for the world-wide tragedy of it all, one could almost be amused at the attempts of those who are trying to pierce the veil of the " beyond," whilst they are still ignorant of the discoverable human potentialities within their grasp. Is it not reasonable to assume that the knowledge of the *means whereby* these potentialities may be continuously developed and employed to the best possible advantage should be the stepping-stone to satisfactory activities on other planes of life? Surely mankind should at least come into the great earthly inheritance—the conscious plane of evolution—before time and energy are devoted to those fields of speculation and doubt in connexion with the " undiscovered country from whose bourn no traveller returns."

for the majority of unreasoned acts and beliefs, and is generally found to be associated with fear in some form or other. The confused state into which man was thrown in his first attempts to find a " cure " for his psycho-physical deterioration was naturally linked up and associated with his original fears. For fear had been man's constant companion from very earliest times, and whether the fear was a healthy or an unhealthy fear depended upon the conditions involved; in either case it was a form of illness for which the lowly evolved creature could not find a " cure." The primary law which ordains that one creature should feed upon another, the shock of new experiences, and ignorance of even simple laws of Nature were responsible for this. There was no escape. Every creature, human or otherwise, lived in constant expectation of an attack from its natural enemy. Our little canary, whose great-great-great-grandparents were caged birds, still looks from side to side with anxious rapidity after picking up each seed, just like the earliest of its kind.

It is easy to understand what would be the effect of thunder, for instance, when heard for the first time by the primitive creature, whose very existence depended upon a proper reaction to the stimulus of fear, and to imagine his terrified aspect when lightning first flashed before his eyes. There can be no doubt that from the very earliest stages man's reaction to such fears as these had been to seek refuge in the supernatural. Indeed, civilized men who have not prayed for years, who may even have ridiculed the practice of prayer, have been known in the circumstances of shipwreck to kneel down and pray instinctively. In such cases fear overrules their convictions, the old primitive subconsciousness holds sway, and they probably fall on their knees without being aware of it.

So it would be with primitive man. Dazed and terrified by the thunder and lightning, he would drop down, and hide his face in his hands, mumbling, incoherently perhaps, to " something." Sooner or later, when the paroxysm of fear had begun to pass, he would take his hands from his face, and it is conceivable that the first tree or stone to meet his terrified gaze would impress him as being the power which had rescued him from some awful fate. From this there would develop the worship of images of wood and stone, and the various religious rites with which we are familiar.

We will not stop to consider all the intervening stages in this development, but will pass on to the time of the Christian Era, and see in what form the primitive fear now manifested itself.

Here we find that though man's fears were modified in the case of thunder and lightning, and other terrors with which he had now become familiar, they were no less acute in new and unfamiliar spheres. And beyond this original fear of the unknown, a new form of fear had come upon him, associated with the one-sided development which had taken place in the human organism. For unbalanced psycho-physical development connotes unsatisfactory equilibrium in all spheres, and unsatisfactory equilibrium is ever associated with fear. As we have seen, since man's entry into the civilized state he had been developing more rapidly on what is called the mental side, whilst on the so-called physical side there was actual deterioration. He had thus been building up within himself two forces, as it were, the one working against the other, until it was almost as if he had developed two separate entities, the "physical" and the "mental." It was the conflicting demands of these "separate entities" which caused the interference with psycho-physical equilibrium and produced in him the condition of inward fear to which I refer, and which to-day is too often called "nerves." [1]

This new fear—*actually a fear of himself*—gradually developed until its presence was recognized as an urgent problem, and it is in man's solution of this problem that we are faced with a conception which will be seen to be a most harmful one when considered in relation to his evolutionary progress.

The conception to which I refer is that of the separation of the human organism into the parts which have been named soul, mind, and body. Those who were bent on this separation attempted, in obedience to their own arbitrary and unreasoning conception, to develop each of the three parts named soul, mind, and body, specifically, nay, even to make a class-distinction, as it were, between them, this last procedure being a reversion to a "habit of thought" associated with

---

[1] The presence of fear always means a condition of conflict. The man who is inwardly afraid puts on an outward show of bravery by an assumed manner. Similarly, it is doubtless this inward fear which induces in certain nations a mania for carrying arms and for the massed attack in accordance with their horde instinct.

other spheres. Surely, even to those who believed in this separation, their knowledge of the process of Nature should have indicated the place which the body should occupy in order of importance, and its relationship to the other parts in the series named body, mind, and soul.

Those who have followed our argument to this point will be cognizant of the following facts :—

(1) that the rules of moral, social, and other conduct already established at the period designated the Christian Era were the result of human conceptions;

(2) that the human beings responsible for these conceptions were themselves the product of the psycho-physical experiences involved in a subconscious attempt to pass from a very low stage in the evolutionary process, which we call the uncivilized stage, to a much higher stage, which is known to us as the civilized stage;

(3) that, during this transition, man's use and development on the so-called mental side had proceeded at a much greater rate proportionately than on the so-called physical side, and for the reason that on the so-called physical side his use and development had already reached such a high standard that the possibilities of future development on that side (as development was then understood) were not so great as on the, as yet, almost undeveloped so-called mental side. Also, in the new mode of life there was relatively less demand on the former and an increasing demand on the latter;

(4) that, in the sphere of civilization, with the new and increasing use and development on the so-called mental side, there was a correspondingly gradual decrease in use and development on the so-called physical side, as compared with those earlier periods when man roamed the plains and mountains in search of his daily food and other necessities;

(5) that this was the beginning of a new era in the experience of the creature called man. It was the beginning of an interference with the co-ordinated use and development of the psycho-physical organism.

From all this it will be conceded that up to a certain point the so-called physical processes, as being the more highly developed, constituted the leading and guiding factor in human activity. Yet, in a comparatively short space of time the relatively unused but more rapidly developing interdependent processes called " mind " were exalted to a higher place than the " body " in the human economy, only to be superseded by what those concerned were pleased to call the " soul," of which they knew even less than the little they knew of the " mind " and its workings.

The very conception of a separation and class-distinction between " body, mind, and soul " indicates the presence of a more than usually potent stimulus which could emanate only from a condition of overbalancing in some direction. As far as we can learn, the poor body came into disgrace on account of the " lusts of the flesh," themselves a natural result of a mal-co-ordinated condition, and if we may judge by the special laws and customs which were formulated, the chief results of this unbalanced condition would seem to have manifested themselves in the sexual sphere. Else why should this sphere have been particularly selected for condemnation, seeing that the satisfaction of the needs and desires of the reproductive system is as essential as the satisfaction of the needs and desires of the digestive and assimilative systems to the welfare of the individual and of the race, and that the results of satisfying the sensory desires and needs of these three systems are normal and salutary, as long as moderate use and not abuse is the rule? The evil of over-eating is only equalled by that of over-drinking, and surely in the last analysis the abuse of the sexual act is intensified by one or the other, or by both. A man or an animal placed on a low diet does not evince any particular desires in the way of sex-relations. As a matter of fact, the very reverse would prove to be the rule.

Indeed, this idea of " separation " in the human organism was a purely arbitrary conception formed to fit in with certain stultifying premises which human beings, probably in all honesty and meekness of spirit, had laid down and made a law unto themselves in striving to fulfil what they considered were the essential demands of the religious ideal.

This led naturally to that dreadful and debasing conception which caused men and women actually to castigate the flesh, to cut, as it were, a way to Heaven through the very fundamental of their earthly being.

But the limit of the destruction wrought by this dissecting process had not yet been reached. As the process called education progressed, this principle of a class-distinction within the organism grew and developed. Side by side with the growth of education the idea was cultivated that lack of knowledge in certain specific spheres was the factor which must determine whether a person should be classified as ignorant or otherwise. A man might be a glorified Touch-stone, a person with a prodigious fund of common sense, or even a reasoning, intelligent creature, but if he did not happen to be versed in all the paraphernalia which made up the curricula of the universities, schools, and colleges of his time, he would be classified as ignorant.

Next followed the most stupid of all the conceptions formed by subconsciously controlled human beings in connexion with education, a conception which was the co-mate of the idea of class-distinction—namely, a more or less growing contempt for those who, despite their natural gifts, were thus classified as ignorant, and especially for those whose work made more demands upon their so-called physical than upon their so-called mental selves (that is, from the educationalists' point of view), together with a wholly absurd and exaggerated admiration for those who worked in professions in which it was concluded the demands were almost exclusively " mental." [1]

Need for Unity and Simplicity

We have only to consider these facts to realize how far men had travelled from one of the original fundamentals of life. For, as we have already indicated, in the beginning of things there must have been unity, and it was a strange lack of reasoning that permitted men to make a false division in an organism that can be satisfactorily developed only as an indivisible psycho-physical unity.

[1] This is only one of the many proofs that we possess that the idea of class-distinction lies at the very root of man's make-up, and that despite all efforts that may be made by legislation or other external means to counter this idea, it will surely remain as a conviction, in one form or another, with both its defenders and its advocates, until mankind has reached the reasoning stage of conscious guidance and control of the individual. Until this stage is reached, those ideals which we indicate by the words democracy, liberty, etc., are impossible of attainment.

I was recently discussing this and other kindred matters with a scientific friend, who put the following query to me : " Why have we overlooked these important points for so long ? " In reply I referred to the phrase now in such common use : " Life has become so complex." In my opinion we have here the crux of the whole matter, and I venture to predict that before we can unravel the horribly tangled skein of our present existence, we must come to a full STOP, and return to conscious, simple living, believing in the unity underlying all things, and acting in a practical way in accordance with the laws and principles involved.

In the midst of a world-wide tragedy such as we are witnessing at the present time, a tragedy which seems to have been increasing instead of decreasing in its intensity since the declaration of the Armistice and the work of the peacemakers, surely it behoves every individual to stop—and I mean this in its fullest sense—and reconsider every particle of supposed knowledge, particularly " psychological " knowledge, derived from his general education, from his religious, political, moral, ethical, social, legal, and economic training, and ask himself the plain, straightforward question, " Why do I believe these things ? " " By what process of reasoning did I arrive at these conclusions ? "

If we are even and direct with ourselves in regard to our cherished ideas and ideals, the answer may at first prove a shock to us, to some of us, indeed, almost a knockdown blow. For the truth will be borne in upon us that much of our supposed knowledge has not been real knowledge, and too often the boasted truth a delusion. Many of us may awaken to the fact that the majority of our cherished ideas and ideals are the product, not of any process of reasoning, but of that unreasoning process called impulse, of unbalanced emotion and prejudice—that is, of ideas and ideals associated with a psycho-physical condition in the development of which unreliable sensory appreciation has played the leading part.

Need for Substituting in all Spheres the Principle of Prevention on a General Basis for Methods of " Cure " on a Specific Basis

As we have seen, unreliability of sensory appreciation has been and still is associated with a general deterioration in the standard of the health of mankind. Consequently, in the matter of making decisions, man's conceptions and thoughts have been and still are conditioned by this unreliable sensory appreciation, and still lead him, as in the past, to erroneous conclusions and decisions in the settlement of the new problems with which he has been continually confronted. Nowhere can we find a better illustration of the erroneous conceptions, leading to unbalanced judgment, which are associated with unreliable sensory appreciation, than in man's choice of a specific " cure " on the " end-gaining " principle—namely, " physical exercises." It was his erroneous estimate of the relative value of the principles of prevention and " cure " which permitted him to make this choice, and so to neglect the " means-whereby " principle which is involved in all preventive procedure.

We have evidence of similar unbalanced judgment in all other spheres where the attempted improvement of the individual is concerned, and the erroneous decisions and opinions which result from unbalanced judgment in these spheres are analogous to the error man made in choosing a specific " cure " in his attempts to stem the tide of general deterioration. Each generation has fallen into the same error in this connexion, and in this way has built up a heavy burden for the succeeding one, inasmuch as the necessity for " cure " has increased and still continues to increase at a pace which bids fair to heap upon the individuals of coming generations such a load as will be beyond the power of human endurance. If the methods which have led to this undesirable situation are ever reviewed by the individuals upon whom will devolve the onerous duty of carrying on the scheme called civilization, we shall probably be written down by them as poor, subconsciously directed human beings, rushing wildly from one extreme to another in the howling wilderness of twentieth-century wonders. Such a review will provide abundant proof of the lowered standard of reliability of sensory appreciation in the human beings of our time, which has caused them to become over-balanced in many directions, and consequently has deluded them into experimenting blindly in too many spheres. Disaster has followed such experiments in chemistry and death-dealing machines, for instance, in exactly the same way as it would follow the activities of children well supplied with powder and matches. The historian of a century or two hence will be able to produce evidence of the psycho-physical state of the peoples of the twentieth century which will show that in this regard they have progressed little on the evolutionary plane beyond the man of the Stone Age, whilst, on the other hand, he will only have to refer to human activities during the years 1914–18 and 1939–45 to convince the most sceptical that human beings of our time have developed a new form of devilry and brutality that surpasses the best efforts of pre-historic man.

Should we decide, however, at the present time upon a retrospection such as I have suggested, we can hardly fail to see that a psychological moment in man's experience has undoubtedly arrived for a widespread consideration of the principle of prevention in its fullest application to human needs (in all " physical," " mental," or " spiritual " spheres), as they are presented to us at this present world crisis. Investigation will show that the proportion of human energy devoted to prevention and " cure " in the twentieth century in all these spheres may fairly be said to be as nine to one in favour of " cure." That this is so after some thousands of years of supposed civilization gives food for reflexion. For the idea of seeking and adopting a specific " cure " had its origin, as we have seen, in the experiences of a lowly evolved type of human creature belonging to an earlier period of human development. It goes with a view of life which is narrow and limited, since it represents an attempt on man's part to gain an immediate " end " without consideration of larger issues.

We are, therefore, faced with the fact, hitherto almost unrecognized, that our adoption of the principle of " cure," with its associated " end-gaining " procedures, as the basis of our attempted reforms in all spheres, means that the foundation of too many of our cherished ideals and beliefs to-day is the same as that from which were built up the instinctive procedures of our earlier ancestors when they sought a " cure " in some specific herb or berry.

On the other hand, a scheme of life in which prevention is the leading principle does not involve working for an immediate " end "; its application, rather, is on a broad, constructive basis, without limits, humanly speaking, and is the product of a consciously conceived and consciously executed plan—in short, it is the conception of a highly evolved type of human creature.

Illustration I

I need not detain my readers with the many obvious illustrations of the lack of reasoning associated with all methods of " cure." I will give three instances, beginning with what is called the " liver cure."

A man feels out of sorts and has suffered from certain symptoms for a year or more. He at last consults his medical adviser and is told that his liver is sluggish. He is ordered to take some grains of calomel or some such drug, and goes home with the conviction that all will now be well. He has his " remedy " and the plan is so simple. If the symptoms recur, all he has to do is to swallow the prescribed number of grains of his drug. This applies to the whole list of such " cures."

At this point I would beg my reader not to judge my standpoint until I have placed my evidence before him. We, the people of the twentieth century, pride ourselves that we are a reasoning race; at any rate, that we have employed the processes of reasoning in far more spheres than our forbears of several centuries ago. This being so, why have the reasoning processes been so comparatively little employed in connexion with those problems on the solution of which our present and future well-being depends?

Let us consider, for instance, how the person of our illustration reasons in connexion with his sluggish liver and his calomel remedy. It is quite understandable that, on the occasion of an acute attack, he should follow the instructions of his doctor, take his grains of calomel, and so get clear, as he considers it, of a crisis. But why does the matter end there, as far as he, presonally, is concerned? He has probably been aware of trouble for quite a long time, and now he has it on his doctor's authority that his liver is unduly inactive. As a matter of fact, he has suspected this himself, led to the conclusion by the presence of certain symptoms and by the knowledge that his sedentary life and his over-indulgence in certain foods and drinks, which are particularly gratifying to his none-too-reliable sensory appreciation (in this case, particularly the sense of taste), are liable to have caused the trouble. This being so, one would expect him to show some intelligent recognition of the real situation. It would not require any special degree of reasoning to enable him to grapple successfully with the obvious facts of his case. But unfortunately he does not think beyond the crisis of the moment. He is set only on being " cured " of his specific ill, and so, in the twentieth century, he continues to act on the " end-gaining " principle, a procedure which was excusable in his forbears of four thousand years ago. He has never applied either to himself or to the difficulties encountered in the sphere of his psycho-physical well-being, any other principle than that of working for an immediate " end." In these spheres he has never adopted the plan of reasoning out first the common-sense *means whereby* an " end " may be secured. Why should he do it now? He is simply a subconsciously controlled person in whom, in this connexion, the processes of reasoning are in abeyance.

An interesting fact, however, is that the drug devotee, on discovering that calomel, say, does not relieve his liver trouble, will try another drug and yet another, and so on, in spite of numerous failures. This serves to show that within one narrow groove he is prepared to make changes, actually to reason out, for instance, that even if calomel fails, podophyllin may prove to be the liver elixir. But he is held down to the " cure idea " of the Stone Age by his confidence in drugs, and thus remains true to one of the most harmful habits which he has inherited as race instincts. Think for a moment of the harmful nature of the building process indicated in the foregoing illustration, where you have a man, supposedly advanced, still clinging to primitive methods of " cure," instead of adopting the only principle a highly evolved, reasoning human creature could conceive of or tolerate—the great comprehensive principle of prevention. If in all his decisions his reasoning processes had not been limited within such a narrow groove, it must have dawned upon him that his liver trouble was the sign that something had gone wrong with the machinery of the whole organism, a conception which would have tended to cause him to consider the guiding and controlling processes involved.

For when a machine, animate or inanimate, has developed mechanical defects, that machine is not functioning at its maximum, and, with the continued use of the machine, these defects not only become more and more pronounced, but actually increase in number. It is obvious, then, that as soon as the mechanical defects are recognized, all possible means should at once be employed to restore the maximum standard of mechanical functioning. In order to accomplish this, a knowledge of the motive, adjusting, guiding, and controlling principles of the mechanism is needed. In the case of the human mechanisms, a knowledge of the psycho-mechanical principles involved is necessary to their co-ordinated use, and this knowledge implies the possession of a sensory appreciation which is reliable.

For in all cases of so-called mental and physical short-comings there are present imperfections and defects in the use of the psycho-physical organism. If the sense registers in connexion with this organism had continued in civilization to be reliable, how could these imperfections and defects have developed in a satisfactorily co-ordinated person? And if the sense registers are so unreliable and deceptive that a person can develop imperfections and defects in the ordinary activities of life, what may be expected as a result of his activities in remedial and other spheres,[1] if he continues to be guided by the same imperfect sense registers which have deceived and are still deceiving him at every turn?

The time is not far distant when these facts will be widely recognized, and it will then be obvious that, immediately we decide to do something to remove a psycho-physical imperfection or defect, the first thing is to acquire gradually a reliable sensory appreciation during a process of re-education, re-adjustment, and co-ordination on a basis of constructive, conscious guidance and control.

---

[1] Many of my readers may object to these arguments and refer to some defect or imperfection which at some time they have removed, with or without aid, as the case may be. I am quite ready to admit this, but I assert that several other defects and imperfections will have been cultivated in the process. As a matter of fact, I am prepared to prove this, if the objector will submit himself or herself for examination whilst he or she demonstrates the process adopted for the " cure." Incidentally, I may mention that these examinations are made whilst the subject remains dressed.

Illustration II

This important point is unfortunately overlooked in all
curative spheres, so that palliative and " end-gaining " specific
methods prevail, and a good illustration of this may be found
in the field of surgery.   In all that follows on this point, however, I wish to make it clear that I am not lacking in the
fullest appreciation of the value of surgery in special spheres,
or of the good results that may accrue from skilful surgery
within these spheres.   But I should like, if I may, to suggest
that it is possible for the surgeon to confer in the future far
greater benefits on humanity than those which he is conferring
at the present time, if he will extend both his field of operation
and his outlook to include the wider plan of prevention.
Take, for instance, the major operations of the removal of the
appendix or of the colon.   The surgeon's business is to remove
these organs in cases where he finds a condition of deterioration which justifies him in concluding that the presence of
these organs is harmful or even dangerous.   It will be seen,
therefore, that to this extent the sphere of surgery is confined
within narrow limits.   The surgeon is asked to examine an
organ which is functioning imperfectly, and if he concludes
from this examination that a certain stage of deterioration of
the particular organ has been reached, he performs an operation.

Under this method of procedure, little consideration is given
to the cause or causes of the general interference with the
functioning of the whole organism, an interference of which
the *specific* deterioration in the appendix, or colon, is merely
a symptom.   Nor do I find that consideration is given, as a
rule, to the fact that the operation, however skilfully performed,
does not restore that standard of reliable sensory appreciation
necessary to the readjustment and co-ordinated use of the
mechanisms, by means of which adequate vital activity will
be restored and the dropped viscera caused to resume their
normal and healthy position in the torso.

This point is in no way affected by the fact that an operation may be entirely successful from the standpoint of the
successful removal of an organ which, being in a state of
deterioration, is a danger to the patient.   The patient recovers
from his operation, but, even so, what is implied by this?
The patient, it is true, has escaped the result of a crisis which

might have proved fatal, but we are still face to face with the same old "end-gaining" principle. The appendix was diseased, the appendix was removed, and the patient recovers from the operation. Nothing, however, in all this has been done to introduce such a change in the working of the psycho-physical mechanisms and general functioning as would prevent a continuance of the imperfect working and imperfect functioning which caused the specific trouble necessitating the operation. This original imperfect functioning not only continues, but is bound to become more and more imperfect as time goes on, and, sooner or later, some other dangerous symptom (due to increasingly imperfect functioning) is almost certain to supervene, when the same palliative remedy—surgery—will again have to be called upon to give relief in a new direction. In the recognition of these facts lies the surgeon's opportunity to pass from the narrow sphere of curative work to the greater achievements that are awaiting him in the broad and comprehensive field of prevention.

Illustration III

Another form of treatment to which I should like to draw attention in this connexion is psycho-analysis. This method has enjoyed a certain publicity in recent years, but in spite of the "cures" which are claimed for it, I am prepared to demonstrate that it is based on the same specific "end-gaining" principle as the less modern methods which it is claimed by some to supersede. By way of illustration I will take the case of a person who suffers from some unreasoning fear, and goes to a psycho-analyst for help in overcoming it. We will suppose that in the course of the analysis, long or short as the case may be, the teacher and the pupil together unravel the knot and decide that the origin of the fear lies in some event, or train of events, which took place in the past and unduly excited the patient's fear reflexes and established a "phobia." For the sake of our illustration, we will say that a "cure" is made. What does this "cure" indicate, however? Wherein lies the fundamental change in the patient's psycho-physical condition?

Before we can answer these questions, we must take into consideration the all-important fact to which I drew attention at the very outset of this book—namely, that all so-called mental activity is a process governed by our psycho-physical condition at the time when the particular stimulus is received. This being so, it is obvious that the reason a person falls a victim to some unreasoning fear is that his condition of general psycho-physical functioning at the time when he receives the stimulus, to which the fear is the reaction, is below a normal and satisfactory standard.[1] For, if his condition of general functioning were normal, his reaction to the particular sensory stimulus would be a normal reaction, not an unreasoning " phobia."

It follows, therefore, that the patient of our illustration must have been below the standard of normal psycho-physical functioning at the time of the establishment of the " phobia "— that is, he must have been beset with a condition of debauched kinæsthesia, the result of imperfect co-ordination, imperfect adjustment, and unreliable and delusive sensory appreciation. The question, then, I must again ask is, What can be done by the " unravelling " procedure of psychoanalysis to remedy these serious defects of general psycho-physical functioning? Will psychoanalysis as practised restore a reliable sensory appreciation to the patient, and co-ordinate and re-educate his psycho-physical mechanisms on a general basis? Certainly not. The psycho-physical condition which permitted the establishment of the first phobia will permit the establishment of another. All that is needed is the stimulus.

The method of psychoanalysis, therefore, like other methods of treatment on a subconscious basis, is an instance of an " end-gaining " attempt to effect the " cure " of a specific trouble by specific means, without consideration being given to the necessity of restoring a satisfactory standard of general psycho-physical functioning and of sensory appreciation.

Fundamental Defect in Our Plan of Civilization a Lack of Recognition of the Importance of the Principle of Prevention on a General Basis

It is the recognition in practice of the principle of prevention which makes possible man's advancement to higher and

[1] It is common knowledge that a person is more subject to infections (colds, etc.) when he is, as we say, run down—that is, in a more or less lowered psycho-physical condition.

higher stages of evolution and opens up the greatest possibilities for human activities and accomplishment. I have
illustrated and insisted upon this point thus fully because I
wish to emphasize what in my opinion constitutes a fundamental defect in a plan of civilization at least two thousand
years old—namely, that in all attempts at reform or improvement in spheres where the well-being of the creature is concerned, human energy has been and still is expended mainly
on the adoption of plans based upon methods of specific cure,
instead of upon the principle of prevention. For many years
past I have endeavoured to put this point of view before
those who have consulted me, for I have found that in the
case of a new pupil, even after I have made my diagnosis of
the malconditions present, explained their actual cause or
causes, and described the practical procedures I should adopt
to remedy such malconditions, I am still generally asked, " Have
you ever ' cured ' a case like mine ? " In answer I point out
that I do not undertake to " cure " anything or anyone.[1] I

---

[1] As I write these words, I can imagine my readers, sooner or later,
asking this question, "Why, then, if you advocate a plan of life founded
on the principle of prevention, have you yourself continued to work in a
more or less curative sphere ? " The answer to this is simple. In the
first place, the principle of prevention should be applied to children at a
very early age; and, secondly, up to the present it has proved impossible
to create a sufficient demand for fundamental psycho-physical re-
education to induce young men and women to study it with a view to
professional teaching in the preventive sphere. This implies that their
work must be confined to children, and the reader will at once see the
difficulty in which we are placed. We are faced with the inevitable law
of supply and demand. Parents must first be themselves convinced of
the need for fundamental psycho-physical re-education, and of the value
of the technique I have to offer, before they will entrust their children
for the time necessary and in sufficient numbers to create a demand
that will make it possible for young men and women to take up the
work on a sound professional and financial basis. Up till now what the
parents have said is, "We will first come to you ourselves; then, if you
are able to ' cure ' our psycho-physical defects, we will consider the
matter in relation to our children." It is in vain that I protest that I
do not set out to " cure " anything. " You see," they reply, " for us to
accept your work as the basis of our children's education means such a
complete change in all our views and methods; it means practically
beginning afresh, and giving up so much that we have been taught is
true up till now, that we cannot interfere with our children's education
without first having the proof of your work in ourselves." Some of my
scientific supporters are no less insistent on these points. Under these

merely look at the subject before me as a damaged machine, as it were, note the badly used mechanisms, the imperfect sensory direction and control, and in the light of my experience ask myself, " Can one restore this machine, improve the mechanical working, build up a new and satisfactory sensory direction and control, restore a well-co-ordinated condition of the psycho-physical organism as a whole? " In other words, instead of trying to remove specific symptoms directly (method of " cure "), I endeavour to bring about such a readjustment of the organism as a whole that the symptoms in question disappear in the process and are not likely to recur if the new conditions are maintained (principle of prevention). This implies in the case of some pupils a long process, for it means a gradual building-up of new and satisfactory psycho-physical use, and the pupils' co-operation in this process must be based upon a reasoning, rather than a blind acceptance of the principles involved. If, at the end of our talk, I consider that there is any doubt on the part of the prospective pupil, I beg him to read my book, study the principles therein set down, and then, if he comprehends and believes in these principles, I suggest that he should come to me for help, but not other-wise. In all seriousness, I beg of him not to come simply

---

circumstances, my reader will understand that I am forced to work in a so-called curative sphere with adults, in the hope that they may help me in my efforts to gain a wide recognition of the necessity for re-educa-tion on a general basis and for preventive measures for the children For once we have created among parents a demand for teachers of the work in the interests of the children, the first part of the problem wil have been solved, for the supply, the material will be there, and will in time bring the right type of man and woman into the work. I am anxious and ready to devote the rest of my life, and the experience have gained, relatively small though this may be, to preparing teachers to teach the children. To this end we need to establish a school for the education of teachers. Such a plan, however, is not without its diffi culties, if the right type of man or woman is to be induced to take up the work. A number of people in England and America have been working with me to the end of establishing such a school. We are all aware of the harm we can do to the cause if we attempt to gain this end quickly at the cost of training only those people who are able to bear the financial burden involved during the necessary years of training, irrespective of the standard to which those psycho-physical potentialities, which go to the making of a teacher, have been developed in their case. Such an attempt could end only in comparative failure, and in the long run do much to delay the wide acceptance of the principles involved.

because he believes that I can " cure " him of something. I am ready to admit that anything will sometimes effect a " cure," as " cure " is generally understood, but the case of the exceptional " cure," by whatever means—whether by a course of medical treatment, by suggestion, transfer, or by any other method, accompanied as these " cures " are by thousands of failures—cannot justify any reasoning person in attempting or promising a continuance of " cures " on these lines. I hold that we have reached a stage in our development when all attempts to remove the cause or causes of suffering which do not come within the scope of reasoned, practical procedure must, with the broader view, be definitely abandoned, and that we should ere now have passed that stage of ignorance and narrowness which permits the human creature to entertain for a moment the idea of a miracle.

The miracle-worker and the advocates of " cure " methods have had free scope for over two thousand years, but despite this fact there has been a gradual increase in malconditions and in the symptoms and complications connected therewith, and therefore a correspondingly increasing need for " cure."

I would even state that in my opinion the fact that man has not been guided by his reasoning processes in connexion with the problems of his well-being is responsible for the tragedy of his progress in civilization. The crisis of 1914 serves to show us that he has released forces which he is not capable of controlling, and by means of which millions of his fellow-beings have been swept from the earth, and it would seem that man is simply preparing the way for his own extinction unless those energies, which in the past have been directed into harmful channels in the outside world, are in future directed and controlled by reasoning processes which have been primarily employed in connexion with the use of his psycho-physical organism.

This horrible recrudescence of barbarity is for the moment held in check, but, like a fire whose white-heated embers have been cooled by water on the outside—a process which has merely served to intensify the degree of heat of the embers which this drenched crust encloses—it will sooner or later burst once more into flame.[1] Every ember, which in our analogy

---

[1] These words, written after the 1914–18 war, have been borne out by the events of 1939–45.—F. M. A.

represents an individual human being, must be dealt with singly and separately, and if we wish to prevent another fierce outbreak we must treat each ember in such a way that it will be as difficult to fire it as it is to fire a piece of stone.

Similar treatment of the individual human creature on a basis of constructive conscious control will bring nearer that stage of evolutionary development where the masses, when thrown together, will no longer exhibit the inflammable traits associated with the herd instinct.

It is clear, then, that our first efforts to enable man to rise above the depths in which he is now struggling, and from which many people to-day believe he cannot extricate himself, should be devoted to the establishment in the individual of a reliable sensory appreciation by means of conscious, reasoning guidance, so as to prevent the recurrence of the disasters which have hitherto been associated with the activities of men and women whose judgments, opinions, and policies have been based more upon a deteriorated sense of feeling than upon reasoning.

Just stop for a moment and think, for instance, of the lack of reasoning associated with the continuance of a plan of life under which the child, the adult of the future, is permitted gradually to develop imperfections and defects, so that long ere the age of adolescence is reached, some curative method of treatment has to be adopted in an attempt to eradicate imperfections and defects which, under a reasoning plan of life, would never have been permitted to become present. Under such a reasoning plan of life, the principle of prevention would be the fundamental underlying the child's education, which means that *from the beginning* preventive measures would be adopted where the well-being of the child is concerned.

The attempt to deal with a form of education based on a principle of prevention will lead into many fields of discussion and probably force me, by way of illustration, to set down descriptions of technical evolutions, a procedure which, on the face of it, would seem to be an encouragement to people to cling to the " curative " and to neglect the preventive plan of life. But I wish here to free myself from responsibility for any such serious harm as invariably follows the attempt of the ordinary subconsciously controlled human being to follow written instructions for some exercise, drill, etc., with the aim of eradicating a defect or imperfection. I have already pointed out in *Man's Supreme Inheritance* that even though a person may succeed by this means in eradicating some specific defect or imperfection, he will be cultivating in the process quite a number of other defects, and in what follows I hope to make clear the reason for this generally unrecognized fact.

For the fundamental shortcoming underlying all human psycho-physical defects, imperfections, and peculiarities is an imperfect and often delusive sensory appreciation, and until those conditions are restored in which the sensory appreciation (sense register) becomes again a more or less reliable guide, *all exercises are a positive danger*. A reliable sensory appreciation, therefore, is an essential, and we will proceed to consider the part which this invaluable human endowment must play in any reasoned and satisfactory plan of education.

I shall therefore devote the rest of this volume to an examination of the part played by sensory appreciation in the process called education, taking this word in its broadest sense, for it is clear from tragic evidence all around us that, despite the influence of our past education, we have not been enabled to stem the rapid progress of human psycho-physical deterioration.

I shall attempt by practical illustrations to demonstrate that the establishment of a reliable sensory appreciation must be the foundation of education of children and of adults in what we call the act of learning and learning to do, or in the performance of all the activities which make up the daily round of occupations and recreations.

PART II

SENSORY APPRECIATION IN ITS RELATION TO LEARNING AND LEARNING TO DO

I

EDUCATION AND RE-EDUCATION

AT no time in our history has the same general interest been shown in education (taking this word in its widest sense) as is manifested at the present day. The experiences of the War and of the world-wide unrest which has followed it have caused all thinking men and women to put to themselves searching questions as to the validity of long-cherished beliefs in every sphere, and nowhere has the searchlight been more vigorously used than in the sphere of education. Articles dealing with defects in educational methods appear with regularity in our newspapers, and because of this prevalent dissatisfaction, all kinds of new methods are being advocated, so that the state of confusion and uncertainty, of which we are all so conscious in the world outside, is equally apparent in the educational world.

This state of confusion and uncertainty, experienced in the practical application of educational theories, has its parallel in that which is experienced in our attempts to decide as to the merit or demerit of any particular system, and for the reason that until now such decisions have remained within the doubtful range of individual opinion, which is too often formed subconsciously and based chiefly upon results.

In the endeavour to make plain what, in my opinion, constitutes the fundamental cause of this generally chaotic condition, I should like to begin by drawing attention to a fact which, though well known, has been practically disregarded in all forms of past and present education, and, indeed, in all our dealings with our fellow-beings in every sphere. This fact is that whenever we wish to convey to anyone a new idea, whether by the written or spoken word, that is to say, to teach him something, the person wishing to make use of it

64

by that psycho-physical activity which we call learning something must first get his or her conception of what is indicated
by those written or spoken words, and his practical use of the
new idea will be conditioned by this conception.   This applies
equally when similar attempts are made by any process of
self-instruction (auto-education).   It then follows that in the
sphere of acquiring knowledge, especially psycho-physical
knowledge, this matter of the particular person's conception of
written or spoken words is all-important, for it is the construc-
tion which the learner, adult or child, places upon what he
hears or reads which determines the course of his actions or
the trend of his opinions.   Yet the ordinary teacher acts and
the ordinary teaching methods are based on the assumption
that the pupil's conception of a new idea is identical with that of
the teacher, the words " teacher " and " pupil " being here used
in the widest possible sense.   Anyone who has had practical
dealings with children will know how frequently disappointment and failure in their studies, or anything else, are due to
their not understanding exactly what is required of them.
The daily experiences of life are studded with instances of misunderstanding, not only in trivial matters, but also in matters
of great importance, and, if the broad view is taken, I think
we may justly say that the great majority of these experiences
constitute one long series of specific and general misunder-
standings and lead us to the conclusion that, where misunderstanding occurs, there is present some impeding factor (or
factors) which interferes with the process of reasoning, a process inseparable from what is called understanding or " mental
conception."

The significance, however, of the fact that a person's attempt
to make practical use of a new idea is conditioned by his conception of the written or spoken word cannot be fully realized
until we connect it with the further fact, that this conception,
in its turn, is conditioned by the standard of the psycho-
physical functioning of the individual, this standard again
being influenced by the standard of sensory appreciation; in
other words, that *the accuracy or otherwise of the individual
conception depends upon the standard of psycho-physical functioning and of sensory appreciation present.*   It is our total dis-
regard of this fundamental fact that, in my opinion, is at the
root of all the confusion and uncertainty so prevalent to-day

in the sphere of education, and, for that matter, in every sphere of practical life.

For, if the foregoing is true, we can see at once how essential it is that in the matter of conveying and imparting knowledge—in other words, in education—we should be able to command a high standard of psycho-physical functioning in the whole organism, associated with that growth and development which makes for the continuous raising both of this standard and of the standard of sensory appreciation; and, further, that in order to arrive at sound conclusions concerning the fundamentals upon which any scheme of education should be based, we must first take into consideration the standard of psycho-physical functioning of the human being whom we are to educate, both to-day and in what we hope is to be a progressive future.

Unfortunately, a satisfactory standard of psycho-physical functioning has not been considered an essential either in the early or subsequent schemes of education which man, whilst depending mainly upon subconscious guidance and control, has adopted in the attempt to make what is known as " mental " progress. Even to-day this essential factor does not seem to be considered an essential, for in this regard modern methods of education are as lacking as those which have obtained for generations.

The seriousness of this position is at once apparent when we take into consideration the fact that, during the past two hundred years, the standard of sensory appreciation in the great majority of people has become harmfully lowered, with the result that mankind has generally become more and more imperfectly co-ordinated and has developed serious defects. Yet, in spite of this, the teachers and originators of modern systems, like those of an earlier date, are still trying to help individuals to progress towards a higher state of " physical " and " mental " development, whilst leaving them dependent on subconscious experiences for guidance and control, without any consideration or, indeed, understanding of the harm that results from attempts to obey instructions made by people who are guiding themselves by an unreliable and often delusive appreciation.

The problem, then, with which we are faced is that the human beings to be educated to-day are already saddled with a more or less debauched kinæsthesia, a condition in which psycho-physical reactions are abnormal and harmful. Satisfactory education is incompatible with abnormal and harmful reactions, and a teaching technique, therefore, to be satisfactory, must be one that will meet the needs of those who are beset with the varying and more or less serious defects in the employment of the psycho-physical mechanisms which are responsible for unsatisfactory and harmful reactions. We shall now attempt to outline some of these defects and to indicate the difficulties they present to both teacher and pupil in any attempt to teach or to learn something, and we will start by considering them in connexion with the child's activities at school.

I should first like to point out that, though there may be a large increase in the number of parents who do not need compulsion in the matter of sending their children to school, the idea that a child should go to school is too often a preconceived idea with them, not a reasoned conviction. It is probable that very few parents have given due consideration to the effect of sending a child to school, other than that it should be educated. To most people the educational process is one by means of which the child is to acquire knowledge and be put right in all matters where he is judged to be wrong. This judgment is usually the outcome of the combined experience of his teacher and parents, the former being influenced by the latter, as all parents have more or less fixed ideas in regard to the present and future needs of the child, and choose the school in accordance with their ideas in this particular.[1] They also have very definite ideas concerning the processes which should be involved, in spite of the fact that they have never had the experience that might have justified them in holding these fixed opinions. Further, it occurs to very few of them to consider whether, in this process of " education " (*i.e.*, in certain specific directions), the child's fear reflexes will not be unduly and harmfully excited by the injunction that it must always try ·to " be right," [2] indeed, that it is almost a

[1] Incidentally, I should like to say that in a properly constituted civilization based on a principle of conscious control, parents would be qualified by training and experience to know their child's needs, and, what is more to the point, they would know how to satisfy these, if need be.

[2] The idea of " right " is almost always associated with *product* or result, not with *method* of operation. We have only to listen to any

disgrace to be wrong; that the teachers concerned do not even know how to prevent the child from acquiring the very worst psycho-physical use of itself whilst standing or sitting at its desk or table, pondering over its lessons, or performing its other duties; that on account of the methods of cramming and other means adopted in the act of learning, there is being cultivated a harmful psycho-physical condition—one result being recognized in a loss of memory—which in our time has developed to such a serious point that it has paved the way for the exploitation of educated people by means of various methods, such as " memory systems," etc.[1]

In this matter of sending children to school, we must realize that any undue excitement of the fear reflexes in the daily routine of school work has a very serious effect upon the respiratory processes,[2] which are so closely linked up with the emotions, and when in addition we consider the detrimental effect upon these processes of the defective use of the organism [3]

---

lesson from this point of view to realize that the directions the child receives, such as " sit up straight," " speak out," " take a deep breath," " see how quietly you can walk," etc., are all specific " end-gaining " instructions which rarely include the correct *means whereby* he can carry them out. It is only when instructions include the correct " means-whereby " that the process of carrying them out involves the satisfactory use of the psycho-physical mechanisms concerned.

[1] All these systems, being framed, however, on the " specific " or " end-gaining " principle, are devoid of the fundamentals of satisfactory psycho-physical development. Incidentally, in connexion with failing memory, the following is exceedingly interesting. We are all aware that a sluggish liver does not make for the best use of the " mental " powers, and we know people who, through bad habits of over-indulgence, have reached a stage of liver and kidney disorder when their reasoning processes are seriously interfered with and they are conscious of a temporary comparative loss of memory. Facts such as these serve to remind us of the interdependence of " mental " and " physical " activity. If the vital functioning of the " physical " mechanisms and organs is inadequate, the organism becomes gradually more or less poisoned, and the " mental " machinery gradually less and less efficient. In such a case it is very difficult to understand in what mysterious way the ordinary memory system can enable one to remedy the " physical " disorders indicated, and if it does not, a successful result is highly improbable.

See, further, Chapter on " Memory and Feeling."
[2] As Byron wrote : " Breathless as we stand when feeling most."
[3] This defective use will be even more pronounced when the arms are employed in the ordinary acts of life, particularly in the acts of writing,

during study at school desks and in school chairs (for in study, as in deep sleep, the respiratory processes are reduced to their minimum of activity), in standing, walking, and, in fact, during the assumption of any ordinary posture, we are faced with a problem which no scheme on a subconscious basis will solve. For when harmful conditions such as have been mentioned are present in the child, they will be found to constitute an impeding factor in all its general activities. In the attempt to improve its handwriting, for instance, new faults will be developed in the general use of the psycho-physical mechanisms, and the established defects will tend to become more pronounced. It is obvious that knowledge, acquired in this way, is being acquired at a cost represented by an interference with the general control, and particularly with the use of those psycho-physical mechanisms upon which respiratory control depends. With these conditions present, the child lacks the psycho-physical equipment essential to the best efforts in learning something. The gradual lowering of the respiratory and other vital processes during study is undoubtedly one of the impeding factors which make for the dreamy condition—often amounting almost to stupor—into which people of the student and orthodox " thinking class " drift.

I am ready to admit that there is a steadily growing minority of parents who want more for their children than for them to read and write, do sums, etc., and who will say that what they desire for them is a " complete and all-round development." I also admit that there have been changes and modifications in certain spheres of education, whilst in others attempts have been made to counter supposed evils or defects. These attempts, unfortunately, are too often merely a reaction from one extreme to another. But beyond this, the fatal defect in all such instances of attempted reforms on a subconscious plane is that they have been, and still are, based

---

drawing, etc. The arm resting on the table or desk will be wrongly employed as a support for the body, and the arm, hand, and fingers engaged in the movements necessary for the act of writing will also come in for criticism, the result being harmful to the child's organism *as a whole*, thereby seriously impeding progress in the act of learning penmanship, and, in many cases, making a satisfactory result practically impossible.

on the principle of a specific, not of a general development, and that whatever form the attempt may take in a particular school, we shall find that it has been worked out neither in relation to the child's organism *as a whole*, nor with any recognition of the fact that the child of to-day does not start life with the standard of co-ordination and sensory appreciation enjoyed by the children of, say, two hundred years ago.[1] Its psycho-physical mechanisms are not nearly as reliable, nor its ingenuity at a given age as great as theirs in relation to most psycho-physical acts in the practical way of life. As a result, by the time the ordinary child reaches school age, certain wrong uses of the psycho-physical mechanism have become established, constituting a serious condition which baffles the most thoughtful teachers.[2]

Anyone having a doubt in this connexion will be convinced by visiting any school with an expert capable of pointing out the defects of which we speak, and of indicating the influence of these defects upon the whole organism in daily activity. The head of an important preparatory school came to consult the writer in the hope that some solution might be found for what she rightly considered *the problem* of the school. She said that although all the most recent methods providing satisfactory environmental conditions, outdoor activity, and opportunity for " free expression " had been adopted in this school, the problem still remained unsolved, whilst the urgency for its solution became more and more apparent to all concerned. She admitted that, until she had read *Man's Supreme Inheritance*, she could not understand why the active outdoor life did not serve to prevent or eradicate the physical defects and shortcomings in the children which gave cause for such serious consideration. But of what avail are good hygienic conditions, an outdoor life, a greatly improved environment, " free activi-

---

[1] I have drawn attention to this fact in *Man's Supreme Inheritance*.

[2] As one teacher wrote : " No one who observes carefully the predominant characteristics of the present generation can fail to note :—

" (1) Alarming imperfections of physique, i.e., defects of spine, wrong posture, lack of correct co-ordination of muscles in bodily acts, depressed stature, etc.

" (2) No less great limitations in the purely mental field, e.g., domination by a fixed idea, inability to apprehend and to respect other points of view, failure to grasp the essentials of freedom, etc. All this is symptomatic of some underlying cause."

ties," and " physical exercises," whilst the child that is to be
given an " all-round development " under these conditions is
actually allowed to use himself during his activities in ways
which interfere to such an extent with the psycho-mechanics
of his respiratory processes that these are working nearer to
their minimum than to their maximum capacity, and this in
spite of the fact that his teachers would unanimously agree that
the proper working of these processes is the most vital element
in the child's development ? [1]

The almost universal call for physical drill, or physical exercises, in schools, for training in posture, breathing exercises,
etc., coming from parents, teachers, and all concerned, is an
admission that there is a great need in this direction, but,
unfortunately, these methods will not give the necessary help.
The harmful effects of the child's psycho-physical experiences,
gained whilst at study, cannot be remedied by the performance
of the movements involved in any forms of exercises, drill,
posture, calisthenics, etc., for the defects resulting from these
daily psycho-physical experiences are the manifestations of a
badly adjusted and imperfectly co-ordinated machine, guided
and controlled by a delusive sensory appreciation, and therefore functioning much nearer to its minimum than to its
maximum capabilities.

The problem is further complicated in that there has been
and still is a continual increase in the educational demands
which are being made upon the child, unavoidably, it is supposed, in the present stage of civilization. For the increase in
the degree of mal-co-ordination present in the child continues
in the same ratio as the difficulties to be overcome in any
attempt to eradicate defects, whilst at the same time the
degree of difficulty which the child will encounter in connexion
with its lessons or other activities will be in accord with the
degree of imperfect general functioning. This again means
that the child, to ensure success, must of necessity devote
more and more time to these subjects, with the result that
increasing demands are being made upon him, involving longer

---

[1] I must refer my reader to *Man's Supreme Inheritance* in regard to
the failure of " physical exercises " and drill to eradicate such defects
as are present. It is possible to prove by demonstration that even if a
specific defect should chance to be eradicated, several others, often more
harmful, will be cultivated during the process of eradication.

hours of work and increased effort, and the increasing complications these imply. How can the psycho-physical mechanisms of the children meet these demands satisfactorily, when they are functioning much nearer to their minimum than to their maximum possibilities? And what is to happen if the educational demands continue to increase, whilst the psycho-physical possibilities of the children continue to decrease, as they surely will, unless the defects which make for badly co-ordinated use of the psycho-physical self are eradicated, and instead there is set in motion a process of genuine development on a plane of conscious control in the use of the organism?

We must remember also that every attempt on the part of the child to do something or to acquire knowledge makes a psycho-physical demand, and that the child's efforts, *when judged on a general and not a specific basis*, will always be in accordance with the standard of psycho-physical functioning of its organism. Where harmful conditions such as those we have indicated above are present in a child, the teacher, in any attempt to remedy *specific* defects (such as, for instance, defects in a child's handwriting), must take into account the standard of the general psycho-physical use of the child, otherwise the attempt will result not only in the development of new faults in this use, but also in a tendency to strengthen any old-established imperfect uses.

It follows, therefore, that in those cases where the psycho-physical mechanism is imperfect and functioning more or less inadequately, we cannot expect the best results in the conveyance or the acquisition of knowledge. There is a lack of co-ordination of the parts of the organism involved in the process called education, so that any attempts made to learn something or to learn to do something (and this applies equally to all processes of self-instruction) must tend to the cultivation of new psycho-physical defects and cannot fail to exaggerate the old ones. The child's early efforts in learning any simple subject which forms part of the curriculum are on a *specific* basis; that is, the child's work is planned for him from the beginning on " end-gaining " lines of teaching him to do specific things in specific ways, and of teaching him to try to get these specific things " right," and long ere the stage of adolescence is reached, this " end-gaining " procedure will have become established, associated with a bad psycho-physical attitude towards the acceptance of new ideas and new experiences, and too often with a serious deterioration in memory. When these defects and shortcomings are present, they constitute two impeding factors which could account for the general lack in the majority of adults to link up knowledge.[1] Knowledge is of little use in itself; it is the linking up of what we know with that which comes to us daily in the shape of new ideas and new experiences which is of value, and this ability to link up is inseparable from the processes concerned with remembering. In other words, the value of knowledge lies in our power to make use of it in association with the greater knowledge which should come to us as we increase in years of experience, and as we substitute reasoning for instinct and for what Professor Dewey calls "emotional gusts."

Our first consideration, therefore, in all forms of education must be in regard to securing for the child the highest possible standard of psycho-physical functioning during his attempts to master the different processes which make up the educational scheme. In this way the child will make a fair start, and, what is more to the point, he will continue to improve the conditions involved, hand in hand with his efforts as a pupil in all other spheres of activity.

The plan of education we advocate is a comprehensive one, such as will not only meet the needs of the human creature at the present stage of his evolution, but will also meet his future needs, as he passes from this present stage of subconscious guidance and control through the progressive evolutionary stages which lead to a higher and still higher state of civilization. The test of man's advance in this connexion demands a consideration of

(1) the plane of consciousness reached in his recognition of incorrect psycho-physical use within the organism, and

[1] I fully realize that efforts are being made to link up and correlate subjects in the school curriculum which were formerly taught as separate subjects, or to group various subjects round one central idea, as the teaching of history in connexion with drama, mathematics, and carpentering, nature with the drawing lesson, etc. But this again is *specific* correlation, and does not affect the point I have raised as to the need for co-ordination of the child's organism as a whole and for the co-ordinated use of this organism in every activity and interest in life.

in the employment of that organism in all psycho-physical
activity in every-day life;

(2) the standard of his ability to accept readily a new
and expanding idea, when once he has become convinced
of its value and of its superiority to older and long-
cherished ideas, associated with a keen desire for the new
experiences which go hand in hand with new and expanding ideas, and for that standard of psycho-physical
development which will enable him to profit by the
experiences;

(3) the standard of his ability to adapt himself to the
rapid changes of environment in civilization with benefit,
instead of detriment or injury, to his psycho-physical self;

(4) the standard of his ability to hold in abeyance the
fear of giving up his job, in whatever profession, trade, or
calling this may be, and boldly to make the necessary
change, should he find that the fundamental principles
concerned are defective; and to make the necessary adjustments which are essential to the acceptance and assimilation of new and approved knowledge whilst going on with
his job.

The foregoing serves to outline principles which are worthy
of first consideration in all forms of education which are to
meet satisfactorily the present and future needs of the human
creature. There can be little doubt that the knowledge of the
satisfactory and adequate use of the organism is of first importance, for it is upon this satisfactory and adequate use that
the degree of our success depends in meeting the demands
made upon us in educational and all other spheres of activity.

The consideration of principles in connexion with any plan
of education leads naturally to the consideration of the technique, the *means whereby* these principles are to be carried out,
and in the pages of this book we are concerned with the technique to be employed in putting the principles I have outlined
to practical use in the work of re-education, co-ordination, and
readjustment on a conscious plane.

At this point it is necessary to remember that all teaching
methods on the subconscious basis are formulated on the
principle that if a pupil suffers from some defect, imperfection,
or peculiarity that needs to be eradicated, he must at once *do*

something (usually with the help of a teacher) to eradicate the defect or defects. The teacher on a subconscious basis believes in this system for dealing with defects. It is his business to teach the pupil to do something to eradicate his defects, the " doing " in this connexion meaning to the pupil simply *the performance of a series of physical movements to be carried out in accordance with the pupil's conception of the teacher's instructions.* The fact that the teacher fails in this attempt in the great majority of cases may disturb him, but does not undermine his faith in his methods or change his attitude towards his original premiss. He may point to some successes, but unfortunately he lacks that keenness of observation, he has not reached that desirable state of awareness, which would reveal to him the fact that his success is merely a *specific* one and that, in the process of eradicating the particular defect, he has permitted the pupil to cultivate several others more harmful than the original, and of which teacher and pupil alike remain in blissful ignorance.

On the other hand, the whole procedure of teaching on a plane of constructive conscious control is based on the opposite principle—namely, that those who have developed a condition in which the sensory appreciation (feeling) is more or less imperfect and deceptive, cannot expect to succeed in remedying this condition by relying upon this same deceptive feeling for guidance in their efforts in re-education, readjustment, and co-ordination, or in their attempts to put right something they know to be wrong with the psycho-physical organism. For immediately the child or adult attempts to perform any psycho-physical act, that use of himself which is the manifestation of his inherited and cultivated instincts (i.e., of his habits) becomes the dominating factor. It then follows that if a pupil is more or less badly co-ordinated, the use of his psycho-physical self will be imperfect and therefore more or less harmful. , This means that he will be beset with defects, that his sensory appreciation (feeling) of what he is doing will be deceptive, and that immediately he makes any attempt to correct these defects, he will be at a still greater disadvantage in consequence of the lack of correct guidance through reliable sensory appreciation.

The significance of this in relation to education comes out fully if we follow our argument a step farther. For if the foregoing is true (and I assert that it is capable of practical demonstration), it follows that in the case of a child who is found to experience difficulty in carrying out some simple activity, or to be suffering from certain defects and imperfections, it is of no use, indeed it is unreasoning, for its teachers to ask it to *do anything itself* with the aim of helping it over its difficulty, or of eradicating its defects, because (and this is the point that is overlooked in all schemes of reform or remedial work with which I have come in contact) *the only guidance the child has to rely upon in doing anything to carry out the teacher's instructions is the very same delusive subconscious guidance (unreliable sensory appreciation) that was instrumental in causing the defects to develop and become established in the first instance.* For all defects and imperfections are symptoms of a condition of mal-co-ordination and of maladjustment, a condition which will always be found to go hand in hand with the possession of an unreliable sensory appreciation. In the same way, we shall find that where a condition of unreliable sensory appreciation exists in the child or adult (and all that is written here applies with even greater force to the adult) there will also be present a condition of mal-co-ordination, in some form or other, and some incorrect adjustment. Any attempt, then, made by the child that is imperfectly co-ordinated to use its unreliable sensory appreciation as a guide in its efforts to do something in obedience to directions in order to correct a defect, is bound to result in some form of misdirected activity, accompanied by an increase of the original defect or imperfection, and by the undue development of the fear reflexes.

This brings us face to face with the demand for a teaching technique which will meet this difficulty, and such a technique involves correct manipulation on the part of the teacher in the matter of giving the pupil correct experiences in sensory appreciation, in the spheres of re-education, readjustment, and co-ordination. Furthermore, in order to give these satisfactory sensory experiences, the teacher must himself be in possession of a reliable sensory mechanism and have gained the experience in re-education and co-ordination that is required for a satisfactory readjustment of the organism.

But in this connexion it must always be clearly understood that the correct sensory experiences to be acquired by means of this technique cannot be described in writing or by the

spoken word in such a way as to be of practical value. As a
friend of mine, a well-known scientific man, replied to a query
in this connexion, " We cannot write a kinæsthesia, any more
than we can write the sense of sound. We can only write the
symbols of sound, notes of music, for instance."

It is necessary to emphasize this point, as it is one that is
so constantly overlooked. Many people have said to me, for
instance, with quite a friendly knowing look, " You know,
that book of yours, *Man's Supreme Inheritance*, is quite a
clever piece of work." When I ask them for their reason,
the same answer is always forthcoming : " Because you give
us enough to make us interested in your theory and just lead
us to the point where we realize we must go to you for lessons."
It has happened in my experience over and over again that,
after I have carefully explained to a pupil that he needed re-
education because of his lack of reliable sensory appreciation,
and have even shown him by practical demonstration that he
was actually developing harmful defects, because he was guiding himself in his movements by a deceptive " feeling," the
pupil has turned to me and said, " Please give me some exercise that I can practise at home." Beyond this I have emphasized in my book the point that manipulation is necessary
for the development and establishment of reliable sensory
appreciation in the case of individuals who have developed
defects, because in everything they are doing *themselves* by
the usual methods to remedy these defects they are guiding
themselves by an unreliable sense of feeling, thus adding to
the incorrect experiences which must always result from
guidance by unreliable sensory appreciation. Yet in spite of
all that I have written on this point, I have been criticized for
" keeping things back," because I would not give in my book
instructions and set exercises that people could *do* at home
by themselves ! In all such instances I point out that I will
not be guilty at this stage of my teaching experience of adding
to the mass of literature on the subject of exercises, or take the
grave responsibility for the harmful consequences which are
certain to result from the practice of exercises, according to
written instructions, by people whose sensory appreciation is
unreliable and often positively delusive. The technique, therefore, in which we are interested has been developed throughout
from the premiss that, if something is wrong with us, it is

because we have been guided by unreliable sensory appreciation, leading to incorrect sensory experiences and resulting in misdirected activities.

These misdirected activities manifest themselves in the use of the psycho-physical mechanism in connexion with all the general activities of life, and in many varying ways, according to our individual idiosyncrasies. They are influenced by and associated with our incorrect conceptions, our imperfect sensory appreciation, our unduly excited fear reflexes and uncontrolled emotions and prejudices, and our imperfectly adjusted mechanisms. These psycho-physical derangements in the process of formation are the forerunners of a psycho-physical attitude towards the conduct of life in general which must be considered perverted, and because these misdirected activities are so closely connected with this perverted attitude, they present a problem of great difficulty to both teacher and pupil in any endeavour to convey or acquire knowledge, particularly in regard to the satisfactory use of the psycho-physical mechanisms. I shall now go on to consider this problem in relation to incorrect conception.

II

INCORRECT CONCEPTION

In the matter of conception, the first step is to convince the pupil that his present misdirected activities are the result of incorrect conception and of imperfect sensory appreciation (feeling).

Now, in this regard I would at once warn those who are inexperienced in this matter that the pupil, as a rule, will not be convinced on this point by discussion and argument alone. A pupil will, indeed, often assure his teacher that he sees the argument, and from his standpoint this statement may be true. But in my experience there is only one way by which a teacher can really convince a pupil that his sense of feeling is misleading him when he starts to carry out a movement, and that is *by demonstration upon the pupil's own organism.* A mirror should be used, so that the pupil, as far as possible, can have ocular demonstration as well.

The next point of importance to be impressed upon the pupil is the necessity for listening carefully to the teacher's words, and for being quite clear as to the meaning that these words are intended to convey, *before he attempts to act upon them.* This may seem a truism, but, as a matter of fact, it is at this point that we come up against a rock on which even a highly experienced teacher may make shipwreck. For, in every case, the pupil's conception of what his teacher is trying to convey to him by words *will be in accordance with his (the pupil's) psycho-physical make-up.*[1]

If, for instance, the pupil has fixed ideas in some particular direction, these fixed ideas must inevitably limit his capacity for " listening carefully " (a capacity which we are apt to take so much for granted)—that is, for receiving the new ideas *as the teacher is trying to convey them to him.* In this connexion, therefore, a teacher, in dealing with the shortcomings of a particular case, must give due consideration to the pupil's fixed conceptions, otherwise these will greatly complicate the

[1] In this sense it can be truly said that a pupil hears only what he wants to hear, because what he wants is decided by the standards fixed by his present habits.

problem for both teacher and pupil. Certain of these fixed
ideas are encountered in the case of almost every pupil; fixed
ideas, for example, as to what constitutes the right and what
the wrong method of going to work as a pupil; fixed ideas in
regard to the necessity for concentration, if success is to attend
the efforts of pupil and teacher; also a fixed belief (based on
subconscious guidance) that, if a pupil is corrected for a defect,
he should be taught *to do something* in order to correct it, instead
of being taught, as a first principle, *how to prevent* (*inhibition*)
the wrong thing from being done.

The teacher experienced in the work of re-education can
diagnose at once, by the expression and use of the pupil's
eyes, the degree of influence upon him of such conceptions,
and at each step in the training he should take preventive
measures to counteract this influence. It is absurd to try to
teach a person who is in a more or less agitated or even anxious
condition. We must have that calm condition which is
characteristic of a person whose reasoning processes are
operative.

The list of fixed conceptions given above might be increased
a hundredfold. The peculiarities of fixed conceptions, like
peculiarities of handwriting, differ greatly in different people,
and the form they take depends, as in the case of handwriting
again, upon the individual psycho-physical make-up.[1]

A teaching experience of over twenty-five years in a psycho-
physical sphere has given me a very real knowledge of the
psycho-physical difficulties which stand in the way of many
adults who need re-education and co-ordination, and, as the
result of this experience, I have no hesitation in stating that
the pupil's fixed ideas and conceptions are the cause of the major
part of his difficulties.

I will now take certain of these fixed conceptions from my
teaching experience, because they are so widespread and have
such far-reaching and harmful effects upon life in general, and
I will begin with the habit which has become established in
most pupils trained on a subconscious basis, and to which we
have already referred—viz., *that of trying to correct one defect by
doing something else.*

[1] All that is written here about fixed conceptions applies equally
to the teacher as to the pupil.

Illustration I. " Doing It Right "

Let us suppose that a person decides that he will take lessons in re-education from a certain teacher and comes for the first lesson. The teacher proceeds to indicate to the pupil, firstly, the results of his diagnosis of the pupil's psycho-physical peculiarities, delusions, and defects which he proposes to attempt to eradicate; and, secondly, the *means whereby* the eradication is to be effected.

It invariably follows that by the time the teacher has concluded his statement, the pupil will have formed his own conception (often diametrically the reverse of his teacher's) of the facts disclosed, and unless he is a very unusual person, he will already have come to a decision in accordance with his preconceived ideas,

> (1) as to the cause or causes underlying the facts disclosed;
> (2) as to the ends that will be gained by the removal of these causes; and, most important of all,
> (3) as to the means he will adopt in order to gain these ends.

In this last decision he will be influenced by his fixed belief that in order to secure the end he desires his first duty is *to do something* (as he understands " doing "), and *to do it right* (as he understands " doing it right "). This is not surprising, as it is probable that all his former teachers will have instilled into him from his earliest days the idea that when something is wrong, he must do something to try to get it right. Beyond this, he will have been told that, if he is conscientious, he will always try to be right, not wrong, so that this desire to " be right " will have become an obsession in which, as in so many other matters, his conscience must be satisfied.[1]

---

[1] If we think the matter out, we shall be forced to admit that in such matters a person's insistence on satisfying conscience is too often merely an attempt to unload responsibility. He is aware of certain orthodox ways of dealing with his difficulties. His own experience of these ways is that they have mostly ended in failure. Still he argues that if he tries them and they fail, he at least has done his best. In other words, he tries to satisfy his conscience, not his reasoning intelligence. He embraces this way of going to work because it is the easy

As soon as the teacher observes that the pupil (following out his fixed idea) is setting out to do something he thinks right to bring about the end he desires, he will point out to the pupil that, in trying to remedy his defects by " doing something " himself, he is relying upon his own judgment, but that *his (the pupil's) judgment cannot be sound in this respect, based as it is on his previous incorrect sensory experiences.* The teacher will therefore advise the pupil to stop relying on his own judgment in these matters, and, instead, to listen to the new instructions, and to allow the teacher to give him by means of manipulation the new correct sensory experiences.

The idea, however, of ceasing to do the wrong thing (as a preliminary measure in re-education) makes little or no appeal at first to the average pupil, who, in most cases, goes on trying to " be right " in spite of his experience and of all that his teacher may say.[1]

There are many reasons for this, chief among them being, in my opinion, the fact to which I have already drawn the reader's attention—namely, that in our conception of *how* to employ the different parts of our mechanisms, we are guided almost entirely by a sense of feeling which is more or less unreliable. We get into the habit of performing a certain act in a certain way, and we experience a certain feeling in connexion with it which we recognize as " right." *The act and the particular feeling associated with it becomes one in our recognition.* If anything should cause us to change our con-

---

way. If he once stopped to reason the thing out, and based his judgment on the experience gained from the knowledge of his previous failures, he would have to discard these orthodox plans and seek new ones. This would not be the easy way. It would be the difficult way. It would mean, among other things, a painful dissection of his psychophysical peculiarities, defects, prejudices, sensory excesses, and these are to him just as much a manifestation of his malconditions as are the diseased liver and kidney in the case of the drunkard. To give his liver and kidneys a chance, the drunkard would have to give up drinking wine, but he has not the control to do this. So with the pupil in our illustration. He knows that certain psycho-physical habits are responsible for his condition, but these habits have become a part of him; they appeal to his perverted sense of feeling, and so he will not make the effort to give them up.

[1] He is so possessed with the idea of " specific cure " that the principle of prevention (inhibition) is accepted by him at such a low valuation that, in ninety-nine cases out of a hundred, it will be ignored.

ception, however, in regard to the manner of performing the act, and if we adopt a new method in accordance with this changed conception, we shall experience *a new feeling* in performing the act which we do not recognize as " right." We then realize that what we have hitherto recognized as " right " is wrong.

For instance, suppose the teacher, in trying to change some malcondition in the pupil, asks him to bend his knees. The pupil, thinking only of what his teacher asks him (the " end "), and desiring to do it right (as he understands " doing it right " in connexion with the act of bending his knees), bends his knees, and bends them as he has always bent them—that is, with a great amount of unnecessary tension and pressure, interfering with his equilibrium, shortening his spine [1] (by increasing the curve, etc.), stiffening his neck, and so attains his end (the bending of his knees), but at the cost of undue strain and disadvantage in the use of the organism. I do not mean, of course, that the pupil is conscious of all this. He has probably never thought out how (the " means-where-by ") he has performed such acts as " bending his knees," and though he knows in a general way that something is wrong with him (else it is improbable that he would be coming to a teacher at all), he has not associated this " something wrong " with anything that *he has been doing himself*—that is, with his own misdirected activities. Therefore, when he bends his knees in response to his teacher's request, he is not conscious of anything being wrong in his manner of doing it. He bends them as he has always been accustomed to bend them. This satisfies him, *it feels right to him.*

Now suppose that the teacher, after drawing the pupil's attention to the very disadvantageous manner in which he has been using himself during the process of bending his knees, gives him some help (into the details of which we will enter in the following chapters), and succeeds in inducing him to bend his knees to the best advantage in the general use of his mechanisms. When this occurs, the act of bending the knees *becomes, as far as this pupil is concerned, to all intents and purposes a new act, bringing with it a new feeling.* This time the act is not what he is accustomed to, and so it *feels wrong* to him.

[1] See Chapter : " Illustration."

Henceforward, whenever the conception of bending the knees comes to this pupil (whether in response to his teacher's directions or through his own initiative), the choice lies before him of bending them in the old way (i.e., at great disadvantage to himself) and " feeling right," or of changing the manner in which he performs the act and " feeling wrong." As a little girl said quaintly when this point was explained to her in connexion with something she was doing, " Oh, I see ! If I feel at all, I must feel wrong. If I don't feel wrong, I mustn't feel." Unfortunately, the average adult pupil, unlike the little girl, does not " see," or, if he does, he will not act accordingly. Indeed, we have to face the fact that the adult, as a rule, does not like a new feeling ; in some cases he is positively *afraid* of it. A new " feeling " gives him a sense of insecurity when he experiences it in connexion with acts that he has been accustomed to associate with a different feeling all his life. This sense of insecurity is particularly marked in connexion with the maintenance of his equilibrium in the acts of standing, walking, etc., in accordance with the newly acquired feeling.[1] And so it comes about that, when a pupil is faced with the alternative of using his mechanisms badly and " feeling right," or of using them well and " feeling wrong," he is apt, as we say, to lose his head, does not stop, therefore, to consider (that is, inhibit), and falls back upon " feeling right."

This is only one example of the difficulty which a pupil's incorrect conceptions and misdirected activities in certain directions will present both to him and his teacher in any endeavour to convey or acquire knowledge in the psychophysical sphere. In such a case as the one we have cited, the pupil's fixed ideas as to what constitutes " right " and what " wrong " in certain conditions will produce a deadlock. For how can new and correct experiences be given to a pupil who, in all the movements he makes, is working subconsciously to reproduce certain feelings that he has grown used to and

---

[1] Incidentally, I would point out that, in cases where a person develops a " phobia " in connexion with crossing streets, travelling by train, crossing bridges or open spaces, being alone in a room, being unduly alarmed by ordinary noises, etc., there is already present in that person a serious condition of unsatisfactory psycho-physical equilibrium, which accounts for the susceptibility to the particular stimulus responsible for the " phobia."

likes? The situation is one that no teacher, be he ever so expert, can deal with satisfactorily, one from which the pupil cannot possibly be extricated, until he stops trying to get things right—stops, that is, working blindly for his *ends*, and gives thought instead to the new *means* [1] given to him by his teacher, *whereby* his ends can be attained.

Illustration II. Doing Things " His Way "

I will now take an equally fixed and unreasoning conception which is common to most pupils who need re-education and co-ordination—namely, their fixed ideas *as to what they can and cannot do*.

Their judgment on these points, of course, can only be based on their previous misleading experiences, but, in spite of this fact, they are not ready to change their ideas, even when their teacher has given them practical proof that their judgment on these points is not to be relied on. Now, it would seem reasonable that any pupil who decides to take lessons of a certain teacher because he believes the teacher can help him to overcome some difficulty would take that teacher's word for it as to whether he is capable or not of doing what he is asked to do at a particular point. But too often the opposite is the case. For if a teacher during a lesson should ask a pupil to do something which happens to be among the things which, in the days before he came for lessons, he was convinced he could not do (i.e., his difficulty), the pupil will immediately baulk. He may not openly refuse to follow out the new instructions given to him, but, what amounts to the same thing, he will make a " mental reservation," as we say, when he receives them. The reason for this is that he subconsciously believes that he knows more than his teacher about the things he can or cannot do. So that, when he receives the instructions, he starts to carry them out on a plan of his own—that is, in " his way "— and so intent is he on this plan that the new instructions do not reach his consciousness—that is, they do not make upon him that due impression which is required for carrying them out satisfactorily, or even for remembering them accurately.

Curiously enough, a pupil's confidence in " his way " of

---

[1] The matter of these new means will be dealt with in the next chapter.

doing things is not in the least disturbed by the fact that " his way " has never worked well in the past, and, as his teacher is careful to point out to him, can never work well in the future, for the simple reason that " *his way* " *is essentially wrong for his purpose*, that, in fact, what he thinks of as a " difficulty " is not a difficulty in itself, but simply the result of " his way " of going to work.

Further, the teacher will point out that any reason he may have had in the past for clinging to " his way " of doing things no longer exists, because the practical help that the teacher is able to give him places him in a totally new position in regard to his " difficulty "; so that all he has to do is to stop trying to overcome his difficulty " his way," and, instead, to remember and follow out the new instructions, by which means he will obtain the result he desires.

This cannot be called an unreasonable proposition, if we have once allowed that a teacher should be trusted to know more than his pupil about the particular matter in hand. In my experience, however, the pupil who has been brought up on subconscious methods is not attracted, as a rule, by this form of reasoning when faced with a " difficulty."

And so it comes about that, although a teacher may demonstrate to a pupil over and over again that he will never be able to do what he is trying to do *unless he changes his* " *means-whereby* " (gives up, that is, " his way " of doing it), the pupil will still go on trying to overcome his difficulty " his way." [1]

Similarly, although a teacher may assure his pupil over and over again that, if only he will adopt the new means given to him, *he will be able to do quite easily the thing he has always believed he cannot do*, the pupil will not make any attempt to adopt the new means. He will go on, in fact, trying to be right " his way," and always being wrong. More unreasonable still, after a certain time he will actually begin to worry because he finds that he is not getting on, that " his way." is not working. Could anything be more unreasonable ?

Suppose a man starts out to reach a certain destination and

---

[1] It must be pointed out that in such instances as the one we are discussing, the pupil's " right way " is the wrong way. The right way (that is, the teacher's right way) is the very last that would ever be recognized by the pupil as the " right way," because this right way has never yet come within the pupil's experiences.

comes to a place where the road branches into two. Not knowing the way, he takes the wrong road of the two and gets lost. He asks the way of someone he meets and is told to go straight back to the crossroads and take the other road, which will lead him directly to the place he wants to reach. What should we say if we heard that the man had gone back to the crossroads as directed, but had there concluded that he knew better after all than his adviser, had taken again his old road, and again got lost, and had done this thing not once or twice, but over and over again? Still more, what should we say if we heard that he was worrying dreadfully because he kept getting lost, and seemed no nearer to getting to his destination?

I can see the reader's look of scepticism as he reads this and assures himself that he, at any rate, could not be guilty of the crime of *not really attempting to do* that which he knows he *can* do, or of *not ceasing to try to do* that which the experience of hours, days—nay, of years—has proved to be *the impossible* in his particular case. Yet this is more or less what happens in the case of every pupil, even of those who are accounted the most intelligent, the most highly educated, the most scientifically trained, and this serves to strengthen my conviction that the principles underlying present methods of education are erroneous. Indeed, it would seem that our educational systems, our methods of training in scientific and professional spheres, have tended actually to cultivate and establish the defect to which I have referred. To call it a defect is to use a word that is inadequate to express what really amounts to the loss of one-half of our original psycho-physical endowment by the gradually decreasing use of the invaluable process called inhibition. And I repeat that the comparative loss of this most valuable potentiality is chiefly due to the erroneous principles which underlie our teaching methods in all spheres. Those who are responsible for these methods have not realized the importance of holding the balance true in every sphere of life between the desire to do (volition) and the ability to check that desire (inhibition).

The words "volition" and "inhibition" are in constant use in these pages and I wish at this point to make it clearly understood that they are used merely as names for two respective acts, volition standing for the act of *responding* to some stimulus (or stimuli) to psycho-physical action (doing), and inhibition standing for the act of *refusing to respond* to some stimulus (or stimuli) to psycho-physical action (not doing). In other words, volition is used to name *what we intend to do*, and inhibition to name *what we refuse to do*—that is, to name what we wish to hold in check, we wish to *prevent*.

We are not interested here in any controversy concerned with the problem as to whether or not volition and inhibition are different manifestations of the same force, or even as to what this force is, any more than the engineer who is using electricity as a power to a particular end is immediately interested as to what electricity is.   We prophesy, however, that before we have acquired accurate knowledge as to the latter, we may possibly have solved the former by means of that consciously acquired knowledge which is coming to us through the practical understanding of our psycho-sensory potentialities upon which a higher and higher standard of human psycho-physical functioning depends.

In the sense, then, implied by a process enabling one to stop, a process concerned not with " ends," however good in themselves, but with the *means whereby* these " ends " can be brought about, I maintain that there is a lack of inhibition in all spheres.   In no sphere, however, has the lack of inhibitory development been fraught with such danger as in matters concerned with the actual use of the psycho-physical mechanism in the activities of everyday life, for the lack of this development tends to produce in the individual a state of unbalanced psycho-physical functioning throughout the whole organism.   Indeed, all our methods of educational training make for rigidity rather than mobility in educational use. Small wonder, then, that adults in whom such psycho-physical conditions have become established in childhood, manifest, where their activities are concerned, an almost total lack of the most ordinary common sense, associated with unreliable sensory appreciation.

Illustration III.   *Not Seeing Ourselves as Others See Us*

Perhaps the most striking and at the same time the most pathetic instance of human delusion is to be found in the human creature's attitude towards his own psycho-physical defects, disadvantages, peculiarities, etc., on one hand, and towards his merits, advantages, and natural gifts on the other. " To thine own self be true," is an inspiring incentive when the human creature's co-ordinated psycho-physical development has reached a point where that self cannot be duped by its sensations.

As a striking instance in this field of human delusion, we will take the attitude of the stutterer towards the things he thinks of as " right " or " wrong " in himself, when he is faced with the practical problem of speaking in everyday life. The case to which I refer is just one instance of many that have come within the writer's experience during investigations made in the past thirty years. The pupil, in this particular case, was what is generally called a bad stutterer, but he made rapid progress during his lessons, and in an unusually short space of time was able to speak without any sign of stuttering as long as he spoke slowly. He reached a point where he could carry on a conversation with his teacher without being troubled with the old defects, provided that he enunciated the words slowly and deliberately.

The teacher then said, " I want you to speak in the way that you are speaking to me now, during your conversations throughout the whole day." The pupil at once became agitated, thus disturbing temporarily his new and developing control, and relapsed into his old way of stuttering, as he replied, " Oh ! I couldn't do that ; everyone would notice me ! "

Now, if we try to analyse the condition of a person who can seriously make a remark like this (and the pupil was quite sincere, he meant it), we shall see that his agitation caused him to revert to a condition associated with his previous malco-ordination, in which he had been accustomed to hypnotize himself where the facts of his shortcomings and peculiarities were concerned. We may try to explain his remark by saying that he had become so used to the conditions of his stuttering, that he no longer cared what " the other fellow " thought about it, or else that he had determined to ignore the disagreeable fact that he stuttered, and in this way had deluded himself into thinking that the " other fellow " did not notice his contortions.[1] The fact remains that he had reached such a

[1] This is the opposite delusion of that of the person who becomes self-conscious over a comparatively unnoticeable peculiarity. For example, a pupil will exaggerate to himself a minor, and comparatively

stage of defective sensory appreciation and self-hypnotic
indulgence that his whole outlook was topsy-turvy. He no
longer saw things as they were, and was out of communication
with reasoning, where his consciousness of his defects was
concerned. He was therefore able to persuade himself that
*the normal condition would be conspicuous, whilst the abnormal
would pass unnoticed. In this he was relying almost entirely on
his perverted sense of feeling.* The point on which we should lay
particular stress is that the condition of delusion and self-
deception indicated in this illustration will be found to be more
or less present in all people who are imperfectly co-ordinated
and have an unreliable sensory appreciation.

Illustration IV. " Out of Shape "

In connexion with unreliable sensory appreciation and with
perverted ideas or conceptions of what is " right " or " wrong,"
where the human creature's uses of his own mechanisms are
concerned, the following is a most significant illustration.

A little girl who had been unable to walk properly for some
years was brought to the writer for a diagnosis of the defects
in the use of the psycho-physical mechanisms which were
responsible for her more or less crippled state. When this had
been done, a request was made that a demonstration should
be given to those present of the manipulative side of the
work (the child, of course, to be the subject to be manipulated),
so that certain readjustments and co-ordinations might be
temporarily secured, thus showing, in keeping with the diagnosis, the possibilities of re-education on a general basis in a
case of this kind. The demonstration was successful from
this point of view. For the time being the child's body was
comparatively straightened out—that is, without the extreme
twists and distortions that had been so noticeable when she

---

unnoticeable, peculiarity to such a degree that he becomes self-conscious
about it and imagines that everywhere he goes people are looking at him
on account of it, whereas the defect is so slight that it would not be
noticed by outsiders. I have pointed out in the chapter entitled
" Individual Errors and Delusions," in *Man's Supreme Inheritance*, the
harmful effects that may follow a person's misguided attempts to conceal
or change characteristics which they believe to be very serious
drawbacks to their appearance, but which, compared with other very
serious defects which they completely overlook, are relatively minor
peculiarities.

came into the room. When this was done, the little girl looked across at her mother and said to her in an indescribable tone : " Oh ! Mummie, he's pulled me *out of shape*."

Here, indeed, is food for reflection for all who are concerned in any attempt to eradicate psycho-physical defects ! In accordance with this poor little child's judgment, her crookedness was straightness, her sensory appreciation of her " out-ofshape " condition was that it was " in shape." Imagine, then, what would be the result of her trying to get anything " right " by doing something herself, as she had always tried and had always been urged to try to do, whilst practising remedial exercises according to the directions and under the guidance of a teacher. Small wonder that all attempts to teach her had resulted in failure !

Consideration of the foregoing cannot but lead us to a full realization of what would have been the psycho-physical condition of such a child when she reached adolescence, if the orthodox methods of teaching in all spheres had been employed to help her. The child's remark is proof positive that, where her defects were concerned, her ideas and conceptions were dominated by her sensory appreciation, and that this sensory appreciation was not only unreliable, but actually delusive. Her experiences in connexion with the functioning of her organism were consequently incorrect and harmful experiences, and as her judgment in these spheres was the result of these experiences, little wonder that her judgment of what was right and what wrong in her case was not only practically worthless, but constituted a positive danger to her future development. Unless in such cases a child is re-educated and co-ordinated on a basis of conscious control, it cannot acquire a new and reliable sensory appreciation, and, lacking this, it will grow up employing guiding sensations which are delusive and which tend to become more and more so with the advance of time. Incorrect experiences and bad judgment will be associated with this delusive guidance of the mechanisms in the functioning of the organism, and all its efforts in the different spheres of the activities of life will be in accordance with this functioning.

* * * * *

The point that comes out clearly in all these illustrations is *that conceptions which are mainly influenced by unreliable*

*sensory appreciation, acting and reacting subconsciously and harm-
fully on the processes involved, are incorrect conceptions, and
that in these cases unreliable sensory appreciation goes hand in
hand with incorrect and deceptive experiences in the psycho-
physical functioning.*

And when we remember that (as we saw in the case of the
little girl of the last illustration) our judgment is based on
experience, we must also see that, where this experience is
incorrect and deceptive, the resulting judgment is bound to be
misleading and out of touch with reality. *We have to recognize,*
therefore, *that our sensory peculiarities are the foundation of
what we think of as our opinions, and that, in fact, nine out of
ten of the opinions we form are rather the result of what we feel* [1]
than what we think.

Our emotional defects also are linked up with our sensory
peculiarities, so that, given the slightest disturbance in these
directions, we must be temporarily thrown into a danger zone [2]
where serious and uncontrolled psycho-physical conditions
prevail.

We can now see how far this line of thought has brought us.
For the fact that emerges from all these considerations is that
our approach to life generally, our activities, beliefs, emotions,
opinions, judgments in whatever sphere, *are conditioned by the
preceding conceptions, which are associated with the individual
use of the psycho-physical mechanisms and conditioned by the
standard of reliability of our individual sensory appreciation.*

This is the great fact which must be realized by our leaders

---

[1] It is only reasonable to conclude that it is because the opinions of
most people are much more the manifestation of their sensory peculiarities (feeling) than of their reasoning processes that we find so many
varied and conflicting opinions held by people about a single simple
point, or serious subject. It is positively alarming that reasoning plays
so small a part in most of the opinions we hold, and in our judgment
with regard to things that matter. It is for this reason that we find
ourselves in such a fearful muddle after two thousand years of struggle
towards a better standard of psycho-physical functioning, struggle which
it was hoped would bring in an era of goodwill, universal unity, tolerance,
and mutual understanding.

[2] It only needs a certain number of repetitions of harmful experiences,
such as are alluded to above, to produce one or other of the different
phases which we place within the borderland of insanity. Many phases
of this development of temporary insanity are accompanied by violent
physical manifestations.

in educational, religious, moral, social, political, and all other spheres of human activities before there can be any " uplifting " of the human creature out of the present chaotic conditions. We all think and act (except when forced to do otherwise) in accordance with the peculiarities of our particular psycho-physical make-up. We read a particular paper each morning because the policy of that paper is the one we believe in and we can read there what we want to read; we cultivate friendships with people who think as we think, and we ignore or are antagonized by those who do not; the preacher attracts to church only those who want to go to church; we start to read a book, but immediately we reach a point with which we disagree our more or less debauched kinæsthesia cannot control the impulses which, when set in motion, put us out of communication with our reasoning. Yet in spite of all this, books are written, lectures given, sermons preached, speeches made in the belief that ideas which are given out by these means can be satisfactorily assimilated by hearers or readers, and that good ideas may thus be passed on for the uplifting of mankind in social, religious, political, and other spheres of activity.

Here we have a great delusion. For, as we have shown, our degree of ability to assimilate a new and unfamiliar idea, or to overcome our prejudices in connexion with our cherished ideas and beliefs, depends upon our individual conception of such ideas and beliefs, and this conception is conditioned by the standard of individual psycho-physical co-ordination and of reliability of the sensory appreciation. Had this fact not been overlooked, writers, lecturers, preachers, orators, etc., would long since have shown some practical interest in the *means whereby* their hearers and readers could reach such a standard of functioning of the psycho-physical organism that they would be able to assimilate satisfactorily new ideas and teachings. For how, I ask, can those who have developed a condition of unreliable sensory appreciation (with all the incorrect experiences, beliefs, and judgments that we now know to be inevitably associated with this condition) assimilate satisfactorily ideas that do not fit in with these experiences? Correct apprehension and reliable sensory appreciation go hand in hand.[1]

---

[1] As a friend, a member of the medical profession, wrote to me recently : " I am getting more and more convinced that people can learn only what they know."

The mass is made up of individuals, and reliable sensory appreciation cannot be given on the mass-teaching principle or by precept or exhortation. This can be done only by individual teaching and individual work. Moreover, people who are massed together are apt to be governed by the " herd-instinct," and we need to help man to evolve beyond that influence as soon as possible, and to this end we must have conscious and individual development.

III

IMPERFECT SENSORY APPRECIATION

THE problem, then, before us is to find a *means whereby* a reliable sensory appreciation can be developed and maintained throughout the organism, and the basis for my argument is that both in education and in re-education this must be brought about in every case by the reliance of the individual, not upon subconscious, but upon *conscious, reasoning* guidance and control.

For we find that the human creature, subjected to the present processes of civilization, develops defects and imperfections in the use of the organism, even in cases where a reliable sensory appreciation *has already existed* on a subconscious basis, whilst in the much larger number of cases, where defects have already been developed, we find that satisfactory results cannot be secured unless during the process a new and reliable sensory appreciation is being gradually acquired. Almost all civilized human creatures have developed a condition in which the sensory appreciation (feeling) is more or less imperfect and deceptive, and it naturally follows that it cannot be relied upon in re-education, readjustment, and co-ordination, or in our attempts to put right something we know to be wrong with our psycho-physical selves. The connexion [1] between psycho-physical defects and incorrect sensory guidance must therefore be recognized by the teacher in the practical work of re-education. This recognition will make it impossible for him to expect a pupil to be able to perform satisfactorily any new psycho-physical act *until the new correct experiences in sensory appreciation involved have become established*.

I will now endeavour to outline as clearly as possible the general scheme which I advocate in connexion with the development of reliable sensory appreciation, first setting out the principles on which the scheme is based, then giving an illustration which will show the application of these principles to the practical work of co-ordination and re-education.

[1] The recognition of this vital connexion marks the point of departure between methods of teaching on a conscious and on a subconscious basis.

First, then, this scheme demands in particular on the part of the teacher a recognition of the almost alarming dominance of the pupil's psycho-physical processes by an incorrect sensory appreciation during the attempted performance of any psycho-physical activity. It is therefore of primary importance that the teacher should recognize and endeavour to awaken his pupil to the fact of his (the pupil's) unreliable sensory appreciation, and that during the processes involved in the performance of the pupil's practical work he should cultivate and develop in him the new and reliable sensory appreciation upon which a satisfactory standard of co-ordination depends.

To this end the mode of procedure is as follows. The teacher, having made his diagnosis of the cause or causes of the imperfections or defects which the pupil has developed in the incorrect use of himself, uses expert manipulation to give to the pupil the new sensory experiences required for the satisfactory use of the mechanisms concerned, the while giving him the correct guiding orders or directions which are the counterpart of the new sensory experiences which he is endeavouring to develop by means of his manipulation.

This procedure constitutes the *means whereby* the teacher makes it possible for the pupil to *prevent* (inhibition) the misdirected activities which are causing his psycho-physical imperfections. In this work the inhibitory process must take first place, and remain the primary factor in each and every new experience which is to be gained and become established during the cultivation and development of reliable sensory appreciation upon which a satisfactory standard of co-ordination depends.

With this aim in view—that is, the prevention of misdirected activities—the teacher from the outset carefully explains to the pupil that his part in this scheme is very different from that which is usually assigned to pupils under other teaching methods. He tells the pupil that, on receiving the directions or guiding orders, he must not attempt to carry them out; that, on the contrary, *he must inhibit the desire to do so in the case of each and every order which is given to him*. He must instead project the guiding orders as given to him, whilst his teacher at the same time, by means of manipulation, will make the required readjustments and bring about the necessary co-ordinations, in this way performing for the pupil the particular movement or movements required, and giving him the new reliable sensory appreciation and the very best opportunity possible to connect the different guiding orders before attempting to put them into practice. This linking-up of the guiding orders or directions is all-important, for it is the counterpart of that linking-up of the parts of the organism which constitutes what we call co-ordination. The aim of re-education on a general basis is to bring about at all times and for all purposes, not a series of correct positions or postures, but a *co-ordinated use of the mechanisms in general.*

The second point to be noted in connexion with the technique we are advocating is that the directions or guiding orders given to the pupil are based in every case on the principle of ceasing to work in blind pursuit of an " end," and of attending instead to the *means whereby* this " end " can be attained. We have already considered this principle in its general application, but I am anxious to lay stress upon it again at this point, because it is of the utmost importance that the pupil should both accept this principle and apply it to his work in the sphere of re-education, for by no other method can he get the better of his old subconscious habits and build up consciously the new and improved condition which he is anxious to bring about.

If we consider for a moment, we shall see the reason for this. For if the pupil thinks of a certain " end " as desirable and starts to pursue it directly, he will certainly take the course of action in regard to it that he has been accustomed to take in like conditions. In other words, he will follow his habitual procedure in regard to it, and should that procedure happen to be a bad one for the purpose (and the fact that he needs re-education proves this to be the case), he only strengthens the incorrect experiences in connexion with it by using this procedure again. If, on the other hand, the pupil *stops himsel* from going to work in his usual way (inhibition), and proceeds to replace his old subconscious means by the new conscious means which his teacher has given him, and which he has therefore every reason to believe will bring about the desired result, he will have taken the first and most important step towards the breaking-down of a habit, and towards that constructive, conscious, and reasoning control which tends towards a mastery of the situation.[1]

[1] This applies equally to the breaking of habit in every sphere of activity.

It is therefore impressed on the pupil from the beginning that, as the essential preliminary to any successful work on his part, *he must refuse to work directly for his " end," and keep his attention entirely on the means whereby this end can be secured.*

In the illustration which will shortly be given it will be noticed that it is left to the teacher's discretion whether, in the case of a particular evolution, the pupil shall or shall not be told beforehand what the " end " is for which he and the teacher are working. But in either case everything possible is done to convince him that the " end " does not matter, because given : —

(1) the teacher's knowledge of the correct *means whereby* the particular " end " can be secured;
(2) the pupil's correct apprehension and conscious repetition of the guiding orders or directions relating to these " means-whereby ";
(3) the manipulation by the teacher, who, with his expert hands, gives to the pupil the reliable sensory appreciation which should result from such directive orders,

it is then merely a matter of time[1] before the desired end will be secured. In other words, the pupil is asked to take care of the " means," and the " end " will take care of itself.

In this way all responsibility for the final result is taken off the pupil. He has no " end " to work for, and therefore nothing to get right. All that is asked of him is, when he receives a guiding order, to *listen and wait*; to wait, because only by waiting can he be certain of preventing himself from relapsing into his old subconscious habits, and to listen, so that he learns to remember gradually and connect up the guiding orders which are the counterpart of the *means-whereby* which the teacher is employing to bring about the desired " end." In other words, he is asked to adopt consciously a principle of

[1] In this connexion the length of time that may be required in the process of re-education before the new and correct experiences can become established has proved a stumbling-block to some enquirers; but here again, if we reason the matter out, we shall see that the ability to break with habits that are sometimes very long-established must depend upon certain natural aptitudes and qualities in the pupil, and especially upon the standard of acuteness of his sense perceptions, and of the development of his ability to inhibit.

prevention as the basis of his practical work, and in every other way to leave the teacher a free hand.

Now it would seem that this procedure, by relieving the pupil from all responsibility as to results, should, from any common-sense point of view, relieve him also from strain and anxiety; and those pupils who are satisfied that they do not know how to put themselves right, and are therefore willing to remain quietly giving themselves certain guiding orders or directions at the prompting of the teacher, but leaving to him all responsibility in the matter of enabling them to bring about the desired result, are able to gain the new and correct experiences without strain and with a gradually increasing sense of power and control.

But the teacher experienced in the work of re-education on a general basis is well aware of the difficulties which pupils actually make for themselves in this procedure, for the immediate call of instinctive habit is so insistent that unless the pupil learns to resist that call by bringing into use and developing his power to inhibit, he is almost certain to fall back into his old and harmful habit of blindly pursuing his " end," which means that he forgets to project his directive orders (the " means whereby ") and falls back again for guidance upon his unreliable and delusive sensory appreciation (feeling).

And it is rare in my experience to find adult pupils who are awake to the necessity of *preventing* themselves from falling back into their old subconscious habits, even though the necessity for this is proved to them over and over again. Very few, moreover, have any idea of giving themselves a guiding order or direction without making an attempt to carry it out. They do not separate the order they are asked to give from the act or acts of which it is the forerunner. Therefore, as soon as they are asked to give a certain continuous order, they rush impulsively into action according to their habitual subconscious use of the parts concerned. This relapse into old habits is exactly what the teacher asks the pupil to prevent, because it renders a successful result impossible from the outset, and reinforces all the incorrect experiences, associated by the pupil with this use of the parts, the very experiences that the teacher is endeavouring to replace by new and correct ones.

Let us take, for example, the case of a pupil who has been accustomed to stiffen the muscles of his neck in all his daily activities. His teacher points this out to him, and explains that this habit of stiffening his neck has come about because he is endeavouring to make his neck perform the functions of other parts of his psycho-physical mechanism, so that it is not an isolated defect, but connected with other harmful imperfections in the use of himself. His stiffened neck, in fact, is merely a symptom of general mal-co-ordination in the use of the mechanisms, and any direct attempt to relax it means that he is dealing with it as a " cause " and not as a " symptom," and such an attempt will result in comparative failure unless a satisfactory co-ordinated use of the mechanism in general is restored. The teacher further explains that, as the pupil's sensory appreciation is unreliable,[1] it is unlikely that he will be able to do anything himself to remedy these defects, but that if he will inhibit his desire to stiffen his neck, and give himself the guiding orders or directions to relax it, the teacher will be able by means of manipulation to bring about such a general readjustment of his body that, as a result, his neck will be relaxed.

If, after this explanation, the pupil gives himself the order to relax his neck (i.e., inhibits his desire to stiffen it), his teacher, provided he has the necessary knowledge and experience, will be able to assist him to bring about *those general conditions upon which relaxation of the neck depends*. If, on the other hand, the pupil forgets to inhibit, and so, when he is asked to order his neck to relax, tries to relax it *by direct means* (i.e., according to his own idea of relaxing it), he will in this attempt either do exactly what he has always done with his neck (i.e., stiffen it), or else bring about in one or more parts, or perhaps in the whole organism, a more or less collapsed condition, and until he stops trying to relax it by direct means, the teacher, be he ever so expert, will be able to do little towards bringing about those conditions which make for a satisfactory state of relaxation of the neck.

[1] In this regard, it is significant that the pupil whose sensory appreciation in connexion with the use of his organism is most unreliable (the pupil, for example, who " feels " that his head is going forward when he is carefully putting it back) is the one who is most unwilling to believe that he really does not know what he is doing with himself, and who, in spite of all remonstrances, will persist in trying to carry out the orders himself, instead of inhibiting this desire and allowing the teacher to assist him in carrying them out.

Another difficulty which pupils make for themselves is in connexion with the giving of guiding orders or directions. They speak sometimes as if it were a strange and new thing to ask them to give themselves orders, forgetting that they have been doing this subconsciously from their earliest days, else they would not be able to stand up without help, much less move about. The point that is new in the scheme we are considering is that the pupil is asked consciously to give himself orders, evolved from a consideration of the requirements, not of a subconscious, but of a conscious, reasoning use of the organism, orders and directions, moreover, the satisfactory employment of which depends on the pupil's clear understanding (1) as to which of these orders are primary, to be given, but not to be carried out (inhibition), and (2) as to which are to follow and to be actually carried out.

To make this clear let us suppose that a pupil is asked by his teacher to sit down. Now if he obeys this order at once and sits down, he will be guided in doing so by the unreliable sensory appreciation established in connexion with the performance of the act in his case; that is, he will simply repeat his usual faulty subconscious manner of sitting down. The object of his re-education is to eradicate such psycho-physical faults, and so, as soon as he is asked to sit down, he immediately says " No," *and gives himself the order not to sit down,* thereby inhibiting the misdirected activity hitherto connected with the act, a procedure which prevents indulgence in the old subconscious faults.

The old faulty activity being prevented by the processes just indicated, the pupil will then proceed to give his attention to the different guiding or directing orders which the teacher considers essential to the correct direction and control of those psycho-mechanics (the correct " means-whereby ") concerned with the satisfactory use of the organism as a whole in the act of sitting down. *These are the orders to be ultimately carried out by the pupil.*

It follows, then, that the orders which are to be given, but not to be carried out, are those which, if carried out, would result in the habitual faulty use of the mechanisms. They can therefore be referred to as " preventive orders." All orders which follow preventive orders are to be carried out (at first by the teacher), for if the teaching technique is reliable, such orders will be concerned with the correct *means whereby* the new and co-ordinated use of the mechanism can be secured.

I have already pointed out that children from the first moment of school life onwards manifest a lack of inhibitory development, and the fact that in most cases they learn to obey orders at once,[1] without stopping to consider the "why and the wherefore," is a contributing factor to this harmful condition.

As a result of this early training, many pupils have become so accustomed to react quickly and subconsciously to any directions they receive, or to any idea that comes to them, that this quick and unthinking reaction has become a habit with them that they find hard to break.

And so, when pupils insist that giving orders is a difficulty, what they really mean is that because of their long-established habit of reacting quickly and unthinkingly to a direction, a habit fostered by years of training, they find it difficult to stop, to wait, to be content just to give orders and to say "No" when the impulse comes to carry out the orders. In other words, they find it difficult not to want to be obedient, not to want to be right, not to work directly for their end. The difficulty, however, as in the case of most human difficulties, lies, not in the thing itself, but in the "breaking of a habit," the indulgence of which not only impedes the pupil's progress, but, if persisted in, makes it impossible for him to achieve his desired end.

It will be found that in every case a pupil's success in achieving an end will depend upon his practical recognition of the fact that only by continually attending to the "means-whereby" essential to the successful achievement of his "end" can a satisfactory result be secured. This applies equally,

> (1) whether the pupil is in the early stages of his work, where he is asked merely to give orders and to leave the carrying-out of these orders to the teacher;

[1] I know that I shall be told that if children are to be taught to inhibit in the sense in which I use the word, i.e., the prevention of misdirected activities, so much time will be taken up in this part of the work that they will not be able to get through their studies. Children have said to me more than once in this connexion : "I could not stop l'ke this at school. They tell us to hurry." In answer I can only say that time spent in teaching children to inhibit impulses to unreasoning activity to which otherwise they must later on become slaves is time not lost, but actually saved.

(2) whether he has reached a later stage where, under his teacher's supervision, he is gradually developing a reliable sensory appreciation upon which he can rely in carrying out the orders himself; or

(3) whether he is working by himself at his ordinary activities outside.

Our discussion of inhibition in the foregoing leads us to the consideration of the individual's ability to wait (inhibit) [1] before reacting to a stimulus (or stimuli) to pursue some " end " in the ordinary way of life, and it may be of interest to give some facts in regard to the experiences in this connexion of people taking lessons in speaking, breathing, singing, etc.

Most people who need lessons in speaking have a tendency to speak too quickly, and they fail to pause, to wait between their sentences. This tendency, of course, has to be checked, but in the work of re-education on a conscious plane we do not try to check the tendency directly, but rely instead on the use of certain " means-whereby " which will indirectly bring about the desired result. Therefore, instead of telling the pupil directly to pause at certain places, the teacher points out to him that he is gasping at the end of his lines or sentences, and that he is sniffing or " sucking in air " through the mouth, and he endeavours to make the pupil realize that these bad habits are the result of his incorrect subconscious conceptions in connexion with the act of breathing, and with the incorrect use of the psycho-physical mechanisms upon the correct use of which satisfactory breathing depends. From this it follows that in all vocal use the pupil must have a correct conception as to the nature of the respiratory act, associated with a conscious, reasoned understanding of the principles underlying the correct use of the psycho-mechanics involved in the act of breathing, before he makes any attempt to put these principles into practice.

When this point has been reached, the teacher will be justified in asking the pupil to stop, to wait at the end of each sentence in speaking or reading (or at the end of each phrase in singing), and to refuse to take another breath until he has inhibited the

---

[1] This " wait " is to give himself time to comprehend and consciously rehearse the orders which are the counterpart of the correct *means whereby* he is to attain his end.

habitually incorrect, subconscious guidance and direction
concerned with the act of taking a breath (which, in his case, is
responsible for the imperfect uses of the mechanism as diag-
nosed by his teacher), and, further, has substituted for these
imperfect uses the new, correct conscious orders which make for
increasingly satisfactory use. The teacher therefore asks him
to perform :—

> (1) *An inhibitory act*, by inhibiting "his way" of
> taking breath—in other words, by *preventing* or holding
> in check, in connexion with the act, the wrong subconscious
> guidance and direction, which constitutes the bad habit he
> has formed when taking breath at the end of each sentence.
>
> (2) *A volitionary act*, by giving himself certain orders
> which are the *means whereby* a more satisfactory act of
> inspiration may be gradually be cultivated *before he
> attempts to go on to the next sentence.*

Now, in connexion with the latter act, the pupil will very
likely raise the objection that if he stops to give the new orders
before going on to speak, he will attract unpleasant attention to
himself, because he will have to wait so long between his sentences that his way of speaking will appear slow and stilted.
This objection only means, however, that he has not realized
that his old habit of breathing audibly through the mouth,
instead of through the nostrils, and of running his sentences
into one another were noticeable defects to other people,
however little he may have been aware of them himself. He is
quick enough to object to the new way of speaking, which, he
believes, will draw unpleasant attention to himself, and also
to the new instructions because in carrying these out he is
forced to break with habits which are familiar and therefore
satisfying to him; but he is not so quick to observe defects in
his own old way. Once, however, he has been taught to act in
accordance with the new instructions, his defects will gradually
disappear, because he will have learned to prevent the wrong use
of the mechanisms responsible for these defects. The time
taken to give, first, the preventive order to stop and wait at the
end of the vocal effort and, secondly, the correct directing and
controlling orders in connexion with the processes concerned
with the respiratory act will constitute the necessary pause
between the sentences. After this, it is merely a matter of

time before the activities, which result from the series of psycho-physical experiences detailed above, become continuously operative, and, because they are now consciously directed, they will be henceforth under the pupil's constructive, conscious guidance and control.

The same difficulty is encountered in any pupil who breathes imperfectly, immediately he begins the actual practice of singing. This pupil also is so intent on his " end " (singing) that he finds it irksome to wait to take breath properly. He also " sniffs " and " sucks in air " through the mouth instead of through the nostrils, and, as a rule, audibly.

It is unlikely that such defects as these can be eradicated or that the cultivation of new defects can be prevented by those processes which we find associated with " breathing exercises " or lessons in " deep-breathing." But if the pupil attacks his difficulties—i.e., his general condition of mal-co-ordination— by means of re-education on a plane of constructive, conscious control, he can be helped to overcome them by learning, firstly, to hold in check his subconscious desire to " take breath " at the end of each phrase (inhibitory act), and, secondly, to give the guiding orders and directions in connexion with the correct psycho-mechanics of respiration (volitionary act).

This pupil also will probably make the objection that he cannot pause, giving as his reason that if he pauses he cannot keep time in his song. This objection, of course, will not hold any more than the previous one, for when once the necessary control has been gained, the pause required for inhibition and for giving the necessary orders will be only momentary.

But even if we suppose, for the sake of argument, that the objection holds, of what avail can it be to keep time, if thereby the primary principles which are essential to good singing— namely, those concerned with the correct and adequate use of the psycho-physical mechanisms connected with respiration— are treated in practice as secondary factors, and are being actually perverted in use?

In all these considerations we must bear in mind that, in the sphere of acquiring satisfactory psycho-physical functioning, though speed will follow as the result of the necessary experience in the correct use of the parts concerned, a correct use can hardly follow a speed which has been achieved at the cost of an incorrect use of those parts.

Now that I have indicated the principles which underlie the general scheme which I advocate in connexion with the development of a reliable sensory appreciation, I will go on to describe in detail one of the technical evolutions [1] which I use in my teaching. It is given as an illustration of what should be the attitude of the pupil towards the practical work in connexion with the cultivation and development of the new sensory appreciation during the processes involved in the performance of the evolution, *but more particularly as an illustration of the means whereby we may develop a reliable sense appreciation of the minimum of so-called " physical tension " ;* for in this sphere of sensory appreciation, the most difficult problem to be solved, in most cases, is concerned with the matter of developing a correct register of the *due and proper amount of so-called " muscular tension " necessary at a given time.*

It is not possible, of course, to tell the pupil in terms of relativity the degree of muscular tension which will be his or her required minimum at any particular moment. Furthermore, even if this were possible, what chance is there that the pupil will be able to register this minimum accurately, when the very factor upon which he will rely for guidance in this connexion (viz., his sensory appreciation) is unreliable, inaccurate, and often positively delusive? I have known cases where a pupil failed to recognize a difference in muscular tension whether his arms were hanging loosely at his sides, as in the act of walking, or were being used for the performance of an act requiring extreme tension.

The question, then, of dealing with the matter of a correct or incorrect degree of " physical tension " is probably, from the teacher's point of view, the most difficult problem to be solved in the scheme that we are considering. It is clear that this problem cannot be solved by the technique involved in the performance of " physical exercises " as such, and the chief danger involved in the performance of exercises associated with systems of physical culture, posture, etc., lies in the fact that this fundamental difficulty concerned with muscular tension has been ignored. If ever a plan of development by means of exercises to be performed according to written or spoken instruction—minus manipulative help—is to be evolved, this problem will have to be satisfactorily solved. I claim, how-

[1] A description of this evolution was first published in 1910.

ever, that in its particular application to the evolution about to be described, this problem has been solved, and in a very practical way, and the unfolding of this part of the technique should prove of great interest to the student. Special attention is directed in this connexion to the instructions given in the following illustration to the pupil in regard to the work to be done with his hands and arms, associated with a more or less co-ordinated body, and particularly to the position of his fingers, wrists, and elbows when placed on the chair as directed.

I would add that the correct performance of this evolution calls for the co-ordinated use of the body, legs, and arms, and of the muscular system in general; it calls, in particular, for their co-ordinated use during the movement of bringing the body forward, and during the act of placing the hands in position on the top rail of the chair, also during the final work to be done with the hands and arms in this position. I want it to be very clearly understood that when I write of the arms, legs, hands, feet, etc., *I always imply their co-ordinated use* with the body as a co-ordinated support. Indeed, we might say that in this sense the body represents the trunk of a tree and the arms the limbs.

It must be clearly understood that in what follows it is taken for granted that the pupil gives special attention to the primary principles laid down for him by his teacher, before he attempts to carry out any instructions given him.[1] If this is done, the majority of the experiences that the pupil receives should be correct experiences, thus making for the development of confidence and for the continuance of the processes involved in the eradication of defects.

[1] It is not possible, of course, to give here all the detailed instructions that would meet every case, because these instructions naturally vary according to the tendencies and peculiarities of the particular pupil. An experienced teacher, however, should be able to supply these instructions in the practical application of the technique to meet the needs of the individual case. We must learn in this connexion to differentiate between the variations of a teacher's art and the principles of the teaching technique which is being employed.

IV

In the technical evolution about to be set down it is necessary to use certain phrases employed in the teaching technique, phrases which I consider call for comment, seeing that they do not always adequately express my meaning and that, furthermore, they cannot be defended as being demonstrably accurate.

My reader may justly ask, then, why I use them. Readers of *Man's Supreme Inheritance* will remember that when I used the phrase " position of mechanical advantage," I pointed out that I did so because a better one was not forthcoming, and I mentioned then that I had called to my aid a number of scientific and literary friends.

I have pursued the same course in regard to the phrases which will follow. As I have already stated, I think them inadequate, but with a teacher present to demonstrate in person what he means by them, they serve their purpose. The phrases are :—

1. *Shortening the Spine*

An objector might justly say that this is practically impossible, but we are dealing with the *use* of the spine, and one of the most common defects among human beings to-day is an undue curving of the spine in the use of the self in the acts of everyday life, and naturally this causes a shortening in stature. As a practical demonstration, take a piece of paper, and after placing it flat on another sheet, draw a line along the extreme ends of the top piece, thereby recording the length by the pencil marks on the paper underneath. Now lift the top piece and curve it slightly and replace it with one end touching one line, and without interfering with the curve. It will then be seen that the other end of the paper does not reach the other line.

2. *Lengthening the Spine*

The foregoing will serve to show that if we modify the curve in the spine, we tend to lengthen it. For instance, to go back to our illustration, if we take the curve out of the top piece

Illustration 109

of paper, and replace it as in the first instance, it will reach both lines, showing that during this experiment a lengthening process has been operative.

3. *Relax the Neck*

There is considerable confusion on the part of the pupil when he attempts to obey directions to relax some part of the organism. In ordinary teaching, pupils and teachers are quite convinced that if some part of the organism is too tense, they can relax it—that is, *do the relaxing by direct means.* This is a delusion on their part, but it is difficult to convince them of it. In the first place, if they do chance to get rid of the specific tension it will be by a partial collapse of the parts concerned, or of other parts, possibly even by a general collapse of the whole organism. In the second place, it is obvious that if some part of the organism is unduly tensed, it is because the pupil is attempting to do with it the work of some other part or parts, often work for which it is quite unsuited.

4. *Head Forward and Up*

This is one of the most inadequate and often confusing phrases used as a means of conveying our ideas in words, and it is a dangerous instruction to give to any pupil, unless the teacher first demonstrates his meaning by giving to the pupil, *by means of manipulation*, the exact experiences involved.

5. *Widen the Back*

This instruction rivals the last one in its shortcomings, when considered as a phrase for the conveyance of an idea which we expect a pupil to construe correctly, unless it is given by a teacher who is capable of demonstrating what he means by readjusting the pupil's organism so that the conditions desired may be brought about.

What really occurs is that there is brought about a very marked change in the position of the bony structures of the thorax—particularly noticeable if a posterior view is taken—also a permanent enlargement of the thoracic cavity, with a striking increase in thoracic mobility and the minimum muscle tension of the whole of the mechanisms involved.

6. *Support the Body with the Arms*

This instruction is given to the pupil when he is holding the back of a chair, whilst sitting or standing, in order to give the teacher the opportunity to secure more quickly and easily for the pupil certain experiences essential at a particular stage of his work in co-ordination. The varying details of the *means whereby* the use indicated of the arms and body is to be gained could not be set down in writing to meet the requirements of each pupil, for they vary with each slight stage of progress. It is for this reason that " correct positions " or " postures " find no place in the practical teaching technique employed in the work of re-education advocated in this book. A correct position or posture indicates a fixed position, and a person held to a fixed position cannot grow, as we understand growth. The correct position to-day cannot be the correct position a week later for any person who is advancing in the work of re-education and co-ordination.

7. *Widen the Arms Whilst Supporting and Raising the Body*

This is the most deceptive of the list of instructions set down in these pages. In the first place, if carried out without manipulative assistance, it is a contradictory instruction, seeing that if you widen the arms, as the act is generally understood, the body would be lowered, not raised. The tendency of the pupil in this movement is to contract unduly the inner muscles of the upper part of the arms, a procedure which interferes with the work the teacher has in view. This must be prevented, and a skilful teacher can employ the above instructions successfully to this end.

We will now pass on to our illustration.

THE PUPIL IS ASKED TO SIT IN A CHAIR IN ACCORDANCE WITH THE PRINCIPLES AND TECHNIQUE SPECIALLY SET DOWN FOR THE ACT OF SITTING AND STANDING IN *Man's Supreme Inheritance*. When he is seated, his body being supported by the back of the chair on which he is sitting, another chair is placed before him with its back towards him.

THE PUPIL IS THEN ASKED TO GIVE THE FOLLOWING PREVENTIVE ORDERS.

Illustration III

In the way of correct direction and guidance, HE IS ASKED TO ORDER THE NECK TO RELAX, TO ORDER THE HEAD FORWARD AND UP TO LENGTHEN THE SPINE.

It must here be clearly understood that in the previous manipulative and other work done in connexion with the technique, the pupil will have been made familiar in theory and practice with Order 1. He is able to give certain orders correctly and also to put them into effect. In the present instance, it is explained to him that the order given is to be merely *preventive*—a projected wish *without any attempt on the pupil's part to carry it out successfully.*

THE TEACHER REPEATS THE ORDERS AND WITH HIS HANDS HE PROCEEDS TO BRING THE PUPIL'S BODY GENTLY FORWARD FROM THE HIPS.

It is important to note here that the imperfectly co-ordinated person tends to *shorten* the stature and *pull the head back* in making this movement forward. Unless, therefore, the pupil remembers this subconscious tendency to shorten, and attends to the new directive orders which will counteract this subconscious tendency, his old habit will prove too strong for him, and at the first touch from the teacher to bring his body forward, though this touch may be so light that it would not move an inch-thick pineboard of the same length and width as the torso of the pupil, the latter will start to move forward at a ratio of, say, seventy-five per cent. subconscious response to his old habit, and only twenty-five per cent. conscious response to the new directive and guiding orders. This latter estimate is, in most cases, too liberal a one, for, as a rule, the slightest touch releases the old sensory activities associated subconsciously in the pupil's conception with the act of " moving forward," this being an " end " which the pupil, in spite of all warnings to the contrary, has already decided upon, and he becomes so dominated by the idea of " moving forward " (his " end "), that the new conscious directive orders are no longer projected. Instead, the old subconscious directive orders associated with his bad habits and with his unreliable sensory appreciation hold sway, and so, in the place of ordering his neck to relax, his head forward and up, in order to secure the necessary lengthening, he will actually throw his head back, stiffen his neck, and tend to shorten his spine by unduly curving it, in accordance with his old fixed habit in moving forward. These particular faults are accompanied, more or less, by an undue and incorrect tension of the legs and other parts of the organism, and also by a stiffening at the hip joints, the defective use of the parts culminating in an expenditure of energy out of all proportion to the requirements of the evolution.

When this happens, the teacher must point out to the pupil that he has not quite comprehended what is required of him, and he must again place the whole position before the pupil, and from as many angles as possible, until he is certain that the pupil understands that the primary orders which he is asked to give are *preventive* orders, and that if he gives these preventive orders (inhibition of the old misdirected activities), and then proceeds to give the new ones, *his spine will be kept at its greatest possible length* (not shortened), whilst the body will be moved forward from the hips easily and satisfactorily, without interfering with the generally relative position of the torso (except in the matter of angle), just as a door moves on its hinges.

THE TEACHER WILL THEN RENEW THE REQUEST TO THE PUPIL TO GIVE THE ORDERS, AND WITH HIS HANDS WILL COMMAND FOR HIM THE ACTUAL PERFORMANCE OF THE MOVEMENT, of which these orders are the counterpart. Sometimes it may be suggested that the pupil shall himself request the teacher to move his body forward for him whilst he (the pupil) gives his orders or directions.

When the teacher is satisfied that the pupil is giving due attention to the directive orders up to this point, and has gained a due appreciation of their relative value as primary, secondary, and following factors; when, also, the correct sensory experiences, made possible by the teacher's help in the way of re-adjustment and re-education, have been sufficiently repeated, the pupil can be taken a step farther in the evolution.

At every step in the work it is essential that the pupil should rehearse his orders from the beginning, because these earlier orders constitute the *means whereby* a further step may be successfully taken. In giving himself orders, the pupil must on every occasion begin with the primary orders before going on to the secondary orders, and so on.

THE PUPIL MUST NOW AGAIN ORDER THE NECK TO RELAX, THE HEAD FORWARD AND UP, WHILST THE TEACHER WITH HIS HANDS SECURES THAT POSITION OF THE TORSO IN WHICH THE BACK MAY BE SAID TO BE WIDENED. These orders should be repeated several times and be *continued* WHILST THE TEACHER TAKES

Illustration 113

THE PUPIL'S RIGHT ARM WITH HIS HANDS, AND MOVES IT FOR-
WARD UNTIL THE PUPIL'S HAND IS ABOVE THE TOP RAIL OF THE
BACK OF THE CHAIR. THE PUPIL SHOULD THEN BE REQUESTED
TO REPEAT THE ORDERS SET DOWN AT THE BEGINNING OF THIS
PARAGRAPH, AND THEN TO TAKE THE WEIGHT OF THE ARM EN-
TIRELY, AS THE TEACHER DISENGAGES HIS HANDS FROM THE
SUPPORTED ARM.

Great care must be taken to see that the pupil has not interfered
with the mechanism of the torso in the effort to take the weight of
the arm. This interference can take place in various ways, but it
always implies that the pupil has forgotten his orders and has
harked back to one or other of his subconscious habits. What is
essential here is a *co-ordinated use* of the arms, and the only way by
which he can secure this is, first, by giving the necessary preventive
orders, and then by rehearsing the series of new orders given by the
teacher, in which the movement of the arms is *linked up* with the
use of the other parts of the body.

If the pupil has not interfered with the mechanism of the
torso in the effort to take the weight of the arm, HE SHOULD
NEXT BE REQUESTED TO GRASP THE TOP RAIL OF THE BACK OF
THE CHAIR GENTLY AND FIRMLY, KEEPING THE FINGERS AS
straight AS POSSIBLE AND QUITE FLAT AGAINST THE WOOD OF
THE FRONT PORTION OF THE TOP RAIL OF THE CHAIR, THE
THUMB ALSO TO BE KEPT AS STRAIGHT AS POSSIBLE, BEING
CALLED UPON TO DO DUTY ON THE BACK PORTION OF THE TOP
RAIL OF THE CHAIR, WITH THE WRIST CURVED SLIGHTLY IN-
WARDS TOWARDS THE LEFT. The teacher will, of course, as far
as possible, assist the pupil with these hand movements.

If, however, as is too often the case, the pupil fails to continue to
give his orders, and so interferes with the mechanisms of the torso
during the movement of the arm towards the chair, *the pupil must be
requested to begin once more at the very first step in the evolution, and
this must be continued until a satisfactory result has been secured. This
principle must be applied in every instance* in this work of re-education
and readjustment. It should be realized here that, during the
course of this work, a process of building is going on, fundamental
sensory building, on a general and not a specific basis. It will
perhaps make this clearer if we use the analogy of building with
bricks, for the processes concerned with this fundamental sensory
building calls for the use of directive orders, just as the process of
ordinary building calls for the use of bricks.

THE PUPIL MUST THEN BE ASKED AGAIN TO ORDER THE NECK TO RELAX, THE HEAD FORWARD AND UP, AND THE TEACHER WILL REPEAT HIS PREVIOUS EFFORT TO ESTABLISH THAT CONDITION OF THE TORSO AND BACK ESSENTIAL TO SATISFACTORY ARM WORK, WHILST HE REPEATS WITH THE PUPIL'S LEFT ARM THE EVOLUTION JUST PERFORMED WITH THE RIGHT, SO THAT THE PUPIL WILL BE GRASPING THE BACK OF THE CHAIR WITH THE LEFT HAND IN THE SAME WAY AS HE HAS BEEN HOLDING IT WITH THE RIGHT, the teacher giving such assistance in this movement as he deems necessary in the light of his experience.

It will be found that at this, as at every other step in the work, one pupil will need more assistance than another. One pupil will need help in one part of the movement, the next will need it at another part, and so on. It may even, in some cases, be necessary for the teacher to give a pupil as much assistance in bringing forward the left arm as he gave him in bringing forward the right arm. In all these matters the decision must be left to the discretion of the teacher. *To command success, correct experiences in sensory appreciation must follow the giving of correct directive and guiding orders. By the repetition of this process the pupil reaches a stage where he can depend on himself with confidence.*

At this point THE PUPIL SHOULD BE ASKED TO RECONSIDER THE DIFFERENT *means whereby* HE HAS BEEN ENABLED TO REACH THIS STAGE OF HIS WORK, AND TO REPEAT ORALLY THE DIRECTIONS AND GUIDING ORDERS EXACTLY IN THE SEQUENCE IN WHICH THEY HAVE BEEN GIVEN TO HIM BY HIS TEACHER, AS PRIMARY, SECONDARY, AND FOLLOWING FACTORS. In this way the teacher will be able to test the pupil's accuracy or otherwise in this connexion. *Whilst the pupil repeats the orders, he must remain in the co-ordinated condition which has been secured during the performance of the evolution.*

When the teacher is satisfied that his pupil has succeeded up to this point, he may go on to give him the additional guiding orders, and proceed to help him to put them into practical effect during the completion of the evolution.

The following are the new directive orders.

The pupil is asked :—

(1) TO CONTINUE TO HOLD THE TOP OF THE CHAIR BY KEEPING THE FINGERS QUITE STRAIGHT FROM THE FIRST JOINTS OF THE FINGERS TO THEIR TIPS, WITH THE THUMBS

Illustration 115

AND FINGERS KEPT FLAT AGAINST THE TOP RAIL OF THE
CHAIR AS PREVIOUSLY INDICATED.

(2) To ALLOW THE WRIST OF THE LEFT ARM TO BE
CURVED INWARDS TOWARDS THE RIGHT, AND THE WRIST
OF THE RIGHT ARM TO BE CURVED INWARDS TOWARDS THE
LEFT.

(3) To ALLOW THE ELBOW OF THE LEFT ARM TO BE
CURVED OUTWARDS TOWARDS THE LEFT, AND THE ELBOW
OF THE RIGHT ARM TO BE CURVED OUTWARDS TOWARDS THE
RIGHT.

In order that the pupil may hold the rail of the chair, keeping
the fingers and wrists in the position indicated above, HE
SHOULD REHEARSE ALL THE DIRECTIVE ORDERS PREVIOUSLY
GIVEN TO HIM AND WHICH HE HAS ALREADY ORALLY REPEATED
TO HIS TEACHER.

The teacher's aim is now to give the pupil the experiences
necessary to a gentle, forearm pull from the fingers, and to this
end HE WILL TAKE HOLD OF THE PUPIL'S ELBOWS AND DIRECT
THEM OUTWARDS AND SLIGHTLY DOWNWARDS, and, following
this, will give the sensory experiences required in DIRECTING
THE UPPER PARTS OF THE ARMS (ABOVE THE ELBOW) AWAY
FROM ONE ANOTHER (THE RIGHT ARM TOWARDS THE RIGHT AND
THE LEFT ARM TOWARDS THE LEFT), IN SUCH A WAY THAT THE
PUPIL WILL BE SUPPORTING THE TORSO WITH HIS ARMS.

THE PUPIL WILL NOW BE ASKED TO CONTINUE TO SUPPORT
THE TORSO IN THIS WAY, CONTINUING TO REHEARSE HIS ORDERS,
whilst the teacher so adjusts the torso that the large " lifting "
muscles of the back will be employed co-ordinately with the
other parts of the organism in bringing about such use of the
respiratory mechanisms that they will function to the maximum
at the particular stage of development reached from day to day.
Success in this part of the evolution will bring about a change
in the condition of the back which would be described by the
ordinary observer as a " widening of the back."

These orders are the *means whereby* such use of the mechanisms may be brought about, associated with a satisfactory
readjustment of the back, as will cause the floating ribs to move
freely, and also tend to develop the maximum intra-thoracic
capacity and to establish the most effective use of the respiratory mechanism during the sleeping as well as the waking hours.

In my opinion, it is expedient here to set down some of the impeding conditions which, in my teaching experience, will be found present, more or less, in the case of every pupil during the attempt at co-ordination at this stage of the movement. The muscular tension, for instance, employed in the use of the fingers and arms is almost always a harmful and unnecessary one. Very frequently this undue tension of the arm muscles will actually prevent the pupil from using his fingers to anything like the best advantage in holding the chair. I have even known instances in which the fingers would actually be kept away from the wood without the pupil's knowing it. This undue tension is particularly noticeable in the case of the contractor muscles of the arm in the region of the biceps and in that of the pectoral muscles in the front of the chest, whereas in a satisfactory state of sensory appreciation these muscles would remain more or less relaxed during the movement, and the greater part of the work would fall on the muscles of the opposite side of the arm and the back (chiefly on the latissimus dorsi). These would thus be the chief factors in the act, factors which make both for the maximum activity of the respiratory processes, with the minimum of effort, and also for an increased intra-thoracic capacity accompanied by a broadening of the costal arch (increased vital capacity).

Other impeding conditions are apt to occur at the pupil's first attempt to pull gently with the arms. In his attempt to do this, either one or other or all the fingers will become bent and the wrists will be curved outwards, *exactly the reverse of the action indicated by the orders* or of the one desired. *This failure to carry out the given orders is due chiefly to the fact that the pupil's sensory appreciation in the matter of due and proper muscular tension is sadly inadequate.*

This leads us directly to a consideration of the means we have adopted whereby a new and reliable sensory appreciation can be developed in the pupil, the *means whereby* he will be enabled to perform this evolution with the *minimum of muscular tension*. In this connexion the reader's attention is specially directed to the following :

If the pupil will carry out the act of the forearm pull and attend to the widening of the upper parts of the arms, whilst continuing to recognize as factors of primary importance the keeping of the fingers straight and the wrists curved inwards, *the minimum tension will be exerted*. Immediately the pupil interferes with the position of the fingers or wrists (in the latter case, tending to curve them outwards instead of inwards), this will indicate that *the point of minimum muscular tension has been passed*.

Illustration 117

It should be remembered here that the pupil's position in this act is an ideal one for watching the hands and wrists. Therefore, if the pupil will watch carefully any tendency to the incorrect movements described above, these can be checked as soon as they show themselves. But here again we have one of the numerous instances where a person will refrain from doing the thing he knows he can do (in this instance, to watch the hands—" means-whereby "), and will prefer to depend instead on the old haphazard method of " trying to do it right " guided by his feeling, and this despite the fact that in every experience in which he has taken " feeling " for a guide he has found it to be unreliable and even delusive.

* * * * *

There has just come to my knowledge an interesting objection to the importance which I attach to the process of inhibition as a primary and fundamental factor in the technique of the scheme I advocate, and the objection is made on the ground that this use of inhibition will cause harmful suppression in the individual concerned. I shall proceed to show that such an objection is the outcome of a total misunderstanding of the fundamental psycho-physical processes concerned with the application of the preventive principles employed in my technique.

There has been and still is a growing tendency to attempt to free children from undue external restraint, both at home and at school, with the idea of preventing those harmful suppressions supposed to be the result of the inhibitions associated with the imposition of the restraint characteristic of less modern methods. The idea concerned is conceived on a specific and curative basis and is generally accepted, particularly in schools where an effort is being made to create conditions of environment and occupation to meet the pupil's needs. The points I wish to emphasize in this connexion are : (1) that the process of inhibition involved is employed in connexion with ideas directly associated with the gaining of " ends," these ideas being the response to a stimulus (or stimuli) arising from some primary desire or need, and (2)—and this is all-important—that the stimulus (or stimuli) to inhibit this response comes from without, and the process of inhibition is *forced* upon the pupil. This means that his desire is thwarted in consequence of compliance with a command from an outside authority, and this could account for the disturbed emotional conditions associated with what is known as suppression.

Now the inhibitory process involved in my technique has little in common with that to which reference has just been made. For the idea concerned with inhibition in my technique is conceived on a general and preventive basis, and the process of inhibition involved is employed primarily in connexion with ideas which are dissociated from any direct attempt to gain an "end," but associated instead with that indirect procedure inseparable from the practical application of the principles concerned with the *means whereby* an end may be gained. These ideas are the response to a stimulus (or stimuli) arising from a reasoned, constructive conscious understanding and acceptance by the pupil of the principles concerned with the "means-whereby," and as the procedure concerned with the application of these principles involves the prevention of "end-gaining" acts, the performance of which is associated with misdirected activities, it follows that the pupil's acceptance of the need for and efficacy of such procedure includes also his acceptance of the principle of inhibition of primary desires concerned with such "end-gaining" acts. This, again, really means that in the application of my technique the process of inhibition—that is, *the act of refusing to respond* to the primary desire to gain an "end"—*becomes the act of responding* (volitionary act) to the conscious reasoned desire to employ the *means whereby* that "end" may be gained.

The stimulus to inhibit, therefore, in this case comes from within, and the process of inhibition is not forced upon the pupil. This means that the pupil's desire or desires will be satisfied, not thwarted, and that there will be present desirable emotional and other psycho-physical conditions which do not make for what is known as suppression in any form.[1]

---

[1] There are many persons who pride themselves on self-control who are really victims of enslavement to a fixed "end"—that is, they do not control themselves by stopping to think out the "means-whereby" to their "ends," but by excluding everything which does not agree with the "ends" which they have set up as right and proper. They themselves may contend that their control is purely self-imposed and not externally imposed, but to other persons it manifests itself as a form of rigidity. On the other hand, control which results from stopping to reason out the *means whereby* desired ends may be secured is unassociated with that rigidity which is inseparable from enslavement to preconceived and unreasoned ideas and beliefs, or to hard-and-fast rules in regard to what is right and proper in conduct and procedure.

Illustration 119

The tendency of people on a subconscious plane to speak and act without adequate thought or consideration is a particularly marked manifestation, when there is present an unusually potent stimulus to those processes concerned with what are known as prejudice and emotional disturbances. We are all familiar with the phrases, " Why don't you think before you act? ", " Think before you speak," and so on. When the human creature's activities are on a plane of constructive, conscious control, he will have reached a standard of development and use of the processes of inhibition (as outlined in the technique which I advocate) which will enable him to apply in practice to his activities in the outside world the very principles concerned with the processes of inhibition which he has applied to the use of his psycho-physical self, with accruing benefit in both spheres of application.

In this connexion I will now give an incident which I think is of particular interest and pertinence as showing the application of the technique employed in the work of re-education on a general basis to the practical ways of life, and also the analogy which exists between the process of " linking-up " (association of ideas) during the lessons, and the process of linking up what has been gained during those lessons with the experience of everyday life. I also give it in proof of the fundamental value of the principle of inhibition involved.

A pupil of mine, an author, had been in a serious state of health for some time, and had at last reached the point where he was unable to carry on his literary work. After finishing his latest book he passed through a crisis which was described as a " break-down," with the result that even a few hours of work caused him great fatigue and brought on a state of painful depression. From the outset of his lessons, therefore, I expressly stipulated that he should *stop* and make a break at the end of each half-hour's writing, and should then either do fifteen minutes' work in respiratory re-education, or take a walk in the open air before resuming his writing.

One afternoon he came to his lesson unusually depressed and enervated, and, in response to my inquiries, he admitted that he had been indulging in his literary work that morning from nine till one without a break, in spite of my express stipulation that he must make frequent breaks. I pointed out to him that if he had been continuing his work for four hours without a break, we could not be surprised at the unfortunate result, for, as I explained to him, during deep thought, as in sleep, the activity of the respiratory processes is reduced to a minimum, a very harmful minimum in his case, owing to the inadequacy of his intra-thoracic capacity, this latter condition being one of the symptoms of his break-down. " But I am unable to stop when once I get into my work," said my pupil. I suggested that if this were so, it must come from some lack of control on his part. " But surely," my pupil objected, " it must be a mistake to break a train of thought? " I answered that my experience went to show that this was not the case, that, on the contrary, as far as I could see, it should be as easy to break off a piece of work requiring thought, and take it up again, as it is to carry on a train of thought, whilst taking a walk with all its attendant interruptions, and that this should be possible not only without loss of connexion, but with accruing benefit to the individual concerned.

In all this I was really preparing the way to a special end— namely, the attempt to show my pupil the analogy that existed between the point in question and his difficulty in accomplishing certain simple parts of the technique in his lessons through his disinclination to stop. I wished to convince him that *the gaining of control in the simple psycho-physical evolutions in which we were engaged during the lessons meant sooner or later the gaining of control in the practical spheres of his daily life.* My pupil had failed to make this all-important connexion between his work in re-education and his outside activities, and therefore the connexion between the difficulty he experienced in " stopping " in his lessons and " stopping " in the midst of his literary work had completely escaped him.

In this, however, he was only in like case with thousands of other well-educated and intelligent people who, in dealing with a situation, fail to make an obvious association of ideas, and so miss most important connecting links between different factors in a case. In this particular instance, had my pupil made the necessary connexion between the difficulty he had in " stopping " in his lessons and " stopping " in his activities outside, this recognition would have given a new meaning, and therefore an added stimulus, to the psycho-physical effort upon which the successful working-out of the technique depends.

V

RESPIRATORY MECHANISMS

WE shall probably find the best practical illustration of the need for correct sensory experiences in guidance and control if we consider sensory appreciation in its connexion with the psycho-mechanics of respiration. It is universally admitted that there are harmful defects in the use of the respiratory mechanisms and a corresponding deterioration in the chest capacity and mobility of the great majority of people. The scientific medical man describes certain types of children as born with a " low respiratory need," and this really means that when the child is born it is more or less imperfectly co-ordinated and its organism is functioning much nearer to its minimum than to its maximum capacity. This condition of inadequate vital functioning is present in the greater number of men, women, and children of to-day, and is one that is commonly associated with what we speak of as " bad breathing." For we say that a person is a " bad breather," or that he " breathes imperfectly." But we must remember that this so-called " bad breathing " is only a symptom and not a primary cause of his malcondition, for the standard of breathing depends upon the standard of general co-ordinated use of the psycho-physical mechanisms. What we ought to say, therefore, in such a case is not that a person " breathes badly," but that he is badly co-ordinated. The truth is that when we refer to this mal-co-ordinated condition as " bad breathing," we are mistaking a general malcondition for a specific defect, and the conception of the respiratory act which makes this error possible, and which affects even our way of expressing it, provides yet another instance of the dominance of our general attitude by the " end-gaining " principle.

This " end-gaining " principle is again dominant when it is decided that a person who is spoken of as a " bad breather " needs specific " breathing exercises " or " lessons in breathing." We shall see that in this, as in so many other spheres, a vicious circle is developed.

In the attempt to make this clear we must give considera-tion to the fundamental principles upon which these breathing exercises (usually called " deep-breathing " exercises) or " lessons in breathing " are based. Take any book on breathing, whether written by a scientific author or by an expert in vocal or " physical culture," and read the written instructions in connexion with the exercises therein advocated. Take the opportunity also, when possible, to be present when the unfortunate children or adults in a gymnasium are being given a lesson in breathing or are performing their breathing exercises. You will then have proof that the whole of the processes concerned are directed towards specific and not general improvement, and though the people who are guilty of teaching " breathing exercises " may differ in detail of method, they all base their work alike on the same specific " endgaining " principle. I shall now proceed to detail the processes involved.

The pupil is asked to take a deep breath. He may also be asked to perform some " physical " movement at the same time as he takes the deep breath, the idea behind this request being that the performance of the movement may help to increase the chest expansion. Yet it is a scientific fact that all " physical " tension tends to cause thoracic (chest) rigidity and breathlessness (lack of respiratory control), two conditions which should be avoided as far as possible by such pupils during their attempts to pass from conditions which are symptomatic of bad breathing to those which ensure satisfactory respiratory functioning.

It will be necessary for the layman to watch the pupil (or pupils) carefully during their attempts to carry out their written or spoken instructions in connexion with " deep breathing." Specific defects and peculiarities to be noted during the process have already been set down in *Man's Supreme Inheritance*. Here we wish to refer only to the defective *general* use of the psycho-physical organism during these attempts. In order to make the point, we must refer to the fact that the pupil or the teacher, or both, must have recognized certain harmful manifestations which called for some remedial procedure on the lines of " deep-breathing," etc. Hence the decision to employ " deep-breathing " as a remedy. These harmful manifestations would be the result of certain incorrect psycho-physical uses of the organism. This would indicate that the sensory appreciation in the sphere of guidance and control of the psycho-physical mechanisms concerned must have become unreliable and defective, and in the present instance, so far as the observation of the teacher and pupil is concerned, certain defects must have been particularly noticeable in the use of the breathing mechanisms.

Here we have a clear case of certain established incorrect uses of the mechanisms, associated with a condition of unreliable sensory guidance and control, and any effort to remedy these incorrect uses by means of such processes as " deeping " or " lessons in breathing " is merely an attempt to correct a *general* defective condition of psycho-mechanics by a *specific* remedial process. In other words, it is an attempt to correct the imperfect uses by the performance of exercises, the guidance and direction in such performance being associated with the same imperfect sensory appreciation which was already established when the lessons began. This means that with the continued practice of the exercises, the original defects in the general use of the mechanisms will become more and more pronounced and, what is more, increase in number.

It may be argued that, as the result of the lessons, the pupil's chest measurements are increased, that he " feels better," and so on. We are quite ready to admit that this may be so, but owing to the unreliability of his sensory appreciation, what he feels is as likely as not to be a delusion. Of what avail, therefore, is it for the pupil to " feel better," if he is still left with a defective sensory appreciation to guide him in all his activities during his waking moments as well as his sleeping hours? It is only a matter of time before the unfortunate pupil will be awakened from his dream by discovering that he has developed certain other serious conditions. I should like here to point out that these serious conditions must result, sooner or later, from the lack in such cases of a reliable guiding sensory appreciation, also from the lack of psycho-physical co-ordination which is associated therewith, and which continues to increase whilst these conditions are present. We have all known people who tell of the improvement in their chest measurement from the practice of exercises. The writer has examined many such in the course of thirty years' professional investigation. In the majority of these cases the supposed increase in chest capacity has been chiefly due to muscular development on the outside of the bony chest, in other cases to some distortion or distortions cultivated during the processes involved, rather than to that co-ordinated use of the psycho-physical system which is associated with a real increase in the intra-thoracic (inner chest) capacity.[1] And it is the same in the case of those who tell you that they " feel better " as the result of these exercises, for to the expert observer it is obvious that the habit of " sniffing " (sucking in air), the contraction of the alæ nasi, the depression of the larynx, and all the accompanying defective use of the organism associated with the practice of the exercises must, sooner or later, cause serious nose, ear, eye, and throat troubles. In other words, the exponents of these breathing exercises act in direct pursuance of their " end," remaining oblivious to the harmfulness of the *means whereby* they are attempting to bring this " end " about, and to the many wrong uses they are cultivating during the process.

This method of procedure, as we have seen, is the very opposite of that which underlies the process of re-education, readjustment, and co-ordination on a conscious, general basis, and we will consider the application of this process to a satisfactory use of the psycho-physical mechanisms.

We will begin by a consideration of the fundamental psycho-physical principles underlying the act of breathing. In the course of this consideration it will be found that breathing is many times removed from the primary principle concerned, and that, therefore, it is incorrect and harmful to speak of " teaching a person to breathe," or of " giving lessons in breathing or deep-breathing." Such a stimulus to the sub-consciously controlled person at once induces projections of all the established incorrect guiding orders associated with imperfect or inadequate breathing processes ; in other words, this stimulus sets in motion all our bad habits in breathing.

Breathing is that psycho-physical act by means of which air is taken into and expelled from the lungs of the creature. The lungs are an extremely interesting part of our anatomy. They consist of two bags containing a network of cells capable of contraction and expansion, with air passages and blood vessels so associated and constituted that the oxygen con-

[1] An interesting delusion prevalent with teachers of breathing exercises is that of mistaking an increase in the muscle development or the outer walls of the chest for increase in intra-chest (thoracic) capacity

tained in the air, when taken into the lungs, can be absorbed through the tissue of the blood-vessels and cells and air passages, whilst carbonic acid gas (poison) passes through this tissue from the blood-vessels into the lung cells to be expelled from the lungs. The thorax (chest) has a bony structure, made up of the vertebræ of the spine, the different ribs, and the sternum (breast-bone), those ribs which are attached to the sternum as well as to the spine being much less mobile than those which are not attached to the sternum, the most mobile being known as " floating ribs." The lungs are enclosed within the cavity of this bony thorax of which the diaphragm is the floor, and the only entrance to which is through the trachea (windpipe). From the very first breath there is a more or less constant air pressure (atmospheric pressure) within the lungs, but not any air pressure on the outside of the lungs. Air pressure is sufficient to overcome the elasticity of the tissue of the air-cells, and to increase their size, when not held in check by the pressure of the walls of the thorax upon the lung-bag itself. The lungs are subject, however, to this pressure exerted by the walls of the thorax during the contraction, and to the release of this pressure during the expansion of the thoracic cavity. The pressure that can be exerted by the walls of the thorax on the outside of the lung-bag is much greater than that which results from the atmospheric pressure (air pressure) within the lungs. Therefore, when we wish, as we say, to " take a breath " (inspiration), all we have to do is to reduce the pressure exerted upon the lungs by the chest walls, and to employ those muscular co-ordinations which increase the intra-thoracic capacity of the lungs (increased chest capacity), thereby causing a partial vacuum in the lung-cells of which atmospheric pressure takes advantage, by increasing the size of the cells and thus the amount of air in the lungs. It then follows that if we wish to exhale breath (expiration), we merely have to increase the pressure on the lungs by contracting the walls of the thorax, thereby overcoming the atmospheric pressure exerted within the lungs, and thus forcing the air out of them. It must be remembered that in all these contractions and expansions, the floor of the cavity (diaphragm) plays its part, moving upwards or downwards in sympathy with the particular adjustment of the bony thorax.

Consideration of the foregoing will serve to convince the reader that if anyone desires, either by his own effort or with the help of a teacher, to secure the maximum control and development in breathing, all that he has to do is to be able to command the maximum functioning of the psycho-physical mechanisms concerned with the satisfactory expansion and contraction of the walls of the thoracic (chest) cavity. *It is not necessary for him even to think of taking a breath;* as a matter of fact, it is more or less harmful to do so, when such psycho-physical conditions are present as call for re-education on a general basis.

The crux of the whole matter, then, is how to gain this control in expanding and contracting the chest, as we say, and thus permanently to increase its capacity and mobility. The answer to this question calls for a comprehensive consideration of the primary, secondary, and other psycho-physical factors involved.

Naturally, the most potent stimulus to the use of the respiratory mechanisms is the necessity for an adequate supply of oxygen, and for the elimination of carbonic acid gas (poison) from the blood. But we must not overlook the fact that in any attempt to gain for a pupil the desired control and the increased thoracic capacity, the pupil's incorrect use of the mechanisms involved is an impeding factor, and so, in attempts to correct such imperfect use, the first consideration must be to *prevent the psycho-physical activities which are responsible for this defective use* by the development and employment of the pupil's ability to inhibit. This demands from the teacher a correct diagnosis of the pupil's numerous bad habits in connexion with the act of respiration in everyday life, and a comprehensive understanding of the imperfections in sensory appreciation, conception, adjustment, and co-ordination which are manifested in these bad habits.

As a result of the diagnosis, the teacher will go on to explain to the pupil why certain readjustments and improved co-ordinations are necessary in his case, and will then give him a reasoned consideration of the *means whereby* these readjust-ments and improved co-ordinations may be secured. To this end the teacher will first name the preventive guiding orders or directions which the pupil is to give to himself in the way of *inhibiting* the deceptive guiding sensations concerned with the defective use of the mechanisms responsible for what we

call bad habits in breathing. The teacher must make certain
that the pupil remembers these guiding orders or directions *in
the sequence in which they are to be employed*. When this has
been done, the pupil may begin the practice in connexion with
the work of prevention. This means a series of repeated
experiences on the part of the pupil in refusing to try for the
" end," and in positively pausing to think of the original faults
pointed out by the teacher, and refusing to repeat them.

For instance, suppose that a pupil has a special desire to
increase his chest capacity. This desire acts as a stimulus to
the psycho-physical processes involved and sets in motion all
the unreliable guiding and directing sensations associated with
his established idea of chest expansion. The only way, then,
by which he can *prevent* the old subconscious habits from gaining the upper hand is for him to *refuse to act* upon this idea.
This means that as soon as the idea or desire comes to him
he definitely stops and says to himself : "No. I won't do
what I should like to do to increase my chest capacity, because,
if I do what I feel will increase it, I shall only use my mechanisms as I have used them before, and what is the good of
that ? I know I have been using them incorrectly up to now,
else why do I need these lessons ? " In other words, he inhibits
his desire to act.

The teacher, of course, must decide when the pupil can proceed from the preventive to the next stage of his work. He
must then proceed to name for the pupil the new orders in
connexion with the satisfactory guiding sensations concerned
with the correct use of the mechanisms involved. The pupil
should recall and give himself these new guiding orders, whilst
the teacher, by means of his manipulation, assists him to
secure the correct readjustment and co-ordination (the desired
" end "), thus ensuring a series of satisfactory experiences which
should be repeated until the bad habits are eradicated and the
new and correct experiences replace them and become established.

Repetition of these correct experiences is all that is required
to establish a satisfactory use of the co-ordinated psycho-
physical mechanisms concerned, when an increase or decrease
in the intra-thoracic (chest) capacity can be secured at will,
with the minimum of effort and with a mathematical precision. The increase in the intra-thoracic (chest) capacity
indicated decreases the pressure on the outside of the lung-

bag and causes a momentary partial vacuum in the lungs. This vacuum is promptly filled with air, in consequence of the atmospheric pressure exerted upon the inside of the lung-cells, and this process increases the amount of air in the lungs, constituting the act of what we call " taking a breath " (inspiration). The marvellous efficiency of the respiratory machine, when properly employed, becomes apparent when we realize that we have only to continue to employ the same *means whereby* we secure the increase (expansion) to secure the decrease (contraction) of the intra-thoracic capacity, which means that in process the contracting chest walls exert such increased pressure on the lungs that the air-pressure within is overcome, and the air consequently expelled, this process constituting " expiration "; the expiration and previous inspiration being the completed act of breathing. When a satisfactory, co-ordinated use of the mechanisms concerned with the acts of inspiration and expiration is established, the teacher may then proceed to help the pupil to employ this co-ordinated use in connexion with all vocal effort. As has been pointed out in *Man's Supreme Inheritance*, this should begin with *whispered* vocalization, preferably the vowel sound " Ah," as this form of vocal use, being so little employed in everyday life, is rarely associated with ordinary bad psycho-physical habits in vocalization.

For this reason, the teacher will begin by helping the pupil to make the expiration on a whispered " Ah." This calls for a knowledge of the psycho-physical " means-whereby " of the use of the organism *in general*, and of the acts of opening the mouth, using the lips, tongue, soft palate, etc., with freedom from stress and strain of the vocal mechanisms, and to this end a definite technique is employed. The process involved prevents sniffing and " sucking in air," undue depression of the larynx, and undue stiffening of the muscles of the throat vocal organs, and neck. It also prevents the undue lifting of the front part of the chest during inspiration, its undue depression during expiration, and also many other defects which are developed by any imperfectly co-ordinated person who attempts to learn " breathing " or " deep-breathing," etc., guided by the unreliable sensory appreciation which is always associated with an imperfectly co-ordinated condition of the psycho-physical mechanism.

VI

UNDULY EXCITED FEAR REFLEXES, UNCONTROLLED EMOTIONS, AND FIXED PREJUDICES

THERE can be little doubt that the process of reasoning tends to develop more quickly and to reach a higher standard in a person whose attitude towards life might be described as calm and collected. In such a person the psycho-physical processes called "habits" are governed by moderation, and his inhibitory processes are adequately developed in all spheres of activity. Their use is not limited to those comparatively few spheres where it was considered necessary to establish taboos during the early and later periods of man's struggle with the problems which arose in the various stages of the civilizing process. In these spheres there has been a harmful and exaggerated development of the inhibitory processes, often causing virtues to become almost vices, whilst in other spheres there has been a correspondingly harmful lack of the development of inhibition, particularly in those spheres connected with the use of the psycho-physical mechanisms in practical activity. This represents an unbalanced use of this wonderful process of inhibition, and tends to produce, as a general result, a state of unbalanced psycho-physical functioning throughout the whole organism, and to establish what we shall refer to as " the unduly excited reflex " process.

This unbalanced psycho-physical condition of the civilized human creature is apparent in most spheres of activity, and the child of to-day is more predisposed to the factors which make for this condition than his parents or their ancestors. This child, therefore, starts his school career with a comparatively poor equipment on the inhibitory side. Now volition and inhibition are invaluable birthrights of the human creature and should be developed equally, as it were, hand in hand, but from the first moment of a child's school life right on to adolescence the training [1] he receives tends to interfere with

[1] The fact of the great number of " don'ts " to which some children are subjected, and the implicit obedience expected of them at school and at home, does not affect my contention that the children of to-day manifest a serious lack on the inhibitory side in all activity involving the use of the psycho-physical organism.

his balanced development, and so is another factor in the cultivation of those psycho-physical defects and abnormalities which make for the unbalanced conditions to which we have already referred.

Unduly excited fear reflexes, uncontrolled emotions, prejudices, and fixed habits, are retarding factors in all human development. They need our serious attention, for they are linked up with all psycho-physical processes employed in growth and development on the subconscious plane. Hence, by the time adolescence is reached these retarding factors have become present in a more or less degree, and the processes thus established in psycho-physical use will make for the continued development of such retarding factors. This is particularly the case when a person endeavours to learn something calling for new experiences.

It is only necessary to watch adult pupils at their lessons to realize that, in the great majority of cases, more or less uncontrolled emotions are a striking feature in their endeavours to carry out new instructions correctly. Watch the fixed expression of these pupils, for instance, their jerky, uncontrolled movements, and their tendency to hold the breath by assuming a harmful posture and exerting an exaggerated strain such as they would employ in performing strenuous " physical " acts. In many cases there will be a twitching of the muscles of the mouth and cheeks, or of the fingers. In each case the stimulus to these misdirected activities is the pupil's idea or conception that he must try to do *correctly* whatever the teacher requests, and, as we have seen, on the subconscious plane the teacher insists upon this. The teacher of re-education on a conscious plane does not make this demand of his pupils, for he knows by experience, and has to face the fact that in cases where there is an imperfect functioning of the organism, *an individual cannot always do as he is told correctly.* He may " want " to do it, he may " try and try again " to do it, but as long as the psycho-mechanics by which he tries to carry out his teacher's directions are not working satisfactorily, every attempt he makes to carry out his teacher's directions " correctly " (trying to be right) is bound to end in comparative failure. For in making these attempts, as we point out elsewhere, the pupil has only his own judgment to depend on as to what is correct, and since his judgment is based on incorrect direction and delusive sensory appreciation, he is held within the vicious circle of his old habits as long as he tries to carry out the directions "correctly." Paradoxical as it may seem, the pupil's only chance of success lies, not in "trying to be right," but, on the contrary, in "wanting to be wrong "— wrong, that is, according to any standard of his own. In this connexion it is most important to remember that every unsuccessful "try" not only reinforces the pupil's old wrong psycho-physical habits associated with his conception of a particular act, but involves at the same time new emotional experiences of discouragement, worry, fear, and anxiety, so that the wrong experiences and the unduly excited reflex process involved in these experiences become one in the pupil's recognition; they "make the meat they feed on," and the more conscientious the teacher and the pupil are on this plan, the worse the situation becomes for both.

It is for this reason that the teacher on a conscious plane does not expect a pupil, as I have pointed out, to perform "correctly" a new act calling for new experiences, but instead, by means of manipulation, gives to the pupil the new experiences, repeating them until they become established. We have seen, indeed, in Chapter III that he asks his pupil not to make any attempt to gain the "end" at all, but instead to learn gradually to remember the guiding orders or directions, which are the forerunners of the *means whereby* the end may one day be gained. This may not be to-day, to-morrow, or the next day, but it will be: the pupil will then be able to repeat the act with mathematical precision at all times and under all circumstances, for such retarding factors as unduly excited fear reflexes, uncontrolled emotions, and fixed prejudices will not have been developed in the process just outlined. Indeed, a process which does not involve a pupil's being asked to perform any act until his teacher has prepared the way by raising the standard of the pupil's sensory appreciation and psycho-physical co-ordination to that satisfactory state which will enable him to perform the act, as we say, easily, will be a process which ensures that the pupil's experiences will be, with rare exceptions, satisfactory experiences, which make for confidence and are not associated with those emotional disturbances which tend towards the minimum instead of the maximum functioning.

The relation of all this to the very important question of the ability to " keep one's head " at critical moments is clear, and it may be interesting to apply the points we have raised in the foregoing to such activities as playing games and to other performances in which skill and so-called " presence of mind " are required. We constantly hear in this connexion remarks like the following : " I didn't do so badly at it at first, but the longer I play the worse I play." One writer in the public Press remarks that it is a curious feature of golf that " the more one knows about it . . . the more difficult it seems to become "; and another writes that a well-known professional had " confessed . . . that golf had become almost too much for him." All this applies equally, of course, to other games, but I have chosen golf for my illustration because it happens that writers on golf, commenting on some of the incidents that have occurred at matches during the past two years or so, have unwittingly emphasized the existence of *the problem* which underlies these admissions and with which I am dealing in the present book. For instance, they have commented on the failure of certain experts to perform some simple stroke when under an unusual stress and at a moment when success depends on their not throwing a chance away; they have pointed to the tendency of some players to become confused and to hurry their strokes through anxiety to " get it over "; " truly heart-breaking " is the description of one such incident, words that will be echoed by many who have had similar discouraging experiences in other matters besides golf.

We are told that this is all a matter of " nerves " and so forth. It is undoubtedly a case of the undue excitement of fear reflexes on the player's part—fear, for instance, that he may miss a shot which he knows he is not in the habit of missing and ought not to miss. As a pupil once said to me at a first interview : " I am always coming up against things that I know I can do, and yet when it comes to the point, I can't do them." The fact is that in all our processes of learning things, the fear reflexes are unduly and harmfully excited by the teaching methods employed, according to which demands are made upon us that we are not able to fulfil. So, for a time, we get bad results, with the undue and harmful development of emotional reflex processes which, as we have seen, inevitably accompanies these unsuccessful attempts. We continue to practise on wrong lines, so that our successful experiences are few and our unsuccessful experiences many. We attempt on a subconscious basis to develop a particular stroke, and in any failure to make the stroke satisfactorily the imperfect use of the psycho-physical mechanisms plays more than its fair share. It is experiences like this which cause disappointment and undue excitement of fear reflexes and serious emotional disturbances, and nothing whatever is done at this later stage of the process to nullify these effects of the psycho-physical experiences cultivated during the earlier stages. These emotional disturbances were part and parcel of an unbalanced psycho-physical condition, of a state of anxiety and confusion, and there can be little doubt that any circumstance that is more or less unusual is likely to bring about a recurrence of the same disturbed psycho-physical condition as was experienced by the subject during his early efforts to make the stroke.

But, beyond this, we must remember that it is only the small minority of experts in any line who really know *how* they get their results and effects,[1] in the case of golf, for instance, *how* they perform their most successful strokes. Therefore directly anything puts them " off their game," they experience considerable difficulty, at any rate, in getting on to it again. It is only by having a clear conception of what is required for the successful performance of a certain stroke or other act, combined with a knowledge of the psycho-physical *means whereby* those requirements can be met, that there is any reasonable possibility of their attaining sureness and confidence during performance.

I would here refer my readers to my earlier volume, where this point was dealt with at some length in connexion with golf, and I have the less hesitation in doing so, as what I have written there has since had the endorsement of such a distinguished golfer as Mr. John Duncan Dunn,[2] a matter,

---

[1] The same thing applies to the expert singer who does not know how he sings, any more than the political and social leaders of our time know how much more they are influenced in their decisions and actions by their prejudices and " emotional gusts " than by their reasoning processes.

[2] Author of *ABC of Golf. Intimate Golf Talks* (Dunn and Jessup).

naturally, of great gratification to me. I there attempted to make clear that the success of any particular process in golf, such as, for instance, " following through," must depend, primarily, on the *general* condition of psycho-physical development and control present, because a player whose sensory appreciation is in any way at fault cannot satisfactorily carry out directions given to him. For the indispensable preliminary to success is a reliable sensory appreciation which will guide the particular player in his efforts to reach and maintain *during the stroke* an adequate standard of co-ordination in the general use of his mechanism. This satisfactory *general* use is essential to satisfactory *specific* use. By chance or good luck a man may make a good stroke without having attained to a good standard in the general use of himself, but he can never be reasonably certain of repeating it, and the experiences associated with this state of uncertainty do not make for the growth of confidence, but rather for the development of undue fear reflexes and serious emotional disturbances.[1]

We must realize that if an individual is to reach that satisfactory stage of progress where he can be reasonably certain of success in achieving his " ends," those principles must be observed which imply reliance in all activities upon the *means whereby* an " end " may be gained, irrespective of whether, during the progress of the activities concerned, the perform-

[1] The following quoted from the *Times*, October 29th, 1921, is a delightful little parable showing the fallacy of expecting pupils to be able to put right some defect unless the *means whereby* they can correct it is first given into their hands :—

" Wandering a little farther along the course, I came across two elderly gentlemen playing a short hole. The first hit a good shot on to the green. The second did not. ' Would any sane man,' he exclaimed, ' believe that such things could be ? ' ' I could put you right in a minute,' said complacent No. 1. ' I wish you would,' replied humble No. 2. ' Well, I will,' said No. 1. And I waited, breathless, thinking that at last I was going to find out the secret of all hitting. ' You don't follow through.' It was yet one more disappointment in a bitterly disappointed life, *for I knew that I, and most other people in the world, very often ' don't follow through,' and that knowledge does not make me play any better.* ' Oh, No. 1, No. 1,' I murmured, ' what the devil is the good of telling me that ? You must tell me *what I do with my confounded arms and legs on the way up, that they behave so ill on the way down.* You are not such a good coach as I thought you, No. 1,' and I went away sorrowful." [The italics are mine.—F. M. A.]

ance is correct or incorrect. The application of these principles in any sphere of learning means that the teacher during lessons must be able to supply the pupil's needs in the matter of reliable sensory appreciation, by giving him from day to day the necessary experiences until they become established. No technique which does not meet the demands herein indicated will prove satisfactory as a means of re-educating a pupil on a general basis to a reliable plane of conscious activity. When this plane is reached, the individual comes to rely upon his " means-whereby," and does not become disturbed by wondering whether the activities concerned will be right or wrong. Why should he, seeing that the confidence with which he proceeds with his task is a confidence born of experiences, the majority of which are successful experiences unassociated with over-excited fear reflexes? This confidence is further reinforced by his confidence in the reliability of his sensory appreciation which ensures that any interference with the co-ordinated use of himself will come to his consciousness as soon as it occurs (awareness). This consciousness is really a state of acute awareness which has been developed in him during the processes of re-education and co-ordination on a general basis, and the confidence associated with it is not likely to desert him in moments of crisis. It is true that he may be put off the right track, but he knows that it will be only momentarily, as he is certain that his awareness, associated as it is with reliable sensory appreciation, will not fail him in such situations or crises, but will prove his protector and reliable guide; for this state of awareness means that he will be able at such moments to remember, to reason, and to judge (that is, to size up the situation, as we say), and the resultant judgment, based as it is upon experiences associated with reliable sensory appreciation and unassociated with unduly excited fear reflexes, will be in its turn a sound and reliable judgment.

This matter of unduly excited fear reflexes has been referred to in the chapter on education, and here I wish to discuss processes used in tests made on children in this connexion.

In some schools special mechanical tests are made in order to discover the potentialities and qualities of the children and to grade them accordingly. The young and undeveloped organism of the child's " mental apparatus " is, as it were, put upon the rack, and his intellectual status and probably his educational fate depend upon the result of these tests which are supposed to be a reliable guide, not only as to the line of procedure to be taken in regard to the details of his school education, but also as to the particular career for which he will be best adapted when the state of adolescence is reached.

A teacher recently told me of an interesting personal experience in this connexion. She visited a modern school where a psychologist was engaged in testing the children for such qualities as accuracy, muscular control, observation, etc. She was taken into a small room set apart for the purpose of such tests. A boy of seven was waiting there to be tested for " control." He had shown various symptoms which were described as " nervous," and the test to be taken was to enable the school authorities to prescribe a curriculum to meet his special needs. The test was made as follows. An apparatus, electrically worked, was placed in front of the child. It consisted of a metal tray in which were sunk two rows of shallow circular holes decreasing gradually in size from that of a shilling to a very small size. The boy was told to touch the centre of each hole with a small metal rod tapering to a point like a pencil. If he made a mistake and touched the side of a hole in his effort to get the centre, an electric flash would be the result.

The child, so I was told, was already in a state of nervous dread, and when he received the instruction, " Now you must try to touch the centre of each hole, and do not touch the side of any hole or else you will make a flash," he at once became so excited *through the fear of making a mistake* that his hand shook and he stiffened and tensed his whole body unduly in making the first try. He was therefore unable to control his hand to find the centre of the first hole, touched the side and produced a flash. Still more frightened by this, still more anxious not to do the wrong thing again, he proceeded from hole to hole, making flash after flash, realizing that every mistake he made was being noted by the " tester," against him, as he thought, so that by the time he had reached the last hole his condition was one of undue excitement. It is obvious that a test taken with such emotional conditions present was not a reliable test of his control or a trustworthy guide to anyone wishing to estimate his potentialities and general qualities. Indeed, I am prepared to prove by demon-

stration that nine out of ten of the children now being sub-
mitted to tests are imperfectly co-ordinated, and that a great
number are beset with very serious psycho-physical defects.

Now in this matter of tests, because the human organism is
an animate machine, I wish to carry the reader on to a consideration of an inanimate machine—say a motor car. Would
any sane person attempt to test a motor car on the road if
he were certain that a number of the important parts of the
mechanism were imperfectly adjusted? And if he happened
to be foolish enough to do this with his badly adjusted machine,
could he expect to judge of the standard of functioning of
that particular make of car by the result of these tests? These
are unreasonable propositions such as no mechanic would
entertain for a moment. But, unfortunately, in the field of
education the same idea in regard to mechanics does not prevail. The " end-gaining " principle holds sway, and in the
sphere of psycho-physical activity under consideration the
process of reasoning takes little part. If it had done so, the
psychological expert in tests would have demanded that a
child should be in a satisfactory state of co-ordination and
adjustment before he would consent to make tests as to the
child's potentialities. He would then be dealing with a
psycho-physical organism functioning satisfactorily, and tests
made with these conditions present could probably be of some
assistance to those concerned with the child's growth and
development and future career.

Where the imperfectly co-ordinated child is concerned, its
first need is to be readjusted and co-ordinated on a plane of
conscious control, until the standard of functioning in psycho-
physical use of the organism is adequate. The organism will
then function as near to the maximum as is possible, and
the potentialities for improved functioning will continue as
the child gradually develops to that standard of conscious
guidance and control in psycho-physical use which makes for
the conditions essential to the fullest development of latent
potentialities.

*　　*　　*　　*　　*

We have all heard instances advanced of wonderful feats
being performed by people in an emotional state, of " faith
cures " being effected when the subjects of these " cures " are

in that uncontrolled and harmful psycho-physical state which is akin to conditions associated with drunkenness, and which at times approximates to mild insanity. For instance, the writer was acquainted with a man who never accomplished anything worth mentioning in his particular sphere of life until he was half crazed with alcohol. He also knows of a carriage painter who is unable to put in the straight lines satisfactorily unless he is well under the influence of alcohol. We can all point to instances of men and women who have performed remarkable acts whilst in an uncontrolled emotional state, in which they have been a danger to themselves and to those around them. Men are sent into battle in a half-drunken condition in order that their " controls " may be temporarily released, and for centuries bands of musicians have been employed in warfare to induce this emotional condition of lowered control. " Muddling through by instinct " is un-intelligent enough, but deliberately to induce in human beings by artificial means (such as the processes involved in methods of " faith cure," auto-suggestion, religious revivalism, etc.) a condition of lowered control, where intelligence and reasoning are superseded by uncontrolled emotions, is a procedure which may be described as an insult to even a very lowly evolved intelligence. All concerned reach the borderland of insanity through the use of such means for the accomplishment of their aims, and the psycho-physical experiences involved have only to be repeated sufficiently to bring madness in their train. In all these instances the " end-gaining " principle is in operation, and the people subjected to these unnatural and harmful experiences are more or less influenced by them in after life, for the uncontrolled forces which run riot on these occasions are rarely mastered again, and recur more or less in other spheres of activity, frequently developing into dangerous manifesta-tions, culminating often in tragedy. Small wonder that after the experience of 1914–18 and 1939–45 we are confronted with dangerous uncontrolled forces in human activity which, before the Wars, were manifested by only a small minority ! When the individual is dominated by his uncontrolled emotions, even a weak stimulus will often cause him to indulge in dangerous activities, leading him temporarily to experiences which are well within the psycho-physical state which we call " insanity." The repetition of such experiences is the beginning of the formation of what we call a habit, in this case the habit of unbalanced psycho-physical activity, and unfortunately, as we all know, it does not take long to establish a bad habit.[1] So-called " mental " tricks are more common than purely " physical " tricks, and we are well aware that, when indulged in, they soon become a habit, and that the indulgence of one bad habit tends to the development of others, with a rapid increase in the degree of indulgence.

In this matter of bad habits, and the lack of control which they connote, we must recognize the fact that the human creature cannot be expected to exercise control in the different spheres of his activity in civilization unless he is in possession of reliable sensory appreciation and of a satisfactory use of the psycho-physical mechanisms involved. People who are lacking in control will be found to be imperfectly co-ordinated, and their sensory appreciation to be unreliable, and no form of discipline or other outside influence can secure that satisfactory standard of psycho-physical functioning without which the individual cannot command a satisfactory standard of control within or without the organism.

Where the human being manifests this lack of control, he needs to be re-educated on a general basis so that reliable sensory appreciation may be restored, together with a satisfactory employment of the psycho-physical mechanisms. The processes of this form of re-education demand that the " means-whereby " to any " end " must be reasoned out, not on a specific but on a general basis, and with the continued use of these processes of reasoning, uncontrolled impulses and " emotional gusts " will gradually cease to dominate, and will ultimately be dominated. The organism will not then be called upon to satisfy those unhealthy cravings which we find associated with unreliable and delusive sensory appreciation (debauched kinæsthesia).

The fact is, the principle of reasoning out on a general basis

---

[1] Worry is one of these bad habits which, once established, are very hard to break. A curious feature of this habit is that, in certain cases, though you may remove the cause for worry, and the subject may admit that the cause has been removed, the removal of the cause does not remove the " mental " state which the subject declared was the cause of the worry. The fact is, the person has developed the worry habit, a state in which he manufactures the stimulus to worry.

the *means whereby* we shall command our "ends" simply implies a common-sense procedure. Common sense is a very familiar phrase and we all have our particular conception of what it means. We know many people who will point out that individual opinion can differ as much in regard to the meaning of common sense, as in regard to religious, political, social, and educational matters. We will therefore put our point of view in regard to common sense by giving an instance in which we consider the human creature does not evince common sense. The man who is convinced that he is suffering from digestive and liver disorders, and knows that this has been caused by his indulgence in alcohol, or by excessive eating, and still continues to indulge in either of these habits, despite the depression and suffering which result, and despite the assurance of his medical adviser that moderation will put him on the road to good health once more, cannot be said to act in accordance with common sense.

My reader may say that the man cannot refrain from taking alcohol or from over-eating, and it may be advantageous to consider this man's inability to act in accordance with the dictates of common sense. In the first place, it is clear that he had recognized the fact that he was ill. The fact that he had consulted his medical adviser is proof that the stimulus (or stimuli) in this connexion had reached his consciousness, and no doubt he was quite ready to take the medicine or carry out the form of treatment prescribed, provided that these did not interfere with his habit of indulging in alcohol or in over-eating. But, of course, the desired return to health could not be secured by such an unreasoning procedure. The habit is always the impeding factor, and in this case the medicine and the treatment were of little importance unless the bad habit of over-indulgence in alcohol, or of excessive feeding, could be eradicated.

This leads us to the consideration of the psycho-physical activities within the organism of which habit, so called, is a manifestation. In the case of a person who is blessed with a satisfactory standard of psycho-physical co-ordination, moderation will be the rule and excess the exception to that rule. With the person who is badly co-ordinated the reverse will be the case, in a more or less degree, in one or more spheres, for the habit of excess will gradually become more firmly established with too frequent repetition of the indulgence of the debauched sensory desires connected, in the case given, with eating and drinking, thus making indulgence the rule and not the exception.

In the continuance of our consideration we will trace the cultivation of the alcohol habit, where the subject of our illustration is concerned. That we speak of the cultivation of this habit presupposes a time in the history of the man when he did not make a habit of taking alcohol in such quantities as would cause liver and other internal disorders. The facts concerned with his reasons, however, for beginning to take alcohol to excess at some particular time of his life would not help us very much, even if we could be certain of them. The important point for us to remember is that his sensory appreciation was unreliable and perverted, and his psychophysical organism in an unsatisfactory state of co-ordination, so that he gradually became dominated by that sensory debauchery which results from excessive alcoholic and other indulgence, and by the depressing and enervating conditions which follow. These latter conditions are among the most potent of the stimuli which make for the repetition of the excesses at more and more frequent intervals, this repetition counteracting again for a time the depressing and enervating conditions brought about by the renewed indulgence. Unfortunately, the process is one that " makes the meat it feeds on," so that the degree of sensory debauchery increases rapidly until the functioning of the organism becomes utterly demoralized.

It is almost certain that in the early stages of his alcoholic experiences the subject was unaware of his lack of satisfactory co-ordination and sensory appreciation. As a matter of fact, it is unlikely that he had ever given consideration to his psycho-physical condition. He had simply taken alcohol occasionally, as he had taken many other things in the way of food and drink, never for a moment meaning that it should become a habit, or even suspecting that he lacked the ability either to continue taking it only occasionally, or to discontinue taking it altogether if he so wished. This reveals the degree to which egotism may be subconsciously developed in the human creature, until it becomes a potent factor in influencing the processes associated with subconscious and unreasoned conclusions, such as the one arrived at by the subject of our illustration in regard to his ability to continue to drink occasionally or to discontinue drinking altogether. If he had consciously attempted to search out the correct premises from which to make his deductions, and if his effort had been attended with success, he would have discovered the unsatisfactory standard of his general functioning, and this would have brought a realization that he must, by some means, make certain that his standard of psycho-physical co-ordination and sensory appreciation was satisfactory, before he allowed himself to entertain even mildly egotistical conclusions regarding his ability to fight his bad habits. If such an analysis of the psycho-physical factors involved had been made, he must have been led to the conclusion that *in the matter of the breaking of habit, the standard of sensory appreciation is the all-important factor*. His increasing desire for alcohol probably came very gradually, as also the corresponding decline in his standard of co-ordination and sensory appreciation. Thus the gratification experienced in satisfying the already abnormal desire would soon dominate psycho-physical processes which otherwise might have been exercised in the field of reasoning and common sense, and he might then have been led to a consideration of the consequences of permitting himself to become a victim of the alcohol habit.

In all such experiences there comes a time at last when the person concerned is forced to recognize the harmful effects of such a habit, and then very often makes an effort to fight the desire and to eradicate the habit. But too frequently it happens that the effort is a feeble one or that it is made along impossible lines. Some well-meaning friend, for instance, may urge the man to use what is called " will-power " to fight and control his desire, *but the desire is a sensory desire, and the processes called " will-power " have in this case long since been dominated by the debauched sensory appreciation associated with this desire*, and therefore his hope of salvation lies in the restoration of his sensory appreciation to that normal condition which we do not find associated with abnormal and unhealthy desire. In *Man's Supreme Inheritance* we have referred to that degenerate state of the organism when the human creature will desire a form of sensory satisfaction through actual pain. In the case of alcoholic excesses, each occasion of indulgence is followed by suffering, often intense suffering, but even this does not act as a deterrent. We must therefore realize the enormous influence of perverted sensory desire on the human creature, and recognize that satisfactory development in the control of his psycho-physical processes is impossible without that reliable sensory appreciation which goes hand in hand with normal sensory desires.

One point more. Fundamental desires and needs must be satisfied; if they are not, serious results must follow sooner or later, and the fact that the attempt to satisfy desires and needs leads many individuals to indulge in abuse and excess does not affect this conclusion. Abuse and excess are always associated with abnormality, and abnormality is due to abnormal conditions in the psycho-physical functioning of the organism, and this applies in the matter of abuse and excess in eating, as well as in drinking and in connexion with any other needs and desires. Abuse or excess is an attempt to satisfy a need or desire which, originally normal, has become abnormal, and as long as this abnormal desire or need remains, it is useless to deny a man the " means-whereby " to his excesses and abuses. Our energies should instead be applied to attempts to eradicate the abnormal conditions responsible for the excess and abuse, and so to restore the normal psycho-physical functioning of the organism and the reliable sensory appreciation which ensures the maintenance of normality in our desires and needs.

VII

PSYCHO-PHYSICAL EQUILIBRIUM

THE lack of a satisfactory condition of psycho-physical equilibrium in all human activities is one of the most striking manifestations of imperfect functioning of the organism. The present faulty subconscious use of the psycho-physical mechanism, in our educational and other spheres, makes for the gradual increase of this condition of defective equilibrium. It would seem that this fact is generally taken for granted, seeing that we expect defective equilibrium at a certain age, just as we expect the development of a flabby and protruding abdomen. This is surely the end of our contention that practice makes perfect; it also seems evident from this that there must be something wrong with the practice in the act of walking.

The fact is that people walk without any clear understanding of the guiding and controlling orders which command the satisfactory co-ordination and adjustment of the psycho-physical mechanism in the act of walking. Hence when one or more defects become present in the functioning of these mechanisms, even though the persons concerned may be aware of their cause or causes, they are incapable of establishing once more that standard of reliable sensory appreciation which would enable them to eradicate these defects. This needs a process of re-education on a general basis, which will restore satisfactory functioning throughout the organism, and so ensure a continued raising of the standard of psycho-physical equilibrium right on through life.

In what follows I shall endeavour to show that, with almost every attempt to correct some supposed or real psycho-physical imperfection, new defects are developed which tend to lower the standard of psycho-physical equilibrium. In this connexion it is an interesting but very unfortunate fact that this unsatisfactory condition develops in the subject hand in hand with the desire to hurry unduly, this being a subconscious endeavour to compensate for the growing lack of equilibrium and lack of control. In extreme cases of lack of equilibrium this manifestation is most pronounced. The subject becomes conscious, first, of a weakness or difficulty which affects his general equilibrium in walking, and, without making any attempt to discover the cause or causes of this newly recognized weakness or difficulty, proceeds, as he would put it, to try to "walk properly"—i.e., to walk without the slight unsteadiness of which he is conscious. But the fact that this weakness or difficulty has developed is proof that the subject's guiding sensations and general psycho-physical co-ordinations of the organism are defective. It is therefore obvious that any subconsciously directed efforts on his part to "walk properly"—i.e., more steadily—will be carried out according to these same defective guiding sensations and imperfectly co-ordinated mechanisms, and cannot therefore succeed.

It must be remembered that during all these "trial-and-error" experiences the fear reflexes are being unduly excited by the fear of falling, and by the general unreliability and uncertainty of the psycho-physical processes which are employed during such subconsciously directed efforts. Taking this process as a whole, we shall find that most harmful psycho-physical conditions will be developed, which soon manifest themselves in other spheres of psycho-physical functioning, and very often culminate at last in some serious crisis.

It is easy to trace the development of this lack of equilibrium in what is usually considered the "purely physical" sphere. Let us take by way of illustration the case of a boy who, in the ordinary way, would be classed as a good walker. We will assume that he has been injured at the age of, say, thirteen by being thrown from a horse or by a fall downstairs, or has met with some other accident which has necessitated his being treated by a doctor and being confined to his bed for some time. It is obvious that his injury and the cessation of his ordinary activities will produce in the patient a more or less weakened condition generally, and also definite specific difficulties in connexion with the injured parts of the organism. The result is that at the psychological moment when the patient makes the first attempt to resume walking, certain impeding factors will manifest themselves which he will immediately proceed to overcome by "trying to walk properly" as he understands it. His attempt to walk "properly" must necessarily be on the subconscious plan of "trial-and-error," for it is almost certain that he has never known how he walked, never had the least idea of the guiding orders concerned with the co-ordinations essential to the act of walking and to the development of satisfactory equilibrium.[1]

It will be necessary here to analyse the psycho-physical processes involved in his effort, for success in such efforts demands quite a high standard of co-ordinated functioning of the organism. Experience has proved to us that this standard of functioning is not at the command of a person who has been through the experiences connected with such an injury, and with the subsequent treatment and gradual recovery to the point when what we call the convalescent stage has been reached. Real success is practically impossible, and for the reasons which follow.

These attempts to walk would be made at a time when the subject was conscious of a weakness throughout the whole organism, of a comparative loss of control, of an interference with the psycho-physical equilibrium, of a lack of confidence, together with a whole series of hopes and fears in regard to what he will or will not be able to do, associated, again, with fears which have their origin in the pain which results from his incorrect subconscious attempts to use parts that have been injured. This whole combination of psycho-physical conditions constitutes a set of experiences which are new as compared with those present at the time of the accident. Each subconscious attempt to walk awakens consciousness of shortcomings, of strange and often alarming sensations, and tends to increase the real difficulties—viz., those concerned with that correct use of the psycho-physical organism in general upon which " walking properly " depends.

It will thus be clear that the attempt to walk properly by subconscious guidance would merely be an attempt to revert to the habit or habits established in the act of walking before

[1] My reader will probably think of the case of some friend who has made an attempt to " walk properly " after an injury, and who is now walking about to HIS OWN satisfaction. My point is, that the subject is not capable of judging whether his use of his psycho-physical mechanisms in walking is satisfactory or not. It is quite certain that anyone with an expert knowledge in this connexion could point to certain harmful defects in the subject's use of himself which are the combined result of the injury, the varied experiences in treatment and recovery, and the attempts " to walk," all of which are indicative of comparative weakness, a sense of interference with equilibrium and a general loss of control.

the accident. This way of walking was instinctive, and a particular instinctive process is the result of certain psycho-physical conditions operating, as we say, by instinct. Change those conditions quickly and you interfere with the reliability of the working of the particular instinct.

This illustration furnishes us with a splendid practical instance of a definite need calling for new experiences in psycho-physical use. The boy wishes to walk. The stimulus to do so produces an immediate response involving the processes concerned with subconscious guidance and control which are habitual, but which depend for efficiency upon a given standard of co-ordinated functioning of the organism. Unfortunately, this standard has been lowered by his experiences associated with the accident, and the psycho-physical machinery does not work as satisfactorily as before; in fact, in the majority of such cases it works very unsatisfactorily. The subject is able to compare the result of his present efforts with those he made before his injury. They compare very badly, and he is conscious of the fact. This merely causes him to " try harder," as he would put it, " to walk properly," and, on a subconscious basis, he has no alternative but to continue the unintelligent method of " trial-and-error."

We will now outline the experiences which the procedure based on the principles of re-education on a conscious general basis would have ensured in the foregoing case. In the first place, we should not allow the subject to try to " walk properly " until he had been given, by expert manipulation, correct experiences in the general use of the psycho-physical mechanisms, and had become well acquainted with the correct guiding and controlling orders which would assist in the securing of the *means whereby* he should use the mechanisms in any attempt to walk properly.

The recognition of weakness or difficulty would be the signal for an examination of the psycho-physical mechanisms involved in the use of the organism as a whole, which in turn would enable us to note the defects and peculiarities in the use of these mechanisms in the specific art of walking. The technique we advocate would demand in practice that the subject should cease to try to improve his walking. We would therefore endeavour to convince him by demonstration that his efforts to improve his walking by " muddling through by

instinct " are not only futile but quite absurd. By the same
process (demonstration) he would be shown that, as soon as he
receives the stimulus to walk, he must begin his remedial
work by employing his inhibitory powers to prevent the use
of the wrong subconscious guidance and direction associated
with his conception of " walking."   In this connexion it is
explained to him that it is the use of the incorrect, subconscious
guiding orders to the mechanisms concerned with the act of
walking, associated with unreliable sensory appreciation, which
has caused the mechanisms to be used imperfectly, resulting
in the weakness and difficulties with which we are contending.

When the subject is more or less familiar with these inhibitory
experiences, we go on to give him a knowledge of the new and
correct directive and guiding orders which, with the aid of
manipulation, are to bring about the satisfactory use of the
mechanisms in a sitting, prone, or other position.   These
experiences must be repeated until the new and reliable sensory
appreciation becomes established, by which time there will
have taken place an actual change in the use of the psycho-
physical mechanisms of the organism in general, making for a
satisfactory condition of co-ordination and adjustment.   When
the required improvement in the general co-ordinations and
adjustments has been secured, the processes we have outlined
will be more or less in conscious operation, and a corresponding improvement in equilibrium in walking will be the result.

The reader must understand that the details involved in
such processes (differing as these do in each case) cannot be
set forth here, and that, moreover, from the very first lessons
the teacher's aim would be to cause the pupil to be conscious
of what he should or should NOT do, and to give such help
to the pupil as would enable him to begin at once to apply
the principles involved, not only to his attempts at walking
but more or less to all the acts of his daily life.   In other
words, the pupil is not taught to perform certain new exercises
or to assume new postures for a given time each day, whilst
continuing to use his faulty mechanisms and unreliable guiding
sensations in his old way during his other activities, but he is
shown HOW he may at once check, more or less, the faulty use
of these mechanisms in the general activities of his daily life.

An increase in lack of equilibrium in what is called the
" physical " sphere will be found, in every case, to go hand in

hand with a corresponding lack of equilibrium in so-called "mental" spheres. And in any consideration of "mental" and "physical" phenomena it must be remembered that in our present stage of evolution on the subconscious plane, the response to any stimulus or stimuli is at least seventy-five per cent subconscious response (chiefly feeling) as against twenty-five per cent any other response, this estimate of the ratio of subconscious response being probably too low.

When these facts are fully realized by all those who are interested in education and in the conduct of life generally, there may be some chance of the realization of those commendable ideals for the uplifting of mankind cherished by leaders in the social, religious, and political spheres.

PART III

SENSORY APPRECIATION IN ITS RELATION TO MAN'S NEEDS

I

" KNOWING ONESELF "

THOSE who give thought to the present trend of human endeavour in political, social, industrial, and other spheres will recognize that our times are " out of joint," and many of them will admit that the masses living in this disjointed time are more or less out of communication with their reasoning. In the midst of this unrest and uncertainty, the individuals composing the masses are struggling blindly for their individual betterment, without any clear understanding of the cause or causes of their difficulties, or of the fundamental principles which constitute in application the satisfactory *means whereby* these difficulties may be prevented or overcome.

" Man, know thyself " is an old axiom, but in my opinion the more fundamental one is " Man, know thy needs." Of course, it may be contended that he who knows himself knows his needs, and that to know one's needs implies knowing oneself, but the contention does not apply to that great majority of human beings whose sensory appreciation is unreliable. We have seen that reliable sensory appreciation is essential to that co-ordinated psycho-physical growth and development of the individual which is fundamental to the satisfactory psycho-physical growth and development of the mass, and this being so, in order to secure this growth and development of the mass, it is essential to command the " means-whereby " of recognizing and supplying the real needs of the individual.

Unfortunately, our attempts to supply and satisfy these needs in the educational, social, political, economic, industrial, religious, and other spheres, have proved, up to now, more or less of a failure, and this is due in a great measure to the fact that our efforts on a subconscious basis have been directed chiefly to evolving methods of teaching, treatment, conduct,

guidance and control to meet the demands of the mass, instead
of making the primary application of the principle or principles
involved an individual application on a conscious basis.   The
foregoing leads us to a consideration of plans for human
development and endeavour on the conscious and subconscious
planes of life, and of the relative possibilities for advancement
on each of these planes.

On the subconscious plane, the orthodox plan has been and
still is to attempt to eradicate " physical " defects and peculiarities by means of physical culture, exercises, etc., " mental "
shortcomings and idiosyncrasies by means of the different
cults for " mental " training, specific systems for the development of memory, will, and so on.   Investigation will show
that the deductions concerned with the adoption of such
methods were made from wrong premisses, the fundamental
principle of conscious guidance and control in the development
and growth of the creature being ignored.   Furthermore, it
will be found that where " physical " and " mental " methods
are employed, any apparent gain will be in a specific sphere,
and accompanied by harmful cultivated defects of which the
teachers and pupils are ignorant, but which, sooner or later,
reveal themselves and gradually become established as habits.

The progress made in recent years in what is called " psychological " knowledge leaves no room for doubt that human
beings are too often unaware of their most striking psycho-
physical defects, peculiarities and tendencies which, in such
cases, have not risen, as we say, to the sphere of consciousness.
Before we can make any real attempt to reach a satisfactory
state of awareness in this connexion—that is, to know ourselves,
we must cultivate, in connexion with our psycho-physical
development, an increasing use of the process of reasoning in
conscious endeavour, and, having reached a satisfactory standard of readjustment and co-ordination through the establishment of a new and reliable sensory appreciation, we must
proceed to put into practice this satisfactory, conscious use of
the psycho-physical mechanism in every act of daily life.

The reader who becomes familiar with the principles of the
special technique which has been evolved to meet these demands
will realize that " knowing oneself " is part and parcel, as we
say, of the process, and a knowledge which will increase and
keep pace with the development in conscious psycho-physical

guidance and control. This knowledge should be the foundation of the act of living in all spheres, and will be so when
the education and general development of children are built
upon the principles of constructive, conscious control. On
this principle we can continue to raise the standard of " knowing oneself," and this is the surest way of raising the standard
of everything else we know,. and of securing satisfactory results
in all spheres of learning.

A friend of mine who wanted to impress me with his right
to be considered an authority on up-to-date psychology
admitted that he based his claim on his intimate knowledge
of human history, which he had acquired by a long and careful study of the works of eminent historians. This belief gave
him such satisfaction that I could not find it within me to
suggest to him that the real history of human endeavour, as
a guide to up-to-date psychology, has not been written by the
historians—in fact, that it has yet to be begun, and that one
does not dare to speculate as to the date of its possible
completion.

When I write of human endeavour, I mean individual
human endeavour in connexion with individual development
and growth, and, therefore, from any real history of human
endeavour we must eliminate the record of man's activities in
wars and other spheres in which he is swayed chiefly by the
herd instinct, where the example, good or bad, or the command
of one person, is immediately followed by the rest as an unthinking, unintelligent, automatic mass. I am quite prepared
to admit that the history of human beings in wars and other
spheres of massed activity is of great interest to many people,
but it is of infinitesimal interest or value, particularly where
man's future is concerned, as compared with that of the individual effort of the human creature struggling daily to find a
solution of the flesh-and-blood difficulties which directly concern his well-being. These difficulties are the natural consequences of his endeavours to adapt himself to ever-changing
psycho-physical conditions and of his attempts to evolve from
the uncivilized to the civilized state in accordance with his
early established subconscious conception of educational and
general development.

This is equally true of the everyday development and
general experiences of ordinary men and women in every sphere

of human activity, for we are beset with contending and dis-
organizing forces in the working of the psycho-physical organism
of each individual, inasmuch as we are developing so-called
" mental " processes at a rapidly increasing pace never before
experienced, whilst attempting to employ them side by side
with so-called " physical " processes which for years have
become less and less satisfactorily controlled and directed, the
result being a lowering of the standard of psycho-physical
co-ordination.

The long line of daily difficulties with which we are now beset
is only equalled by the series of shattered hopes that have
followed each subconsciously directed, specific " end-gaining "
attempt to bring about a solution of these difficulties. Each
failure makes " the meat it feeds on," and the " trial-and-
error " method of the ape has been persistently adhered to,
despite the fact of its failure in most civilized spheres.

I will now deal from this point of view with certain systems
of education and development which hold public attention at
the moment, and which were designed to meet certain difficulties and defects, and I will endeavour to show that the
hopes of those concerned cannot be justified, because these
systems were conceived on a specific basis, and because the
processes involved in their practical application call for reliance
only upon subconscious experience for direction and control.
We have reached a stage in our evolution when we should
refuse to consider the merits or demerits of any new system of
education or development which is not built upon a conscious
basis.

One of these systems has been taken up in recent years by a
number of people in England and America as a new and
valuable form of education, but as the principles involved are
simply those which were employed by the circus trainers of
our grandfathers' time, in training horses to perform evolutions to music and at the change of music to change the step,
etc., in a discussion of general psycho-physical development
on a basis of reasoning control, it can be put out of court and
dismissed without further comment.

Another system has been hailed as a new and progressive
movement and is well known for the special claim that is
made for it in connexion with its value in the development of
the young child's senses of sight, feeling, taste, hearing, touch,

etc. An organized series of materials, or educative toys, provides the technique for this attempted sense cultivation, but
it will be realized by anyone who has watched the classes of
children at work that it is again a *specific* and not a general
development that is aimed at in this technique—a fatal mistake when we consider the interdependence of what have been
differential as " mental " and " physical " in the human
organism. It is quite possible that a child, by using this
material, may gain a certain facility in the use of its hands,
or a specific development, say, of the sense of touch. But if,
in making the movements necessary to the particular occupation in which he is engaged, he is relying upon the guidance
of an imperfect sensory appreciation in the general use of his
organism, it must follow that any specific improvement in the
sense of touch will be accompanied by a use of his psycho-
physical mechanism which, faulty to start with, will become
more and more faulty, the harder he tries or the more absorbed [1]
he becomes in working subconsciously for his end. Although
a specific improvement may take place in one direction, many
more serious defects in the use of his mechanism *as a whole*
will be cultivated in the process. It has been my experience
that children who have had a specialized training such as this
in their early years have exhibited more than the usual number
of psycho-physical defects and imperfections, that their sensory
appreciation has been more than usually unreliable, and anyone who has followed my argument through the earlier pages
will see that this must be the case where any specific development has been sought and achieved on a subconscious basis.

The interdependence of the " mental " and " physical " and
of the muscular mechanism in general in psycho-physical acts
has long since been recognized in theory, and yet methods of
education aiming at specific development remain the vogue.[2]

As a matter of fact, in connexion with this very question of

[1] See Chapter on Concentration.

[2] A striking instance may be mentioned in connexion with re-
education. Some forty years ago well-known scientific men in France
recognized the value of re-education and adopted forms of re-education
on a specific instead of a general basis, and I am informed that this
obtains even to-day. The principle involved has been dealt with in
Man's Supreme Inheritance, and those acquainted with the facts and
arguments employed will appreciate the relative value of general as
against specific development or treatment of any kind.

the specific development of a particular sense, it is now a well-recognized fact that the sense of sight, for instance, is greatly affected by the " muscle-pulls " of the organism in general, and this applies where all the senses are concerned. For many years past we have had practical proof of the improvement that can be effected in the sense of sight of pupils who have been re-educated and co-ordinated on a general basis of conscious control. In every case this improvement has followed a general improvement in the co-ordinated use of the whole organism.

This is the point which must always be emphasized by those advocating the claims of re-education and co-ordination on a general as against the claims of re-education and co-ordination on a specific basis. The person with defective sight will have quite a number of other psycho-physical defects, and re-education on a general basis must precede any attempt at specific re-education. This applies in the case of the person with defective use of the organs of speech, defective use of the arms or legs, or any other defect, peculiarity, or shortcoming.

In the case of children, if they were re-educated and co-ordinated on a plane of conscious control, seventy-five per cent of the ordinary sense imperfections and difficulties with technique would never be encountered by the teachers working in educational and other spheres. It does not require any special degree of intelligence to realize the tremendous amount of time and energy that would be saved if we adopted the comprehensive and constructive principle herein involved and applied it to all forms of human development and general growth in our attempts to ensure a progressive civilization.

The satisfactorily co-ordinated child on a plane of conscious control will be possessed of a psycho-physical mechanism which will tend to function to the maximum in all spheres in accordance with the standard of co-ordination reached. With such conditions present, the teacher can draw from the child the very best that the particular psycho-physical organism, functioning adequately, is capable of giving, and can also be confident of a more or less increasing improvement, without the undue excitement of the fear reflexes and without undue effort.

Think, on the other hand, of what will be the harmful

psycho-physical effect on a child, beset with all the impeding
factors resulting from a condition of bad co-ordination, if,
when learning to write, for instance, it takes up its pencil to
use it for the first time and holds it with strained and cramped
fingers, this being the result of a harmful condition of stress
and strain in the general use of the psycho-physical organism.
Even if the teacher does not point out directly to the child
that its use of the pencil is not what it should be, the child
will probably be conscious of a lack of control and of being
below the ordinary standard of success with its writing.
Sooner or later, however, the teacher will endeavour to improve the child's writing, and he may succeed up to a point,
but it will be a very poor result as compared with the standard
that might be attained if the child were first re-educated and
readjusted, and thus enabled to hold the pencil without the
general imperfections to which I have referred.

I have already stated that I am prepared to prove that
when the usual methods on a subconscious basis are employed
to establish a condition, or to eradicate a fault or defect, quite
a number of others, often more harmful than the one in process of eradication, are developed. At recurring stages, therefore, of our attempted progress and development, we are confronted with new and increasing difficulties calling for eradication, which we have actually cultivated in educational and
other processes. I shall now point out different attempts that
have been made in the educational process to counteract by
specific means the retarding influences of certain peculiarities
and defects, manifestations which have themselves been
developed by this same educational process. A little thought
will enable the reader to discern the developing complications
inseparable from such a process.

In fact, this process becomes operative as soon as the child
goes to school, for the experiences gained at school too often
lead to complications, if from the beginning the child is functioning nearer to its minimum than to its maximum. The
methods of training, etc., actually make for complications, in
consequence of the numerous specific attempts which are made
to remedy the many defects or shortcomings which are recognized in the child's efforts, most of which defects, however,
would not have manifested themselves if the child's psycho-
physical functioning had been satisfactory when it entered the

school. The establishment, therefore, of this condition should be the first consideration in any sound educational plan. To attempt to educate an imperfectly co-ordinated child by dealing in a specific way with specific defects or shortcomings is an unreasoning process, especially when we take into consideration the important part which is played in a child's life by the process of imitation. We will now go on to consider this point.

II

IMITATION

THE psycho-physical process called imitation would seem to be one that is operative in most people to a high degree, as compared with other fundamental processes. We are all aware of this aptitude, as we call it, in our fellow-beings, and subconscious imitation of the characteristics of others is a factor which plays a great part in the development and growth and also in the use of our individual psycho-physical selves. Overwhelming proof is forthcoming in regard not only to the natural aptitude and subconscious inclination to imitate, but also in regard to the harmful consequences which may result from imitation, and we will now consider some of the chief factors responsible for the disappointing results accruing from the exercise of this natural aptitude in civilization.

This book deals with the defects, peculiarities, imperfect uses, etc., of the human psycho-physical organism; furthermore, it is herein contended that the majority of people are more or less beset with these shortcomings, whilst in a certain number these shortcomings are so extreme that they may be said to constitute a condition of deformity in the human creature. Herein lies the cause of the disappointing and harmful results which follow imitation. For the process of imitation remains inoperative unless there is something striking to be imitated, and the chief stimulus to imitation comes from our perception, subconscious or conscious, of some characteristic or striking manifestations of another human creature, and such manifestations are as a rule the manifestations of psycho-physical defects or peculiarities. In all spheres of present-day life the dangers from the individual imitation of others' defects or peculiarities are very great, and it is therefore of the utmost importance that these dangers should be eliminated, or at least minimized, in all our activities in learning or learning to do, particularly where people are associated as teachers and pupils—as, for instance, in schools and gymnasiums, in fact, wherever teachers and pupils are in that close contact which makes possible the operation of the process of imitation.

Most children at school manifest defects in the use of themselves in the ordinary acts of life—in a large number of cases, very serious defects—and all kinds of drills and remedial exercises are employed in the attempt to eradicate these defects. Yet, except in very rare instances, the teachers employed in these remedial and other spheres in our schools are too often themselves beset with exaggerated forms of the same or other defects or peculiarities. If teachers are worthy of the name, it is certain that their pupils will be influenced by them in more ways than one, and that most pupils will tend subconsciously to imitate them. Now, as has already been pointed out, the most striking manifestations of these teachers will prove the most potent stimuli to the pupils' processes of imitation. Such manifestations, for instance, as peculiarities in the qualities of a voice, in the manner of opening the mouth, of using the arms, or in defective utterance, vocal production, or use of the different parts of the organism in standing, walking, sitting, etc.—in fact, all defects or peculiarities manifested as striking characteristics of the teachers—will be found to be the most potent stimuli to the pupil's aptitude for imitation. A realization of the serious consequences involved in the foregoing will bring conviction that all teachers who manifest defects and peculiarities which are the result of their own unreliable sensory appreciation and unsatisfactory use of their psycho-physical organism are a bad example—indeed a positive danger—to their pupils, and that the possibility of satisfactory psycho-physical results accruing to both pupil and teacher is seriously minimized by this impeding factor—viz., the acquisition of defects and peculiarities by imitation.

In any sphere of learning on a subconscious basis we have to face the fact that pupil and teacher are imbued with the erroneous idea that the pupil, by observing the teacher doing something successfully, will be able to copy it and succeed also. The pupil is quite convinced as to this, and the teacher is certain that if he teaches the pupil to do as he (the teacher) believes [1] he does himself, he will succeed in enabling the pupil to succeed.

---

[1] Take the case of a singer who, in consequence of throat trouble, is forced to retire from the public platform and becomes a teacher of singing. I can recall two such instances in which singers were forced to retire through this cause, and having listened to their vocal efforts on several occasions prior to their retirement, one did not need to be a prophet to be sure that this would happen. For no human throat and accessories could withstand indefinitely the abuse to which they were

Yet most of us are aware that if a pupil in some art is sent to watch a great artist, as is so often done, in order that he may learn something which will assist him in his particular art, the pupil is almost invariably more impressed by some characteristics of the artist that may be classed as faults than by his " better parts."

These characteristics are seized upon by the pupil as factors essential to his own improvement in performance, but experience constantly proves this belief to be mistaken.   In the first place, the characteristics may be faults which the genius of the particular artist enables him to defy.   It is possible that the artist succeeds *in spite of them* rather than because of them.[1] But even if the characteristics seized upon by the pupil for imitation were of value, the only way by which the pupil could make practical use of them would be, firstly, by a study of the general employment of the organism of the person to be imitated, of which the characteristics named are but special manifestations, and, secondly, by being himself re-educated so as to be able to command the same general use of the organism for good or ill, according to the standard of such use as that enjoyed by the expert he tries to copy.

---

subjected in the matter of strain and larynx displacement and chest and abdominal distortion, through the imperfect use of the psychophysical mechanisms upon the satisfactory use of which depends the normal condition of the specific parts named.   When these same people took up teaching, they at once proceeded to impart to their pupils, as far as they were able, the methods of singing or breathing in which they themselves believed.   We can only suppose that they believed their methods were correct ones, because they were the ones they had themselves adopted during their days of learning to sing, and had continued to practise up to the time that they took up teaching, and that the fact that they had both lost their voices by remaining faithful to these very methods had not even reached their consciousness.   Otherwise, how could they have ventured to try to pass on to others the methods that had been the cause of so much injury to themselves ?   The power of the human creature to hypnotize himself is nowhere more apparent than in such instances of human idiosyncrasy as this.

[1] Unfortunately, this tendency may be noticed in all spheres of learning.   Take the point in connexion with games, for instance. S. H. Smith indulged in a crouch and whirlwind drive; Gore was noted for his forehand drive; Doherty for his use of the unchanged grip, and so on.   These characteristics have been imitated by other players with the idea of improving their own game, but again experience has constantly proved this idea to be mistaken, and for the reasons given above.

III

CONCENTRATION AND THE SUSTAINED (CONTINUOUS) PROJECTION OF ORDERS

A CONSIDERATION of the experiences outlined in the last chapter in connexion with the conscious use of the process of imitation leaves little doubt that this conception of the employment of imitation involves specific attempts to gain an " end "—in other words, *specific* manifestations are selected for *specific* imitation—and thus the process of imitation becomes one of "fixating on specific points or objects"—that is, of what is known as " concentration."

This conception of concentration is a disastrous and narrowing one, if we may judge by the use of the word as revealed in practice, and by the harmful manifestations which follow the intention of a person to " concentrate·"; these harmful manifestations becoming more and more exaggerated according to the degree with which the teacher finds it necessary to urge the pupil to develop this doubtful acquisition.

Whence came this idea of " concentration "? At what stage in the process of education was it considered necessary?

There can be little doubt that the conception and use of concentration sprang from a desire for the ease, spontaneity, and healthy enjoyment associated with that use of the organism which is considered a successful one, and which is characteristic of people who are said to " give their attention " to whatever they wish to do. What has not been realized in this connexion, however, is that only those children whose psycho-physical organisms are functioning imperfectly and inadequately manifest such symptoms of " mind-wandering " as lack of spontaneity of observation, of curiosity, etc.—granted, of course, a reasonable approach by the teacher. There is little doubt that the child of, say, two hundred years ago was born with comparatively reliable instincts, adequate respiratory need, and all the necessary psycho-physical equipment which would have made for satisfactory development, if the educational process adopted had been on a plane of conscious control—that is, worked out on the principle of the " means-whereby." Unfortunately it was worked out on a subconscious basis—that is, on the "end-gaining" principle—and the harmful effects of the employment of this "end-gaining" principle grew very rapidly, until at a certain stage in the educational process the child exhibited among other shortcomings a lack of attention, or, as they say, "mind-wandering." When this shortcoming called "mind-wandering" increased to the extent that it called for a remedy, what was more natural than that the educational experts, subconsciously directed and controlled, and dominated, therefore, by the "end-gaining" principle, should attempt to counteract it by some idea which would "hold the mind" (attention) to one subject or to one plan? [1] The word "concentrate," according to the *Students' English Dictionary*, means "to force or cause to move to a common centre; to bring to bear on one object," the latter being the general acceptance of the word.

Here, then, was the remedy. As we all know, it has been applied for many, many years, and to-day it makes a universal appeal in accordance with a universal belief in what the particular person conceives of as "concentration." Make a search for a person who does not believe in concentration, and the results of your investigation will convince you of the truth of the foregoing statement. Introduce the subject to a friend and for the sake of argument tell him that you do not believe in concentration, that, in fact, you believe the practice to be harmful in its effects. You will almost certainly be met with such remarks as, " But surely we should concentrate our minds on what we are doing!" "How can we keep our minds on what we are doing unless we concentrate?" "One is naturally anxious to do one's best, and surely one's degree of success depends upon one's power of concentration." And so on.

Again, people will tell you that they cannot work successfully except in perfect quiet, that any interruption breaks the train of thought, and many other points will be brought forward to support the speaker's belief in concentration. There is only one satisfactory way to end such arguments as this. The teacher who has worked on a basis of conscious control employs psycho-physical demonstration in his attempts to convince,

---

[1] The recognition of the defect of "mind-wandering" and the remedy adopted for it has its parallel in the first recognition of "physical" deterioration and the remedy applied. The false principle underlying both remedies is the same.

and in this particular sphere we are prepared to convince anyone who can and will trust his or her eyes during such a demonstration. Statements and arguments in connexion with psycho-physical activities should not be accepted unless the persons making them can give a practical demonstration of their truth, whilst evidencing at the same time that they themselves are in communication with their reasoning. By way of proof by demonstration, then, note the psycho-physical manifestations of the person who believes in concentration during the act of reading, writing, thinking, or during the performance of any other of the numerous daily activities. First observe the strained expression of the eyes, an expression of anxiety and uneasiness, denoting unduly excited fear reflexes; in some cases the eyes may be distorted, and the whole expression one that is recognized as the self-hypnotic stare. Then turn your attention to the general expression of the face, and pass on to the manifestations of the body and limbs. You will notice that there is an undue and harmful degree of tension throughout the whole organism. How could it be otherwise when the subject, instead of consciously reasoning out the cause (or causes) which has tended to develop his defect, is making a subconscious effort (on the method of " trial-and-error ") to overpower one set of imperfect so-called " mental " projections and " physical " tensions by a still more powerful set?

For example, suppose a person is in the habit of performing a certain act—the act of sitting in a chair, for instance—with a great deal of unnecessary tension, and suppose his teacher points this out to him, and reasons out with him the *means whereby* the act can be performed without this unnecessary strain, giving him the necessary directions (series of orders) to this end, and the reliable sensory appreciation which the satisfactory carrying-out of the orders demands. Suppose, further, that the pupil, instead of following these directions quite simply in the order in which they are given to him, starts, as he calls it, to " concentrate " upon them. What will he really be doing? In a specific way, he will be concentrating upon one order and comparatively neglecting the others, whilst, in a general way, he will be overpowering the new set of conscious orders which he is asked to give in connexion with the act of sitting in a chair, by a still more powerful set of orders which are in accordance with his conception of the requirements of *the act of concentration*. This last proceeding being an unreasoned one on his part, all he accomplishes by it is to reinforce all the old misdirected activities subconsciously connected with the act of sitting down, whilst the new reasoned directions concerned with the act go by the board. He sets up what I have described elsewhere as a state of civil war within the organism, with the greatly added tension and strain that always accompany this condition. The point is most clearly brought out in the case of the pupil who is asked to sit quietly and do nothing whilst the teacher moves some part of his body for him. In my experience, as soon as the pupil is asked not to do anything, he will immediately show all those signs of strain and fixity of attention that he shows when he is asked to do something, and which we have learned to associate with any attempt at concentration. Point this out to the pupil, and he will answer, nine times out of ten, " I am trying to do nothing ! " He actually believes that he has something *to do* to do nothing. To such a point can we be led by our belief in concentration !

This whole matter is most instructive, as showing the danger of applying a specific remedy to a psycho-physical defect like " mind-wandering," which has its basis in an imperfect use of the psycho-physical mechanism in general. When a person has developed " mind-wandering," there is present a condition of unreliable sensory appreciation and that undue stress and strain during psycho-physical activities, which is always associated with imperfect co-ordination. To a subject in this condition any attempt to supply a specific remedy is fraught with danger. On a plane of conscious control such dangers can be escaped, but practically never on a subconscious basis.

Now as to the narrowing effect of so-called " concentration." Those who are fortunate, or unfortunate, enough to undertake to act as teachers are well aware of the difficulty of finding an adult who can, as we say, think of more than one thing at a time, or perform satisfactorily any evolution requiring the co-ordinated use of even two parts of the organism. Co-ordinated use of the different parts during any evolution calls for the continuous, conscious projection of orders to the different parts involved, the primary order concerned with the guidance and control of the primary part of the act being *continued* whilst the orders connected with the secondary part of the

movement are projected, and so on, however many orders are
required (the number of these depending upon the demands of
the processes concerned with a particular movement). Ordinarily, in attempts to use two or more parts in remedial work,
the primary projection *ends* with the correct or incorrect use
of the parts concerned with the primary movement. This
applies to all other projections concerned with other parts of
the movement, and is another instance of concentrated effort
connected with a procedure based on the " end-gaining "
principle. The projection of continued, conscious orders, on
the other hand, calls for a broad, reasoning attitude, so that the
subject has not only a clear conception of the orders essential
(" means-whereby ") for the correct performance of a particular
movement, but he can also project these orders in their right
relationship one to another, the co-ordinated series of orders
resulting in a co-ordinated use of the organism.

It follows that an imperfectly co-ordinated use of the human
organism is not associated with the broad, reasoning attitude
and the accruing benefits just indicated. And as most people
have developed a more or less imperfectly co-ordinated use
of the mechanism, which involves reliance upon the " end-
gaining " principle, it is not surprising that so many pupils have
the habit of projecting unconsidered and *disconnected* orders—
orders, that is, that have not been reasoned out from the point
of view of the co-ordinated use of the different parts concerned,
and which therefore result in a mal-co-ordinated movement.
When, therefore, such a pupil comes for remedial work on a plane
of conscious control, and is asked to project a series of connected orders continuously, he naturally finds great difficulty
in breaking the habit he has formed of discontinuous attention
and of haphazard and subconscious guidance and direction.
In fact, it will be found that, as a rule, a pupil has no conception of linking up the different parts of the movement and
the orders relating to these. He may, as I say, give the primary
orders or directions required for the first part of the movement,
but, as soon as that point is reached, he no longer attempts to
carry on the primary order in association with that required
for the secondary part of the movement, although the essential
connexion between these two parts may be pointed out to him
over and over again. The chief reason is that he believes that
he cannot " bring his mind to bear " on more than one point

at a time.   As he expresses it, " I cannot think of so many things at once."   This is entirely in line with the definition of concentration given above, but it represents a delusion on his part, because, of course, he has been " bringing his mind to bear " on several things at once subconsciously all his life, else he could not have carried out the simplest of his daily activities.

A simple illustration will make this clear.   Suppose a person who has been sitting down rises to speak to a friend who comes into the room.   The stimulus to rise from the sitting position comes to him, and his response to this is his decision to stand up. Immediately this decision is made, the orders connected with the well-established habit of rising from the sitting to the standing position are projected to the psycho-physical mechanisms involved, and the act of rising is performed, ending in the assumption of what is called the " standing position." Suppose, further, that this person engages at once in an ordinary conversation or a scientific discussion with his friend for, say, half an hour.   As far as our subject is concerned, he is absorbed by the requirements of the discussion ; in fact, he will tell you that he must concentrate on the matter of the discussion in order to do his best.   The point of interest for us is the consideration of the *means whereby* he remains standing, and *of which he is not and never has been conscious*.   We have already referred to the projections which were associated with his decision to stand up, and these projections must be sustained until he makes a different decision, as, for instance, to move to some other position.   It will be clear, therefore, that during the process of subconscious development the human creature has also developed the ability to sustain continuous projections of orders.   Insistence, therefore, on the necessity and importance of sustained projections in the work of co-ordination and re-education is based, not on a new, but on a very old and fundamental principle in human development.

The point of interest in all these considerations lies in the fact that this prevalent belief in concentration goes hand in hand with the acceptance of the " end-gaining " principle, as against the principle of thinking out clearly and *connectedly* the *means whereby* an " end " can be secured, and of " bringing the mind to bear " on as many subjects (continuous projections of orders) as is necessary for the purpose.   The whole psycho-physical tendency of the person who believes that concentration is essential to success, and adopts and develops it as a practice in his efforts in different spheres of activity, is " to bring the mind to bear on one object." This exactly fits the " end-gaining" principle, and is antagonistic to the " means-whereby " principle which calls for the ability " to bring to bear on " a dozen or more objects if necessary, and which implies a *number* of things, all going on, and converging to a common consequence (continuous projection of orders).

In the sphere of every-day life it will be found that in the opinion of ninety-nine persons out of a hundred, the consideration of " means-whereby " in connexion with the use of the psycho-physical self will prove a hindrance or an interference. These people are confident that they cannot attend to two things at once—that is, to themselves and to their work, business, or profession at the same time. It never seems to occur to them that their psycho-physical self is the instrument or machine by means of which they carry on their business or profession, and that their standard of success, therefore, in this sphere of their business or professional activity will be in accordance with the standard of functioning of this instrument or machine. This instrument or machine being the *means whereby* they will be able to carry on their business or profession successfully, it follows that due attention to the functioning of this instrument or machine is essential to the due and satisfactory attention to their business or profession. The confession, therefore, that they are incapable of carrying on, hand in hand, as it were, these two all-important and interdependent psycho-physical processes is tantamount to an admission that due attention to the *means whereby* they can gain their " ends " will render them unable to attend to these " ends "; which is absurd ! Such a confession, indeed, fixes the stage on the evolutionary plane where mankind, as a mass, stands to-day. It certainly is not a very high stage, when we take into consideration the potentialities of the human creature and the fact that in the development of the animal and the savage the two processes concerned with the use of the creature's self and the use of that self in the activities of life were interdependent.

In a world where the ordinary person not only believes in but practises what is called " concentration," the conception of the word itself and of its practical application will be in accordance with the psycho-physical defects of the individual concerned, who, on becoming conscious of certain defects, believes that what he understands as " concentration " will remove them. Once he has adopted this narrowing process, it is not surprising that he finds it impossible to do or think of more than one thing at a time. The harmful psycho-physical condition thus established does not make for a satisfactory condition of all-round functioning.

On the other hand, those of us who have watched the progress of pupils who have been re-educated on a general basis, have had conclusive proof that it is possible for a person to learn to give due attention continuously to—i.e., to " keep the mind " on the " means-whereby " of the satisfactory use of the psycho-physical mechanisms, whilst employing these mechanisms in the round of daily life, whether this be a business or professional life or any other, and with the desirable result of a continuous development in general psycho-physical health. The human machine is capable of doing many things at the same time, and, in those cases where a condition of unified psycho-physical co-ordination is operative (a condition in which the process of true concentration is present), the subject is as unaware of the operation of the process of concentration as he is of that of the process of co-ordination. As a matter of fact, it is unlikely that such a person will have given thought to the necessity for concentration ; he will not have recognized the need for it, and, this being so, he will not have considered it in the light of a process requiring special attention in its application.

The satisfactory conditions of co-ordination and the manifestations of the co-ordinated creature to which I have referred represent a form of concentration which cannot be secured by " thinking of concentration " or by telling another to think of it (which also means that one cannot be " concentrated " in that sense of the word). This whole book is devoted to the exposure of the fallacy of asking any imperfectly co-ordinated person to attempt to eradicate a defect or peculiarity by some written word or spoken instructions. It is certain that any person who fails to concentrate, in the sense of giving due attention to the matter in hand, is an imperfectly co-ordinated person. To ask such a person to overcome his failure to concentrate by

" concentrating " or " by learning to concentrate " in accordance with his conception of these acts, is to cause a harmful and artificial division of personality. What is needed is the restoration of a satisfactory condition of psycho-physical coordination on a general basis which will involve the use of the true processes of concentration.

IV

MEMORY AND FEELING

TEACHERS in most schools of to-day, if we are to judge by the opinions they express, are fully awake to the growing lack of attention on the part of the children; they seem to be unusually disturbed by this lack of attention, that the children, as they say, " cannot concentrate "; but they do not seem to be so disturbed by the increase in what is called " loss of memory." Possibly they are not yet as aware of it as they should be. Be this as it may, there can be little doubt that these teachers are not aware of the fact that learning to " concentrate," and the subsequent psycho-physical efforts in connexion with the act of " concentrating," tend to interfere with the processes of remembering (taking this word in its broadest sense), with the result that unequal, narrowing, and often inadequate impressions are registered.

Many people nowadays acknowledge their growing " loss of memory," and many attempts are being made by means of memory systems, courses of " mental training," etc., to help educated people to make good a certain loss in this connexion. Here again the point of interest for us lies in the fact that all these systems are based on the " end-gaining " principle, and that no attempt has been made in any of them (any more than in the case of " mind-wandering ") to associate the particular defective manifestation—in this case, " bad memory "—with other psycho-physical defects which will be found to be associated with it.

At a stage of our development when what we call " loss of memory " is more or less a general defect, it behoves us to consider the psycho-physical conditions involved and also the various imperfect uses of the psycho-physical mechanisms which make for the development of these conditions.

Memory is the impression which is registered as the result of some stimulus or stimuli.   The lasting quality of the impression depends upon certain psycho-physical processes concerned with registering impressions, and the effectiveness of these processes in their turn upon the general psycho-physical condition, and especially upon the standard of sensory appreciation present in the particular case. Environment also influences these conditions in accordance with the standard of psycho-physical functioning present at the time of the registration of the impression, whilst a further factor in the case is the degree of ability possessed by the individual concerned to link up the knowledge or the experience, conveyed by a given stimulus or stimuli, with the knowledge and experiences already acquired. As we are aware, our habits of life are the manifestations of our psycho-physical functioning, and this functioning governs our habits in the matter of registering impressions in connexion with memory, just as it influences all our other activities.

There can be little doubt that the growing habit of news-paper-reading and light literature, and the accompanying decline in the reading of books or matter which is to be retained as valuable knowledge, have been accompanied by harmful psycho-physical habits which to-day are seriously affecting the human memory, in a more or less degree in accordance with the standard of psycho-physical functioning of the individual concerned. People study and commit to memory printed matter contained in certain books, because by this means they hope to acquire lasting knowledge. As a rule, they merely read hastily the printed matter in newspapers, magazines, etc., without making any attempt to memorize it. In the same way, they simply glance at the news of the day and register only the faintest impression. This probably serves them for that day or a week, but in a month's time they will probably be hazy about it, and in a year's time the impression may be completely effaced. This habit of taking faint impressions in reading is repeated daily by millions of people who rarely read a book in the way of study, a form of reading which would make for the registering of definite and lasting impressions. " Skimming "—that is, receiving only faint impressions of what is read—is a harmful habit which, if indulged in, rapidly becomes established, and very soon the person concerned is aware of a growing loss of memory in all spheres.

We are all aware that what we term " loss of memory " is a more or less general defect in the process of remembering and recalling knowledge which has become more and more marked during the past twenty or thirty years, and it would seem that, like insanity and other besetting evils, it is a defect which, unless checked in time, must undermine the usefulness of our psycho-physical processes.

For reasoning is dependent upon the association of remembered facts with other facts, which are the stimulus or stimuli to the processes concerned; hence, when the memory fails, the process of satisfactory reasoning will be suspended.

As we are to deal with the effects of certain sensory habits in connexion with memory, it will be useful to consider the interdependence and the action and reaction of sensory appreciation and so-called " mental " activity. The idea conveyed by the voice of one person reaches the consciousness of another through the sense of hearing, the written word through the sense of sight; then we have all the stimuli received through the senses of touch (feeling), taste, smell, etc. In a general way it will be seen that our senses play the leading part in all the processes of remembering and reasoning—in fact, in the great round of psycho-physical activity. The standard of functioning in the foregoing processes of reasoning and remembering depends, therefore, directly or indirectly, upon the standard of functioning of sensory appreciation.

My readers may, of course, point to instances of remarkable feats of memory performed by people in specific spheres, but the writer's experience of these cases is that excellence in one sphere will be found to be equalled by lack of it in all others. In fact the cases to which I refer are simply abnormal.

One of the most interesting in my experience was that of a young man whose abnormality was manifested in dealing with time-tables and the like. If you asked him to look up a train to a particular place at, say, three o'clock, he would turn up the page, look for the particular train by running his eyes up and down the list of times of departures, and during this apparently cursory glance at the time-table he would memorize the whole list. Three months later, if you asked him to name the trains in the list departing between any two hours you liked to name, you would be certain to receive a correct answer. But this same young man would continually leave his umbrella in the bus, go out to purchase some ordinary article for domestic use, and, forgetting what he had gone to fetch, return without it. In fact, in the general way of life, and judged by the ordinary standard of human intelligence, he was quite a hopeless person.[1] We have here a fine instance of a remarkable feat of memory in a specific sphere accompanied by defective remembering and reasoning in general activity, a condition which, as I am able to state, in consequence of personal acquaintance, was, in this case, associated with delusive sensory appreciation.

There is little doubt that most of the early bad habits which result in what we call " loss of memory " are actually cultivated during the different processes in all forms of education. This cultivation is most marked in those teaching processes where the pupil is called upon to perform some " physical " act. Therefore, now that we have been unreasoning enough to force every unfortunate school child, irrespective of his individual standard of sensory appreciation, to learn " physical " drill or to perform exercises, we must expect among the majority a more rapid development of " loss of memory " than during the previous years. As the writer is prepared to demonstrate the truth of these statements before any scientific or intelligent body of men and women, he has decided to take his illustration from this sphere of teaching.

If the reader takes the trouble to be present in the school or gymnasium or during any outdoor teaching in connexion with exercises, drill, or games, he will note, if he observes carefully, that each of the children or adults is occupied chiefly in endeavouring to learn the teacher's instructions by the " physical " performance of some small part of these instructions which has specifically appealed to him, and is so concentrated and absorbed in this part of the performance that he

[1] I should like to urge here that we must beware of placing an exaggerated value upon intelligence which manifests itself only in some specific sphere. Judgment must always be made upon the human creature's intelligent activities on a general basis in the process of living and all-round usefulness. The genuine specialist, for instance, must always be primarily a proficient general practitioner in the sphere of trade, profession, or general activity, for satisfactory growth as a specialist demands a continuous growth and development of those experiences which only the general practitioner can command. This important matter of correct relative values is of the utmost importance, and if we are to establish a sound basis for judgment in the future, we must first give consideration to the " means-whereby " of the act rather than to the act itself. What useful part does the performance of an act play in a man's so-called " intellectual " or " physical " development, if the man is injured thereby ?

is oblivious to any other part of the instructions that are being given by the teacher. He will only have to question the pupil to find that this is true; an expert in psycho-physical re-education has only to observe the expression in the pupil's eyes, and certain other manifestations, to be quite certain.

The following is an incident in this connexion which occurred recently during a lesson in re-education in the writer's own experience. The pupil was asked to listen to certain simple instructions which involved the use of the lips, tongue, and jaw, in the order named. (Of course, the necessary work in regard to the general co-ordinated use of the organism during such teaching had already been given.) The first time the instructions were given it was obvious that, before the teacher had finished speaking, the pupil was trying to memorize them, as they were given, by a "physical" (sensory) process—i.e., by trying to "feel" the instructions as they were spoken, rather than to acquire them by a process of remembering ("committing to memory," as we say).

The pupil was again asked to listen to the instructions, and not to attempt to make any movements of the parts concerned. He was asked merely to concern himself with the process of remembering the instructions. Before the instructions had been given to him a second time, however, the pupil was again very busily engaged in making certain movements of the neck, lips, and jaw. He was then asked why he was making these movements. He promptly answered, "I am trying to make certain of the instructions." It was then explained to him that the method he was pursuing was not the correct and satisfactory way of making certain of instructions; that, instead, the instructions should first be memorized, and that only when this had been done would there be any chance of his carrying them out in the psycho-physical sphere, and then, only provided that the instructions included the correct *means whereby* the act was to be performed.

Spoken instructions reach our consciousness through the sense of hearing, written instructions through the sense of sight, the resulting action and reaction being influenced by the standard of general psycho-physical functioning of the organism. But as the standard of psycho-physical functioning in the ordinary child or adult of our time is inadequate, the creature is brought within a danger zone directly he attempts to carry out any activities which call for new psycho-physical experiences. In a very large number of cases the standard of this functioning has been so lowered that the individuals concerned may be said to be perpetually within this danger zone, for their guiding sensations are unreliable and often harmfully delusive.

It is quite conceivable that any stimulus, as it is conveyed by sensory appreciation to the consciousness, is influenced by the psycho-physical conditions present, and there is not the least doubt as to this influence on the reaction which follows. We are all aware of the different reactions of different people to the same stimulus or stimuli. Now, where the psycho-physical conditions are such as we find associated with unreliable defective or delusive guiding sensations (sensory appreciation), we cannot surely expect a proper standard of psycho-physical functioning in the general round of so-called "mental activities." Sound and comprehensive reasoning is rare in a person whose sensory appreciation is unreliable—in other words, whose kinæsthesia may be said to be debauched.

To return to our illustration. The facts set down serve to show that the pupil, in going to work in the way he did, was following out a preconceived plan in regard to the attempt to memorize instructions. In his conception, the act of memorizing was much more a "physical" than a "mental" act, and if in his case the psycho-physical functioning had been up to that standard which commands a reliable sensory appreciation, the pupil's plan might have proved successful; and in this connexion the most interesting fact in the whole experience remains to be stated. For on the morning following the lesson, when he was asked to repeat the instructions, he said, "I can't recall them now." Here, then, was the proof that the pupil's preconceived plan of memorizing his instructions by trying to feel them had failed, as how could it be otherwise, considering the very imperfect sensory appreciation that he had at his command? The habit of attempting to perform an act before the directing and guiding orders concerned have been memorized is, in such a case, associated with an inadequate use of the processes of inhibition as compared with those of volition; therefore, when the pupil is brought face to face with the new psycho-physical experiences, his inhibitory processes are ineffective. This means that he is gradually cultivating within himself an unbalanced psycho-physical condition in which the so-called "mental" impressions he receives during the act of learning are unduly faint and unreliable.

In order to restore balance in such a case, it is necessary first to develop a conscious, reasoning inhibition (prevention). To this end, the person concerned must learn to say "No" to every stimulus to psycho-physical activity until he has taken time to consider what are the reasonable *means whereby* the end he desires can be achieved, and he must then repeat and memorize the orders relative to these means before employing them in guiding and directing the mechanisms essential to the particular psycho-physical act to be performed.[1]

[1] We have recently seen the rise and fall in reputation of a system which, it was claimed, could restore failing memory and by specific means bestow "mental" blessings which were, however, quite beyond the most sanguine expectations of any person who still enjoyed even a temporary state of sanity or who possessed even a reasonable knowledge of the fundamentals of the psycho-physical processes which are essential to satisfactory memorizing. In this particular instance, the rapid rise and fall of this system affords food for reflection in connexion especially with the eulogies which the proprietors of this system published from time to time from the pens and over the names of men and women, some of whom are recognized leaders of thought in our time. It is unfortunate that we cannot call these men and women to account and force them to justify these eulogies of a system, which after all was but a piece of "mental gymnastics" or series of gymnastics carried out in accordance with definite instructions, which totally ignored those general psycho-physical conditions of the person concerned, which were the cause or causes of the "mental" shortcoming and of which these leaders of thought were themselves totally ignorant. The blind continue to lead the blind in the twentieth century as in the days of the cave-man, but the process brings with it more disastrous results in our time than was possible in those early days of man's more limited spheres of psycho-physical activities.

V

COMPLEXITY AND COMPLICATIONS IN RELATION
TO STRESS AND STRAIN

VERY frequently we are told that the cause of most of our difficulties is the increasing complexity of the demands of living in the present stage of civilization. It is much more to the point to say that our real difficulties arise from the almost universal adoption in practical life of the lowly evolved " end-gaining " principle in our attempts to meet these demands, the result being that we cultivate within ourselves a condition of stress and strain (which in our ignorance we look upon as something apart from ourselves), in a subconscious, unintelligent effort to adapt ourselves to the ever-changing environment of what we designate as an advancing civilization.

First, we have stress and strain within ourselves—that is, in the functioning of the psycho-physical mechanisms as we employ them to satisfy the needs of the organism in the maintenance of health conditions and in general activity. The errors and defects in the sphere of psycho-mechanics indicated by the foregoing are the result of the dependence upon unsound and misleading principles concerned with our individual development and growth.

Then we have the stress and strain of what we so often describe as the " fight for life," " the complexity of life," and so on; in other words, the stress and strain occasioned by our endeavour to make the wheels of the complex man-made machinery of life go round in social, industrial, political, educational, religious, and moral spheres.

These two spheres of stress and strain, which we have indicated, must always be considered as inseparable, seeing that our social, educational, industrial, political, religious, and moral life depends for its being on the experiences of our individual psycho-physical life. The false principles which are applied to the act of living in both instances are entirely responsible for these harmful conditions of strain and for the unsettled state which holds sway at this very moment. Had the prophets, philosophers, and leaders of the past recognized this fact, they would have shown proof of clear analysis and foresight. That they did not do so is most unfortunate, and to this fact we may attribute the growing tendency towards disunion instead of unity, towards dissatisfaction instead of satisfaction, towards enmity and discord instead of good-fellowship and peace, the sum total of these present conditions constituting an unsatisfactory instead of a satisfactory stage in human evolution. We have unrest everywhere, unrest in men, women, and children, which is attributed to " nerves " or some such symptom, and the alarming feature of it all is that it is an increasing unrest. The venomous and penetrating roots of the cancer of disunion continue to spread and have already caused to deteriorate, and in many instances have actually demoralized, the vital parts of our psycho-mechanical life as well as our social and industrial life, and the difficulties in application of the principles which make for unity are already alarming. It is universally contended that we need unity in all spheres, and we are all familiar with the cry " united we stand, divided we fall," and this has a universal application to satisfactory human endeavour. Yet in almost every sphere of human activity—in religion, in education, in the social plan, in politics, in trades unionism, etc.—we find a growing tendency to disunion. Review the history of human endeavour during the past few hundred years, and consider the cause or causes of the increase in the number of different sects in the sphere of religion, in the number of different systems of education, social reform, in the number of political parties, and, probably most striking of all, in the increase in the tendency to adopt, under the banner of trades unionism, measures and principles which impede unity. Surely it is fair to conclude that the cause or causes of the growing disunion in all these spheres is due to some serious defect or defects in the fundamentals of these man-made institutions. If the principles involved had been sound, their application would have tended towards unity, and the fact that the people immediately concerned failed to remain in agreement as to the relative value of the principles they had decided to apply, is surely an admission of their unsoundmess. Be this as it may, we cannot fail to recognize the important fact that an alarming growth of disunion leading to complications in human activity is herein indicated, and complications are ever associated with misdirected activity. If we keep to our present system of life, living will be still more complicated in a hundred years from now, and so on, until possibly such a degree of complication will be reached that we shall not even have time to live !

The foregoing serves to indicate that the unreasoned processes which lead to harmful complications in the educational sphere are paramount in every other sphere of life. The parallel to the failure in our teaching methods is to be found in our attempts to progress in social, political, industrial, religious, and other spheres, where the remedy is often more harmful than the disease. How absurd, for instance, are the attempts for the " uplifting of man " in the industrial sphere, when these are associated with that demoralizing conception which has led to the lowering of the standard of man's daily efforts to that of the less capable, and so to the lowering of the standard of individual psycho-physical functioning in the sphere of labour. We are all aware of the psycho-physical effect of giving our best in our daily labours, and there is little hope for the person who is no longer able to gain satisfaction and happiness from this source. Again, in the sphere of politics, what can be more stupid than the ordinary party attitude, leading, as it does, to undesirable individual manifestations of deception, prejudice, egotism, and " emotional gusts " ? It is an unreasonable and dishonest course to withhold support from or denounce measures which one believes to be right and of value to humanity, simply because they chance to be advocated by the political party to which one does not belong. Under the present plan politics and deception are interdependent. The individual seeking re-election will resort to forms of deception to which he would not stoop in other walks of life, particularly in the matter of making promises which he has not the least hope of fulfilling, and which his electors, if they used their reasoning powers, would often know he cannot fulfil. They are still at a stage of evolution where reasoning is dominated by the herd-instinct, and so they are carried away by his oratory or personality or both. The harmful effects of the activities of individuals beset with serious and often abnormal psycho-physical defects are present in every sphere of life, and we have to face the fact that it is not the people who are out to do harm to their fellow-beings who are setting back the clock of civilization to-day, but, on the contrary, those misguided people who are devoting themselves to the uplifting of their fellow-men, whilst remaining themselves under the influence of perverted emotions and prejudices. The history of our social plan in the spheres of industrialism, politics, religion, education, medicine, etc., for the past three hundred years is of the greatest interest in this matter of the attitude of those concerned with attempts at reform, organization, advancement, and unity, for these attempts will invariably be found to be specific and " end-gaining " attempts, resulting, even where the specific " end " is gained, in new complications leading to social conflict and harmful diversity. If we are to check the present over-balancing in these directions, and to advance satisfactorily, we must gradually raise the standard of individual psycho-mechanical co-ordination, and pass to a stage of constructive conscious control which would be associated with the establishment of " means-whereby " principles instead of " end-gaining " principles.

PART IV

SENSORY APPRECIATION IN ITS RELATION
TO HAPPINESS

THE characteristic note of true happiness is struck when the healthy child is busily engaged in doing something which interests it. It may be the little girl washing and wiping her tea-cups, or dressing and undressing her doll, or the little boy setting to work to make a toy train or cart with the aid of a piece of wood and a string, or piecing together some modern toy which, when completed, will be a house, or a bridge, or a working model of some machine. The child is always attracted by machinery; indeed, to find out " how it works " is the natural desire of every healthy child, and it is therefore very significant that in schools where experiments have been made in re-education on a general basis, the children have become more interested in this work than in any other of their school activities. They are not slow to recognize that they are themselves the most interesting machines, and their natural interest in mechanics finds full scope in the process of their own re-education. Our experience has been that this interest, an intelligent interest in the working of their own psycho-physical mechanisms, is one that grows steadily and comprehensively. For the psycho-physical processes which precede and accompany the child's desire to acquire a knowledge of the mechanical working of inanimate machinery are the same as those which are called into activity in connexion with the acquisition of the knowledge of the satisfactory use of its own mechanisms. It should be obvious to all concerned that in any process of growth or development of the child or adult, experience in employing the mechanics of the psycho-physical organism should precede all other mechanical experience, and that any experiences gained later in the sphere of inanimate mechanical experimentation would thus be materially increased in value.

One can recall the expression of interest, happiness, and satisfaction exhibited by the child when one has enabled him to understand [1] for the first time that his unduly stiffened neck—with perhaps his head too far pulled back—is really not the fault of his neck at all, but is due to the fact that he is trying to do with the muscles of his neck what should be done by other mechanisms.

One cannot forget either the unfamiliar but satisfactory manifestations of the child when he becomes able to inhibit [2]— that is, to say " No " to some stimulus to misdirected activity (which in the case of the last illustration would be to say " No " to his subconscious desire to throw back his head and stiffen his neck)—and then, with an expression born of confidence, to give the orders or directions, which are the result of a reasoned conception of his correct " means-whereby," the whole process tending to prevent the over-excitement of the fear reflexes. Experience has proved to us that children are unusually interested in the working of their own psychophysical machinery when the processes employed are concerned with re-education on a general and conscious basis.

[1] Of course the teacher's manipulation will have given him previously the reliable sensory appreciation in this connexion. For a detailed statement, see Chapter " Imperfect Sensory Appreciation."

[2] The demeanour of the child changes when he learns to inhibit his desire to respond to a certain stimulus, before going on to give the new orders or directions which are the forerunners of the new *means whereby* the particular " end " he desires can be achieved. This change of expression was very noticeable in the case of a little girl who had developed the most pronounced bad habits in the use of her psychophysical organism, and had what we call a " dour " expression when her lessons started. At a certain stage in her re-education she developed a conscious recognition of the new and correct experiences secured by the teacher's manipulation, and she became able to inhibit—i.e., to say " No " to the stimulus which had previously started up the whole train of movements that were incorrect and harmful. When she discovered this—viz., that by saying " No " to herself she could PREVENT her troublesome and long-established bad habits from gaining the upper hand—her whole demeanour changed, and, with a confidence that was quite new to her, she proceeded to give herself the directions which would enable her to make in the new and co-ordinated manner (correct " means-whereby ") the very movement which she had stopped herself from making in her old mal-co-ordinated manner. The fact that she could not only think out but CONTROL THE MEANS WHEREBY she could attain her " end " (instead of rushing at it blindly in her old subconscious way) robbed her of the diffidence which had been such an over-developed trait in her case, and with the gradual development of control the old " dour " expression gave place to one of confidence and happiness.

They find a new interest in all activities to which they can apply an improving use of themselves, and their happiness in finding, for instance, that they can improve their games by a conscious *general* direction of themselves (a very different thing from the usual *specific* directions they receive in coaching lessons) is a happiness which increases with their psycho-physical improvement.

I shall now endeavour to show that the lack of real happiness manifested by the majority of adults of to-day is due to the fact that they are experiencing, not an improving, but a continually deteriorating use of their psycho-physical selves. This is associated with those defects, imperfections, undesirable traits of character, disposition, temperament, etc., characteristic of imperfectly co-ordinated people struggling through life beset with certain maladjustments of the psycho-physical organism, which are actually setting up conditions of irritation and pressure during both sleeping and waking hours. Whilst the maladjustments remain present, these malconditions increase day by day and week by week, and foster that unsatisfactory psycho-physical state which we call " unhappiness." Small wonder that under these conditions the person concerned becomes more and more irritated and unhappy. Irritation is not compatible with happiness, yet the human creature has to employ this already irritated organism in all the psycho-physical activities demanded by a civilized mode of life. It stands to reason that every effort made by the human creature whose organism is already in an irritated condition must tend to make the creature still more irritated, and, therefore, as time goes on, his chances of happiness diminish. Furthermore, his experiences of happiness become of ever shorter duration, until at last he is forced to take refuge in a state of unhappiness, a psycho-physical condition as perverted as that state of ill-health which people reach when they experience a perverted form of satisfaction in the suffering of pain—that is, in " the enjoyment of bad health," as we say. This perversion links up with those purely animal traits which are apt to accompany morbid conditions, and which become unduly and harmfully manifested in those states of unusual excitement and marked depression, when the individual's reasoning is in abeyance and he is dominated by his emotional impulses.

We have merely to consider the experiences of the human creature, afflicted with the conditions of irritation and pressure already referred to, in his attempts to employ this irritated organism in a general way in the activities of life, to recognize that even his occasional experiences of happiness will be of unduly short duration, and will tend to become more so with the progress of time. It matters not whether these experiences are gained in the sphere of rest, work, recreation, pleasure, games, or general education; in all these activities impeding factors, such as irritation and pressure, remain more or less unchanged. This means that experiences that would only tend to irritate a person in possession of a comparatively high standard of sensory appreciation and of satisfactorily co-ordinated psycho-physical mechanisms, would be certain to irritate most harmfully a person who is already beset with irritation and pressure, in consequence of the harmful condition of unreliable sensory appreciation in the use of the organism which we have indicated. Furthermore, such a person will be irritated by experiences which would not have the least effect upon one whose sensory appreciation is reliable.

The psycho-physical condition of the person afflicted with irritation and pressure is such that all his efforts in any direction will be more or less of a failure as compared with the efforts of those who are not so afflicted, and there is probably no stimulus from without which makes more for irritability of the person concerned than failure (either comparative or complete) in accomplishment, nothing which can have a worse effect upon our emotions, self-respect, happiness, or confidence —in fact, upon our temperament and character in general. Just note the expression and general demeanour of one who is a success in life, then of one who is a failure; of one who has just succeeded in some simple act, in work, games, or learning something, then of one who has failed comparatively or completely. If we note any of these people on days when comparative success has attended their efforts, the least observant among us must be convinced of the striking influence of success and of how conducive it is to happiness. Watch the child in its earliest efforts before and during school days, or the experiences of adults in the activities of daily life in any sphere, and it will be observed that when either is employing his organism successfully, happiness and satisfaction rule supreme. Confidence is born of success, not of failure, and our processes in education and in the general art of living must be based upon principles which will enable us to make certain of the satisfactory *means whereby* an end may be secured, and thus to command a large percentage of those satisfactory experiences which develop confidence, as against a small percentage of those unsatisfactory experiences which tend to undermine our confidence and make us unhappy.

A well-known medical specialist sent one of his patients to me for a diagnosis. He then called upon me to discuss the details of my conclusions, and when I pointed out to him that his patient would be a difficult pupil to re-educate, in consequence of his unusually unbalanced emotional condition and state of harmful irritability, he remarked, " I must tell you that he has been soured by comparative failure in his professional work."

In order to illustrate these points, we will deal with the practical experiences of the human creature in the fields of recreation and games, because we may assume that here, at any rate, he will be acting in accordance with the dictates of his own wishes and desires, in the anticipation of those psycho-physical experiences which make for happiness.

We are all aware of the pleasurable anticipation, and even joyous mild excitement, associated with the early experiences of our men and women friends who take up golf, tennis, cricket, football, and other games and forms of recreation. This pleasurable anticipation arises from the fact that they associate the manifestations which we call happiness with indulgence in these activities, and there can be little doubt that we should be able to command a continuance of happiness, and an increasing satisfaction with the increase of our experience in any game or form of recreation, as far as our personal efforts, at any rate, in the practice of the game are concerned. But despite this fact we know that in the great majority of cases, manifestations of happiness, contrary to expectation, tend to decrease rather than increase with the accumulation of practical experiences in these forms of recreation. That this is the case with most of us is surely proof that something is radically wrong with the use of our psycho-physical mechanisms, and with the application of these mechanisms to the demands of the particular game or recreation.

The reason for this will be clear if we try to set down the psycho-physical experiences in action and reaction which result from a person's decision to play, say, golf. Let us take the case of any ordinary person (not some person exceptionally well-equipped for golf) and watch him at his first lesson with his teacher, professional or otherwise. It is safe to conclude, firstly, that this pupil's sensory appreciation is more or less unreliable, and associated with an imperfectly co-ordinated use of his psycho-physical mechanisms, and, secondly, that he has never been re-educated on a general basis. Unfortunately, this applies equally to the teacher, and means that, in both cases, their knowledge of the use of the psycho-physical mechanisms which they are about to employ in the lesson is the result of unsatisfactory and even harmful subconscious experiences. It is safe to assume that they have little conscious knowledge of the use of these mechanisms either in the field of theory or in that of practice, and even that little will be on a specific basis. The true relation of " cause and effect " on a general basis in connexion with the working of these mechanisms will not be given due consideration and, as we shall see, the majority of effects (symptoms of some " cause " or " causes ") that they chance to recognize will not be treated by them as such, but as " causes," and dealt with in accordance with the " end-gaining " principle.

We are all familiar, for instance, with the type of instructions which the teacher will give to the pupil in regard to " holding the club," " keeping his eye on the ball," and all the other things which the pupil should or should not do with the different parts of his organism at a particular time. Now it will be clear to any spectator with a knowledge of the satisfactory employment of the psycho-physical mechanisms on a general basis that the particular pupil will be psycho-physically incapable of carrying out satisfactorily quite a number of the specific instructions given to enable him to meet his difficulties, and, indeed, that any attempt on his part to carry out these instructions on the " end-gaining " principle will result with practice in an increase, not in a decrease of his difficulties. It is a matter of common knowledge that the majority of players fail to keep their eye on the ball, but neither the pupil nor the teacher is aware of the fundamental impeding psycho-physical factors concerned with this failure.

It is impossible, within the scope of this book, to discuss these factors in detail in relation to golf, and I intend instead to deal with the pupil's attempt to carry out the teacher's instructions from the standpoint of reliability of sensory appreciation and of co-ordination on a general basis. And as a preliminary I want to point out that in the teaching plan, of which the lesson we are watching is an example, nothing is given in the way of practical help to the pupil in these directions. The teacher is certainly unable to make a satisfactory diagnosis in the matter of reliable sensory appreciation, and probably does not know whether a pupil is well co-ordinated on a general basis or not; in any case, it is a fact that he does not attempt to make a diagnosis in either connexion. He merely assumes that if he gives the pupil certain instructions, tells him what to do and what not to do, he has conscientiously carried out his duties as a teacher. Yet, he should know perfectly well that in the course of the " up and down swing " of the club, for instance, quite a number of separate instructions that he has given his pupil have to be carried out by quite a number of different parts of the organism. Further, he should know that all these instructions must be linked together (that is, the pupil must be able to think of and put into practice more than one thing at a time), and that all the different parts of the organism must be employed " sympathetically "; must, as he would say, " work together." In other words, the teacher should know that there must be co-ordination in the employment of all the mechanisms involved, yet he gives his pupil no *means whereby* he can achieve this necessary co-ordination of a *general* basis in the use of his psycho-physical self.

Now, we have already pointed out, and we are prepared to prove, that the great majority of people of our time are more or less imperfectly co-ordinated. If this is so, how is it possible for a pupil to co-ordinate this psycho-physical organism on a general basis for the carrying-out of the golf-teacher's specific instructions, on that first day or any subsequent day of lessons, until he has been restored to a satisfactory standard of general co-ordination by some process of re-education which will restore a reliable standard of sensory appreciation?

It is clear, therefore, from the foregoing that the pupil whose lesson we are watching is ill-equipped to carry out the teacher's instructions successfully, and we will now follow him through the experiences which result from the different efforts he makes to carry out these instructions in his ill-equipped condition.

It will be safe to assume that after the performance of the first stroke the teacher will have noted some particular fault or faults, to which he will draw the attention of the pupil, and it is equally safe to assume that the pupil (working on the " end-gaining " plan, and indulging in that process which he calls " concentration ") will start to concentrate upon the different corrections suggested by the teacher in connexion with the fault or faults pointed out to him, after which he will make another shot—i.e., " try again." It will be found that in this attempt the pupil has already decided that one or other of these corrections is the all-important one, and so he will proceed to concentrate specially upon it, to the practical exclusion of the others, and he will repeat this process with each subsequent attempt.

Now, although it is quite possible that by this plan of concentrating on the corrections he may succeed in eradicating some specific fault or faults, the point I wish to emphasize again is that he will have gained this end at the expense of overlooking some other equally important corrections in consequence of his having concentrated upon one at a time. By this process of concentration, therefore, as we have pointed out in an earlier chapter, he will probably have added to his list of faults. Not only this, but the psycho-physical process involved is inseparable from the over-excitement of the fear reflexes, and gradually builds up an emotional state which impedes the pupil's progress in the game, and becomes an established phobia which will not only influence his play harmfully, but will impede him in all his other activities. One thing is certain, that if an imperfectly co-ordinated person makes a subconscious effort to carry out such specific instructions as we are now dealing with, the result *as a whole* must be unsatisfactory. The majority of his psycho-physical experiences will be harmful experiences, inasmuch as they must tend to undermine his confidence in himself, and this lack of confidence, arising from a consciousness of complete or comparative failure, will serve to add still another impeding factor to the situation, in the over-exciting of the fear reflexes and the development of harmful emotional conditions which are associated with a state of comparative unhappiness.

One of the greatest factors in human development is the building up of a form of confidence which comes as the result of that method of learning by which the pupil is put in posses- sion of the correct *means whereby* he can attain his end before he makes any attempt to gain it. By this method the attempt he makes will be more or less successful from the outset, and a series of satisfactory instead of unsatisfactory psycho-physical experiences will follow, and with them that intelligent con- fidence and state of happiness associated therewith which is the " consummated conquest " of the human being on a conscious plane.

In a civilization such as ours, where unrest, unhappiness, and lack of interest in the real things of life are strikingly manifested by mankind, all our efforts should be to enable the human creature to retain the interest and satisfaction exhibited by the healthy child when employing his organism success- fully; further, to create conditions in which satisfactory growth, with all that this process connotes in fundamental psycho- physical manifestations, will continue right on through life, and in which the stagnation which accompanies fixed psycho- physical habits and specific " end-gaining " uses of the psycho- physical organism will be impossible.

Conscious employment of the psycho-physical mechanisms on a basis, not of a specific, but of a general co-ordination in all the acts of living constitutes a real and never-ending intel- lectual problem of constructive control, which, instead of destroying, develops the interest and general intellectual pleasure in even such ordinary acts as those of " sitting down " and " standing up."

Take, for instance, the oft-repeated act of " sitting down." In this act, the subconsciously controlled person, as soon as he touches the chair, instead of allowing it to support him, pro- ceeds, as he would say, to " sit down "—that is, to make cer- tain unnecessary movements and alterations in the adjustment and general condition of the organism, involving that imperfect use of the mechanisms which he subconsciously employs in order to seat himself (" sit down ").

This means that he has performed the act of " sitting down " in accordance with his subconscious conception of it. In other words, he has " slumped," as we say, and when this imperfectly co-ordinated condition is brought about, the process of seating himself is completed, as far as his awareness is concerned. He remains oblivious to the misuse of the mechanisms involved and to the irritation and pressure associated with the harmful posture which he has subconsciously assumed, and which, unfortunately for him, *feels* natural and comfortable. Likewise, when he stands up, he " feels " the way to stand up, and repeats the same subconscious indulgence of his automatic habits connected with the act of standing up, and once he has " stood up," the process again is completed, as far as his awareness is concerned. In both instances he ends a psychophysical process which, in reality, should never be finished. His standard of awareness, indeed, in such connexions is as inadequate as his sensory appreciation is unreliable, and the psycho-physical conditions here indicated are inseparable from lack of interest and lack of general pleasure in the ordinary acts of life.

On the other hand, when a person sits down or stands up in accordance with the demands of constructive conscious control, the process involves an adequate and continuous state of increasing awareness in regard to the use of the mechanisms, so that immediately there is a wrong use of these mechanisms, the person concerned becomes aware of it, and at once substitutes a satisfactory for the unsatisfactory use. Increasing awareness in this connexion makes more and more for successful accomplishment in accordance with reasoned and satisfactory " means-whereby," and connotes a continuous process which introduces a special interest and pleasure into the most ordinary acts of life.[1]

Conscious fundamental psycho-physical processes do not end; they are continuous, and therefore connote real growth and development. This applies to all the acts of life, and the establishment of the psycho-physical uses which are associated with the processes of constructive control and continuous growth herein involved is inseparable from that psycho-physical

---

[1] As I wrote in *Man's Supreme Inheritance* : " When real conscious control has been obtained a ' habit ' need never become fixed. It is not truly a habit at all, but an order or series of orders given to the subordinate controls of the body, which orders will be carried out until countermanded."

manifestation which we call " happiness." They are processes which result from the application of " means-whereby " principles, and not from the application of " end-gaining " principles associated with those specific attempts which are characteristic of human endeavour on a subconscious plane and which are adopted in the pursuit of what we call " pleasure." Here we have the explanation of the growing need among subconsciously controlled people for *specific* pleasure, with all its attendant shortcomings of unrest and excess, as compared with that enduring happiness, with its accompanying sense of satisfaction and contentment, which is associated with moderation and general control.

Unfortunately, we have been taught that all the ordinary, most necessary, and therefore most oft-repeated acts of life should be automatic and unconscious; for this reason they have become indifferent. The psycho-physical condition here indicated is one that induces stagnation in the organism, and, as it is a condition which becomes more and more pronounced with advancing age, we gradually lose the capacity to take conscious interest in and derive pleasure from those normal and useful activities of life in the sphere of doing, hearing, seeing, etc. Small wonder, then, that sooner or later we seek satisfaction in less normal and less useful activities, and create an undue and harmful demand for specific excitements and stimulations or for some other *specific* pleasure !

All our efforts in the way of education should be to create conditions in which growth will continue through life, conditions in which the stagnation which accompanies fixed habits will be impossible. We shall not then find men and women, as we do now, actually afraid to retire from the business or profession in which they have gained their livelihood and earned a competence, because they have no interest in doing anything else, and cannot adapt themselves to a new way of life. This tragedy is one of the most common and most poignant features of our modern life, and it will be found that, in such cases, the individuals concerned have so little control over their psycho-physical mechanisms (except within certain limited spheres) that they cannot employ them in an entirely new sphere without experiencing the most distressing forms of psycho-physical functioning.

A study of this question will show us that the processes of

reasoning and of action in the ordinary subconsciously controlled person who has reached the age when he is about to retire from his business or professional work, reveal a tendency to fall back and depend more and more upon automatic methods of procedure. By the time that the greater number of men and women have reached this age, they have become mere automatons, repeating day by day the same round of psychophysical activities, and gradually limiting themselves, more and more as time goes on, within certain specific spheres of activity, whilst, at the same time, the defects and imperfections in the general use of the mechanisms upon which this activity depends become more and more pronounced. This means that with the approach of age a condition of deterioration and stagnation is being gradually cultivated throughout the organism generally, the very worst possible preparation for the new way of life which is entailed [1] when a man or a woman retires from his or her business or profession. This explains why so many people break down when they stop work.

Someone has said, in referring to the monotony of the environment in which the human creature lives and moves, that monotony is the deathbed of existence. But what of the monotony *within* the human creature's psycho-physical self, a monotony caused by the gradual cessation of those sensations concerned with new experiences which have accompanied growth and mobility within the organism since birth? This is, indeed, monotony in its most harmful form, for it goes hand in hand with an increasing degree of stagnation throughout the whole psycho-physical organism. We recognize, for instance, the danger of stagnation in our cells, when the processes concerned with repair of wasted tissue cease to be operative; when this occurs, the stagnation which ensues is analogous to that which follows the cessation of sensations concerned with new experiences referred to above, both forms of stagnation making for monotony and unhappiness.

Yet another form of monotony results from " knowing,"

[1] One has only to note the attitude of people in general towards circumstances, even within the domestic sphere, which enforce changes in their habits of life, to realize what an exaggerated and even harmful conception they have of the sufferings or discomforts they are called on to endure on account of this disturbance of the automatic round of their domestic existence.

from having grown up; from the consciousness that we have ceased to grow. When a man reaches the point where he concludes that he " knows " his subject, he decides, consciously or subconsciously, that he has nothing more to learn, and he promptly begins to lose what he does know; when he becomes aware that he has " grown up," he has reached a stage where he has already begun to stultify those potentialities for growth which once were his, and which might have been his to the end. Boredom, monotony, and discontent follow swift upon the establishment of this condition.

We also find that the people who are satisfied that they " know " are the least observant people, and at the same time the most unhappy and discontented. Most people will admit that realization too often is not equal to anticipation, but this again is in consequence of the psycho-physical conditions present. If realization is not only to equal but even sometimes to surpass anticipation, our psycho-physical plan of development must be fundamentally one of continuous growth and of new experiences, and consequently we never reach the point when we may be said to finish learning. This connotes a continuous anticipation of new experiences in growth and development, so that the realization of some new experience in psycho-physical functioning does not bring a sense of finality, with the consequent loss of interest, but is a clear indication that a step forward has been made in growth and development, which is again a stepping-stone to the next stage of advancement, and so on.

The new experiences concerned with the gradually improving functioning of the human creature, indicated in the foregoing, are primarily dependent upon a growing understanding, *consciously developed*, of the operations concerned with the direction and control of the psycho-physical organism in general during the waking and sleeping hours.

William James suggested to us that we should get up every morning looking for health. We hope to go farther, for we have a technique to offer in this connexion which will command for the human creature an increasingly high standard of that condition of psycho-physical functioning which makes for health, and the experiences resulting from the use of this technique bring conviction that the all-important duty of the human creature, in our present stage of evolutionary vicissi-

194 Sensory Appreciation in its Relation to Happiness

tudes, is that of the *continuous* individual cultivation of fundamental, constructive conscious control of the human psycho-
physical organism and its potentialities.

It is true that man has made a specific application of so-
called conscious control in the employment of his powers of
reasoning in relation to " causes and effects," " means and
consequences " outside of the human organism, but this
attempt at specific control of environment has not resulted
in a really reliable control of actual consequences; our experiences seem to show, rather, that the longer we continue to
apply this form of unreliable " conscious control," the worse
off we are likely to be. My experience in connexion with the
practical application of the technique I have described con-
vinces me that if we are ever to command a reliable constructive control of environment and satisfactory reasoning in
relation to " causes and effects," " means and consequences "
in this connexion, we must be able primarily to command
fundamental constructive conscious control of the individual
psycho-physical organism. This calls for a higher and higher
standard of psycho-physical functioning, which in turn demands
a satisfactory and growing understanding and conscious use
of the wonderful mechanisms concerned. This process provides the human creature with a sphere of psycho-physical
activity, almost unlimited in its possibilities, where hitherto
he has evidenced the worst forms of unreasoned and subconsciously directed activity.

CONCLUSIONS

PSYCHO-PHYSICAL ATTITUDE

In the course of this book I have dealt with various human defects, peculiarities, shortcomings, and imperfect uses of the psycho-physical organism, which tend to increase during the process of growth and development, and too often become established as "bad habits" long ere adolescence has been reached, the sum total of the experiences involved being the foundation of what is called "mental attitude."

The attitude of the human creature towards the functioning of his psycho-physical self, and towards the employment of this self in the activities of daily life, is the "be all and end all," and only those who possess the key to this storehouse of their psycho-physical experiences, inherited or acquired, can reach that stage of understanding of their psycho-physical reactions to stimuli which justifies an optimistic view of any efforts that may be made for man's uplifting.

The understanding to which I refer is that understanding of the psycho-physical processes, present at the varying stages of the human creature's growth and development, which are responsible for manifestations, the proper understanding of which is essential to any satisfactory consideration of "cause and effect," primarily, in connexion with the activities concerned with the development of the human creature himself and, secondly, in connexion with his activities outside himself when applied to the act of living in the complex round of social, religious, political, moral, educational, industrial, and other experiences in civilization. The human creature continues to rush from one extreme to another on the "end-gaining" principle in his attempts at reform or "physical" improvement, and the point just made as to what is necessary for the primary and secondary understanding of "cause and effect" is of the utmost importance in this connexion, and in any estimate of schemes for the uplifting of the human creature that are likely to prove permanently satisfactory. What probability is there that any one of these schemes of reform will do anything but make conditions more chaotic, until the individuals concerned have been re-educated on a general basis and reorganized as a psycho-physical unity? For, in the last analysis, it is the creature's individual reaction to the stimuli resulting from the individual conception of that scheme of reform that matters, even if the scheme, taken by itself, might be considered a satisfactory one.

This leads us back to the theme of conception which has been outlined, and in connexion with which we have endeavoured to show that only in a state of *co-ordinated activity*, in which the organism is functioning near its maximum, can we hope for anything approaching a satisfactory conception of new and unfamiliar ideas or experiences. Hence the necessity of having an understanding of "cause and effect," primarily, in connexion with the functioning of the organism itself.

For it is only after we have solved this problem in the individual that we can safely pass on to the secondary consideration of "cause and effect" in connexion with the problems of everyday life. Only then shall we be justified in asserting that individual reactions to stimuli will be the reactions of a controlled human creature, whose employment of the processes of reasoning in the activities of life prevents the undue and harmful excitement of the fear reflexes and emotions, especially when he is called upon to deal with those new and unfamiliar situations or problems which are the natural outcome of all processes tending towards advancement on the evolutionary plane.